I0605901

# CROMWELL'S SPY

DENNIS SEWELL is a writer and broadcaster. He spent twenty-two years on the staff of BBC News, latterly as presenter of *Talking Politics* and as a reporter for *Newsnight*. His previous books include *The Political Gene: How Darwin's Ideas Changed Politics* and *Catholics: Britain's Largest Minority*. He lives with his wife and twin daughters in London.

# CROMWELL'S SPY

## From the American Colonies to the English Civil War: *The Life of George Downing*

DENNIS SEWELL

PEGASUS BOOKS
NEW YORK LONDON

CROMWELL'S SPY

Pegasus Books, Ltd.
148 West 37th Street, 13th Floor
New York, NY 10018



First Pegasus Books cloth edition February 2026



ISBN: 979-8-89710-050-7

10 9 8 7 6 5 4 3 2 1

Printed in the United States of America
Distributed by Simon & Schuster
www.pegasusbooks.com

*To Laura, Hilla and Thea – with everlasting love*

# Contents

# Dramatis Personae

*George Downing* (1623–84) – scholar, preacher, spy, diplomat, politician, American Roundhead, member of the Cavalier Parliament, Envoy Extraordinary, property developer, antihero.

*Emmanuel Downing* (1585–1660) – George's father. Puritan, barrister-at-law, New England pioneer, entrepreneur, shameless opportunist, crook.

*Lucy Downing* (*née Winthrop*) (1600–79) – George's mother. Stalwart promoter of the interests of her many offspring.

*John Winthrop Senior* (1588–1649) – George Downing's uncle. Leader of the Great Migration to New England. Twelve times elected governor of the Massachusetts Bay Colony between 1630 and 1649. Puritan, intolerant, politically savvy.

*John Winthrop Junior* (1606–76) – George Downing's favourite cousin, friend and collaborator. College drop-out, alchemist, metallurgist, founder of Saybrook Colony, governor of Connecticut Colony, markedly more liberal than his father.

*Hugh Peter* (1598–1660) – Puritan pastor noted for his theatrical style of preaching. A radical political activist during the English Civil Wars. A close ally of Oliver Cromwell and George Downing's early mentor.

*Oliver Cromwell* (1599–1658) – Parliamentarian, Civil War general, man of destiny, Lord Protector, political and spiritual sphinx. George Downing's most important patron.

*Thomas Scot* (n.d.–1660) – Commonwealth spymaster and George Downing's overseer in the intelligence office at Whitehall.

*Archibald Campbell* (1607–61) – 1st Marquis of Argyle, leader of the Whiggamore or Kirk Party in Scotland. Covenanter, unreliable friend, one of the spied upon.

*Lord Wariston* (*Archibald Johnston*) (1611–63) – Presbyterian zealot, Covenanter, Argyle's political sidekick, instinctively suspicious of George Downing.

*George Monck* (1608–70) – professional soldier, general, reliable in a crisis, indulgent of and avuncular towards George Downing, ultimately Earl of Albemarle.

*John Thurloe* (1616–68) – Thomas Scot's successor as spymaster, Secretary of State, George Downing's boss under the Protectorate and his match in intellect and energy.

*Charles Howard of Naworth* (1628–85) – Cumberland aristocrat, religious and political chameleon, commander of Oliver Cromwell's Life Guard, George Downing's brother-in-law, eventually Earl of Carlisle.

*Frances Howard* (1625–83) – Charles Howard's sister, George Downing's wife and mother of his children. Woman of mystery.

Johan de Witt (1625–72) – Grand Pensionary of Holland, dominated the States General – the parliament of the Dutch Republic – and was effectively political leader of the United Provinces of the Netherlands. De Witt was the champion of the merchant class and an anti-monarchist. He and George Downing tried constantly to outsmart one another. Another of the spied upon.

*Lord Clarendon* (*Edward Hyde*) (1609–74) – Courtier and adviser to King Charles II, appointed Lord Chancellor after the Restoration and consequently became George Downing's political master. Clarendon despised Downing and sought to sink his career.

# Introduction

George Downing was a spy, a diplomat and a shameless turncoat. He worked in both darkness and light. A secret agent for Oliver Cromwell, an MP and ambassador abroad, he might have seemed the model servant of Protector and Parliament; but one day he would abruptly shift sides to scheme in support of the Stuart Restoration.

Born in 1623, Downing spent his formative years in America as a pioneer in colonial Massachusetts. Travelling to the Caribbean just as the use of African slaves was expanding in the English colonies there, he cheered on the wider adoption of slavery with unselfconscious glee. Back in Britain, he played a part in making slaves – of a sort – out of a bedraggled army of Scots, taken prisoner during the Civil War. After switching to the King's side, Downing pioneered the state-sponsored kidnapping nowadays known as 'extraordinary rendition'; had a hand in starting two major wars; and is credited with a crucial role in extracting Manhattan and Long Island from the Dutch, thereby helping to found New York. He was a crafty Janus in a life filled with political intrigue. Yet he is chiefly remembered – when he is remembered at all – for a single speculative property venture, undertaken late in life, to build a street in London that came to house generations of British prime ministers. In truth, developing Downing Street was one of the less interesting things that George Downing turned his hand to.

A scion of one of the founding families of the Massachusetts Bay Colony, Downing was in the first class ever to graduate from Harvard. Three years later, following other New England Puritans, he sailed back to Britain to take up the Roundhead cause in the English Civil War. Impressed by his abilities, Oliver Cromwell soon appointed Downing head of military intelligence, rewarding his two signature traits: resourceful competence and ruthlessness. Cromwell remained George Downing's patron through the Commonwealth and the Protectorate, sending him on missions around Europe doubling as diplomat and spy; and Downing in turn remained loyal to the republic, until the day for treachery arrived.

When Charles II was restored to his kingdoms in 1660, it was as if George Downing had simply swapped one patron for another. He surprised friend and foe alike by keeping all the generously rewarded posts he had acquired during the interregnum and adding a few more under the new dispensation. As it turned out, he had been working both sides of the street for some time. He went on to play a part in the frenzy of Royalist revenge that followed the king's return, helping to hunt down the regicides who had signed Charles I's death warrant. Some had been among Downing's friends, patrons and colleagues, yet he was prepared to propel them callously towards the most gruesome executions.

History views George Downing through narrowed eyes. When not censuring his moral turpitude, it tends to shoo him into the footnotes, like an embarrassing relation.

Scour the indexes of Civil War histories – from venerable Victorian to the latest revisionist take – and Downing rates scant mention.

Contemporaries decried him as 'a sider with all times and changes, well skilled in the common cant', as 'a fearful gentleman' and as a 'Judas'.[1] Downing is guilty on all counts. This book will not advance any contrarian or revisionist line in that respect. Rather, it accepts him as he was: a man who betrayed his former friends and colleagues; not to save his own skin, either, but to further his career. Yet there is more to this strange and darkly knotted character than the sum of his mortal sins.

In 1876, the antiquary Edward Peacock observed that the Leveller Thomas Rainborowe, 'has not found his way into our biographical literature, and in the popular histories of the period there is little recorded concerning him'. Rainborowe's neglect, according to Peacock, was a result of the restricted focus of Civil War historiography. 'The fame of three or four of the leading spirits of the time has eclipsed in the common memory almost all the other people who took an important part in the struggle between Charles the First and his Parliament,' he said. 'There is, we believe, no other great crisis in modern history where the less known have been permitted to remain so entirely *unknown* as the time of which we speak.'[2]

Since Peacock's day there has been a burgeoning of Leveller studies, and our understanding of what happened in that period has been all the better for it. Nevertheless, the three or four leading spirits of the Civil War years still tend to dominate the scene, permitting other players only the occasional cameo appearance. By following the figure of George Downing, moving through the shadows and surfacing at crucial moments, always on the make, we may discover a fresh perspective on this convulsive episode in English history.

Downing always stood close to the people who mattered. The governor of Massachusetts was his uncle; the governor of Connecticut was his cousin. He was at Cromwell's elbow throughout the Third Civil War and was hugger-mugger with the Protector's spymaster, John Thurloe, afterwards. Under the new regime he tried (and failed) to scrape up to Charles II's chief minister, Lord Clarendon, but for a while succeeded in insinuating himself into the affections of the King instead.

As a writer, reporter and documentary-maker, my interest over thirty years has involved three main strands: religion, politics and spying. These are constant themes, plaited together, in Downing's mysterious life from the late 1640s to the early 1670s; but thereafter they abruptly fall away as Downing is exiled from the world of intrigue and confined to more pedestrian politics in the House of Commons. Indeed, his last dozen years in this world were pretty unremarkable by any standard. Consequently, I decided not to attempt a rounded, balanced, definitive account of George Downing's whole life, but rather to keep my focus on his spying and scheming. For these reasons, I touch only lightly upon Downing's public-finance reforms and skirt the intricacies of the great power diplomacy in which he engaged. Other writers have addressed these specialist areas and I point to their work in the Bibliography at the end of the book.

Since espionage is a clandestine activity, leaving few traces and next to nothing by way of documentary evidence, it is a field in which a great deal is necessarily left to conjecture. But when used properly, conjecture is a perfectly respectable analytical tool and should not be confused with being over-imaginative. Examining Downing's letters and reports to work out who his agents may have been, what they would have been in a position to tell him, how he knew what he knew, and who and what he chose to tell at vital moments, opens windows of interpretation. Downing's secret side may also tell us more about the man himself: how he shifted from American Roundhead to English Cavalier, or from Puritan preacher to suspiciously wealthy voluptuary; and whether he truly was a shameless cynic or perhaps a paradoxically principled turncoat.

Throughout the period in which George Downing's story unfolds, the American colonies and England employed the Old Style date system based on the Julian calendar, where the new year began on Lady Day, 25 March, while the continental European countries that Downing visited had adopted the Gregorian calendar and New Style dates that were ten days in advance of the Julian ones. Scotland (where much of the early action of this narrative takes place) employed a hybrid system: a modified Old Style, with the New Year beginning on 1 January. To avoid confusion, all dates in this book (except where otherwise specified) conform to the Scottish model – that is, Old Style, but with a 1 January start. Similarly, when quoting from documents I have adjusted the spelling, punctuation and grammar for the sake of consistency and clarity.

Dennis Sewell

# CHAPTER 1

# An Unsentimental Education

## *Cambridge, Massachusetts Bay Colony, 1638*

HARVARD WAS FOUNDED by Puritans in the pious hope that it would turn out saints, but in George Downing it apparently summoned a demon. Liar, blackmailer, seducer and thief, this double-dealing shapeshifter would betray both friends and principles without a moment's misgiving. Yet as a most artful spy for Oliver Cromwell, as an envoy alternately bruising and charming his way through the chancelleries of Europe, as a politician revamping England's public finances and blowing early wind into the sails of empire, George Downing showed himself to be, by any reckoning, the most successful, significant and fascinating figure in Harvard's first graduation class.

Heaven alone knows to what extent Downing's Harvard years shaped his moral character, but it was perhaps of some salience that during his freshman year, beginning in the summer of 1638, the master of the college was a deranged and brutal sadist. Nathaniel Eaton had come to his new post with all the right credentials: Westminster School; Trinity College, Cambridge; a spell in the Netherlands, studying under an exiled Puritan divine. The Board of Overseers, who knew of Eaton's family, but had not the faintest intimation of his propensity for violence, conferred on this son of a Cheshire vicar the title of professor, with full authority over the construction of the new college, its academic life and the pastoral care of its students.[1]

At this time Newtown – as Cambridge, Massachusetts was originally known – was a frontier community. The line of trees that curtained the northern edge of Cow Common marked the limit of the young colony's mapped territory – beyond lay primeval wilderness. The town had become a scrapheap of abortive schemes. Newtown was originally intended to replace Boston as the colony's capital, until the governor, John Winthrop, realized that the plan was a ruse on the part of a rival to separate him from his political base. He performed a theatrical gesture of repudiation, uprooting the wooden frame of his Newtown house, and then had the whole structure carted three miles east, where he established a country residence beside the Mystic River. Winthrop kept his town house in Boston, which remained the seat of government.[2]

With their political aspirations thwarted, some Newtown boosters reposed their hopes in commercial farming. But the quality of the soil was too poor for wheat, so the only realistic way to make money was by rearing livestock – hence the stockyards and ox pastures in the heart of the town. To be profitable, though, the cattle business needed to be conducted on a scale that the topography of the locality would not allow. The beasts required room to graze, but the cattlemen looked out at the forbidding thicket and saw that it could never be cleared for pasture; not in their lifetimes anyhow. Ultimately it would be George Downing's father, Emmanuel, who would help solve the colony's livestock problems by shipping in animals from England and supervising the erection of cattle pens on grassland further north, near his home town of Salem.

Meanwhile, the people of Newtown concluded that the only thing for it was exodus. In June 1636, one hundred of the town's original inhabitants, led by their charismatic pastor, Thomas Hooker, along with all their cattle, pigs and goats, simply upped and went in search of fresh woods and pastures new. Providence guided them on a journey westwards along a Native American trail that after two weeks deposited them in the Connecticut River valley, where they established a new settlement close to a Dutch trading post. For the eight or nine families who decided to stay behind when Hooker departed, together with many skilled artisans who later came crowding in, the college represented Newtown's last chance to establish itself as a going concern.

Winthrop's Massachusetts Puritans valued scholarship so highly that they founded a university only six years after they landed in America. They barely had enough time to build churches, farms and roads before making higher education their priority. The founding of Harvard was partly brought about by members of George Downing's extended family. John Winthrop may figuratively have been the father of the Bay colony, but he was literally George Downing's uncle. George's mother, Lucy Downing, was Winthrop's sister. She lobbied her brother to develop the colony's educational institutions, making it a condition of bringing her family over to New England. As it transpired, he already had the matter in hand. Lucy Winthrop Downing had spotted that her son George possessed an aptitude for learning and was determined that he would attain 'perfection in the Arts'. 'It would grieve me in my grave,' Lucy told her brother, 'if his mind should be withdrawn from his book by . . . sports; for that were but the way to make him good at nothing.'[3]

Another energetic advocate for a university was Hugh Peter, the pastor of the church at Salem, who was related to the Winthrops by marriage and became an unofficial uncle to young George. When it came to establishing the college, Massachusetts possessed impressive reserves of cultural capital. More than fifty of the colony's leaders – clergymen, politicians and lawyers – had attended Cambridge University in England, including John Winthrop and Hugh Peter, both alumni of Trinity College. The name 'Cambridge' was an irresistible choice for the town where their new university would be established. So it was that, in May 1638, ill-starred Newtown formally became Cambridge, Massachusetts.

Money was tight in the young colony, but providence delivered. In this instance it did so by infecting a wealthy thirty-year-old clergyman named John Harvard, late of Emmanuel College, Cambridge, with terminal tuberculosis; then sparing him for just long enough to make a deathbed bequest of half his fortune, together with his entire library, to the college. Naming the institution after him was, you might think, the least the colony could do, but John Winthrop avoided acknowledging John Harvard's generous gift, always referring to the institution simply as 'the college at Cambridge'.[4] The founders constantly held up the older Cambridge as a pattern for the new. The world's first university press, for instance, had been founded at Cambridge in 1534 by Thomas Thomas (his name so suggestive of a misprint); consequently the New Englanders sighed for a press of their own. Providence delivered once again. This time a certain Josse Glover, on his way from England with a printing press in his baggage, perished of a fever during the voyage.[5] Ownership of his equipment passed to his widow, Elizabeth. She engaged Stephen Daye, a young locksmith whose passage Glover had covered in exchange for help in establishing the press, to operate the apparatus at a house in Crooked Lane, Cambridge in 1639. It was the first press in the American colonies. Two years later, Elizabeth Glover found herself a new husband in Henry Dunster, the brutal Eaton's more irenic successor, whereupon the commercial press became a university press. And despite Winthrop's cussed reluctance, the college adopted the name Harvard shortly after opening.

## *The Peyntree house, summer 1638*

There were curious events in the colony in the spring and summer of 1638 that some read as portents or intimations of divine dissatisfaction. Farmers had to re-plant their corn two or three times in a season, when they found it rotted in the ground. In June an earthquake occurred, making a sound, according to one witness, 'like continuous thunder or the rattling of coaches in London'.[6] It shook the ground violently for four minutes and then rumbled away to Connecticut, though the aftershocks went on for almost three weeks. But nothing more came of it; the sun shone and the corn crops recovered. Young men going up to Harvard were able to set all anxieties aside and begin their new life as scholars with high hopes and innocent cheer.

George Downing, along with a dozen or so fellow freshmen, arrived in late summer at the newly refurbished

Peyntree house on Braintree Street. From the rear windows of this converted farmhouse the students could look out across the ox pastures and the common in the distance; and, more closely, onto Cowyard Row, a series of lots that Nathaniel Eaton was busy transforming into Harvard Yard, which soon became (and today remains) the heart of the Harvard campus.

Immediately behind the Peyntree house, work was beginning on Old College, a pastiche of the Cambridge originals back in olde England, constructed mainly out of wood. A large E-shaped building of timber, faced with clapboard and with cedar-shingle roofs, it included a great hall and library, kitchen and buttery, bedrooms and studies; and from its centre rose an elegant bell tower. In its finished pomp, Old College appeared magnificent – a little too magnificent for some Puritan tastes. But for much of his time at Harvard, George Downing would see it only as partly built, just a frame and a façade to show for itself, a Potemkin college *avant la lettre*; and a startling incongruity planted way out here in a farmyard, on civilization's very edge.[7]

And there were wolves. As George and his fellow students lit their candles to read their Latin texts after dinner, a wolf pack would pad down to the common to sing by the light of the moon. The moment they ceased howling, a litany of spine-chilling shrieks and screeches would start up, as an entire food chain of predators set upon one another in the blackness beyond. There were foxes, martens, otters and deer *in them thar woods.* There were occasional sightings of moose and foraging black bears. Nobody knew it yet, but the real danger for Harvard's freshman class lay not in the red-in-tooth-and-claw world beyond the ox pale; but rather from inside the Peyntree house itself.

*Harvard Old College*

Harvard's curriculum was breathtakingly extensive. Downing and his class studied not only the customary classical languages – Latin, Greek and Hebrew – but also Chaldean and Syriac. Divinity, ethics, rhetoric, politics, metaphysics, logic, mathematics, physics, astronomy and even a little botany crowded into the timetable. The academic day began at seven o'clock in the morning with a passage from Scripture, after which each student would explain to his tutor what he had learned by candlelight the night before. A programme of lectures would follow, with further Bible readings in the afternoon. Instruction in all subjects was delivered in Latin; indeed, theoretically at least, every conversation held on college premises, whether during working hours, at mealtimes or at leisure, was conducted in Latin too. The young Downing quickly mastered conversing in the ancient tongue. It was a skill he would keep up in later life.[8]

Cotton Mather, a Puritan prodigy of the next generation, who went up to Harvard at the age of eleven, described Nathaniel Eaton as 'a rare scholar' who had 'made many more such', but added that 'their education truly was in the school of Tyrannus'. This judgement chimes with the eye-witness testimony of William Hubbard, one of Downing's contemporaries, who compared Eaton to Orbilius – the poet Horace's schoolmaster and a notorious flogger.[9] Eaton would eventually be put on trial for his relentless battery. Of the students brave enough to testify against him, some said that they had received twenty, and even thirty, strokes of his lash. There is no record of whether George Downing gave evidence or was among the teenagers Eaton abused. That he was the governor's nephew may possibly have given Downing immunity. Eaton's egregious defence to the charges brought against him was that in each instance he needed to 'subdue the party to his will'. In the end it was not the professor's brutality to the undergraduates that proved his undoing; his mistake was to assault a member of the academic staff. The magistrates heard that one night, after an argument, Eaton decided to 'reform' his assistant, Nathaniel Briscoe. He armed himself with a cudgel carved out of walnut wood and 'big enough to have killed a horse'. Taking with him two servants to hold Briscoe down, Eaton beat his victim for two hours, delivering more than two hundred blows to his head, neck, shoulders and torso. The ensuing investigation discovered much else to the professor's discredit.[10]

Since moving into the Peyntree house, Downing and the other scholars had been served their meals by an African slave, known only as 'the Moor'. It is likely that this young man had recently arrived in Massachusetts from the island of Providence, a Puritan colony off the Caribbean coast of Nicaragua, aboard a Salem ship, the *Desire*.[11] The exploitation of the Moor by Harvard College was unlawful; the trading of slaves would not be legalized in Massachusetts for another three years. The master of the *Desire* was William Pierce, who later instructed two of George Downing's brothers, Joshua and Robin, in the maritime arts. Pierce had spent the previous six months buying and selling in the Caribbean, visiting Barbados, St Kitts and Tortuga, as well as Providence Island. No surviving record confirms where exactly the Moor was purchased, but if it was Providence Island, as Governor Winthrop's account suggests, then it is probable that he had originally been enslaved by the Spanish and taken from one of their galleons by English privateers. The kingpin of organized piracy in the region was a London merchant, Maurice Thomson, who controlled the buccaneers operating out of Providence Island under letters of marque issued by Charles I. In 1635, the King licensed the seizure of Spanish ships after Spain raided the island of Tortuga. Thomson was a business associate of Emmanuel Downing in a string of enterprises running from fisheries to furs. Later a notorious interloper in the Atlantic slave trade, he would soon become one of the hard-faced merchants who financed the parliamentary side in the coming English Civil War.[12]

Had Nathaniel Eaton's wife not been caught stealing the students' dinner money, the trafficking of this young African might have passed unremarked. As it was, the Moor was made a scapegoat during the investigation into the Eatons' custodianship of the college. They could not blame him for the mackerel brought to table with the guts still in them; nor for thickening the hasty pudding with goats' dung; nor even for stealing the cheese and beef: Mistress Eaton admitted to doing all that herself. But some of the young scholars actually appeared to be envious of a slave, griping that they were denied bread of their own and had to eat 'the Moor's crusts'; or that there were occasions when the Moor had beer, but they had to go without. However, the greatest outrage was occasioned when young Samuel Hough came back to his dorm one day and – like the three bears in the Goldilocks story – found a young trespasser asleep in his bed. Samuel's father, one of the most senior elected figures in the colony, was so distressed that he withdrew his son from Harvard altogether and sued the professor for the fees that he had already paid.

The court banned Eaton from working in an educational establishment ever again and Harvard formally dismissed him in the autumn of 1639. As there was nobody at hand to take his place, the Board of Overseers had no choice but to shut the college for almost a whole academic year. The freshmen were packed off to their parents, who were advised to hire private tutors to keep the scholars' heads in their books until the following August.

George Downing returned to Salem, where he was fortunate to receive instruction from John Fiske – yet another Cambridge graduate. Fiske was proficient in the Scriptures, the classics and medical science. He also preached at the meeting house in Salem as an understudy to pastor Hugh Peter and, as a sideline, dispensed remedies to the sick. Downing was used to interruptions to his education. When the plague ran hot in London, Emmanuel and Lucy Downing would send their son away to board in Kent; when it diminished, he was allowed home.

## *A London boyhood*

George Downing was born in the autumn of 1623 in Dublin, Ireland. From the age of two until he was ten, the family lived at Peterborough Court in London's Fleet Street, hard by the conduit that brought fresh water all the way from Tyburn. The site of Downing's childhood home has in recent times housed the offices of the *Daily Telegraph* and the London branch of Goldman Sachs. His father was a barrister with chambers in the Inner Temple nearby. In 1634, the Downings moved to a new house near the south-west corner of Lincoln's Inn Fields.

George's wide and precocious knowledge of the world owed a good deal to the intellectually stimulating figures passing through the family home. Chief among them was his cousin, John Winthrop Junior. Winthrop became more like a big brother to George, and the pair were closely involved in the details of one another's lives despite an age gap of seventeen years. The Winthrops were country gentry, with an estate at Groton in Suffolk, and the Downings' house became Winthrop's London base. He was a man of many and various schemes, who struggled to keep his focus on any one project for long. His father was disappointed that John did not go up to Trinity College, Cambridge, but to Trinity College, Dublin instead. He was disappointed again when John Junior dropped out of the university without taking a degree and enrolled to study law at the Inns of Court in London. But before long, John was on the move again; this time, sailing off to war.

Emmanuel Downing's brother, Joshua, was Surveyor to the Navy and managed the shipyards at Rotherhithe and Chatham. He used his influence to obtain a place for young

Winthrop on the Duke of Buckingham's 1627 expedition to relieve the beleaguered Huguenots at La Rochelle – a romantic cause for Protestants at that time. The Huguenots were holding out against an army led by the Catholic Louis XIII and his chief minister, Cardinal Richelieu. With a background in divinity and law and no nautical experience, and being too much of the officer class for swabbing decks, the only suitable role Buckingham's fleet could find for Winthrop was as secretary to the captain of the *Repulse*, a forty-gun warship.[13]

The expedition was a shambles, poorly planned and inadequately funded; and it left 20,000 Huguenots dead in the mud on the Île de Ré. Profoundly disillusioned by the experience, Winthrop lit out for Italy and the Levant, visiting Florence, Venice and Constantinople, returning with a thousand stories and a stock of fresh enthusiasms. He turned out all right in the end, becoming the governor of Connecticut and a Fellow of the Royal Society. Though he followed his father to New England, he would frequently return to London on business. For the young George, time spent with his mercurial and impulsive cousin was always an education.

Also resident in the Downing house during George's formative years was Edward Howes, John Winthrop Junior's best friend from his student days in Dublin. Howes too was still uncertain of the right road to take in life and he also decided to read for the Bar, more or less apprenticing himself to Emmanuel Downing, doubling as both his pupil and his clerk – living in Downing's home, eating at the family table and performing any other duties his pupil master might from time to time assign him. Howes shared Winthrop's obsessive interests in alchemy and magnetic engines and had his own special hobbyhorse: the search for the Northwest Passage.

Oddly, Howes was in the habit of encrypting portions of his correspondence with Winthrop. It is possible that he gave the young George a head start in espionage with breakfast-table training in codes and ciphers, for Howes turned out to be a natural teacher. After the Downings left for America, he abandoned the law to become a mathematics master at a school in Stepney, East London. He wrote an arithmetic textbook and dreamed up a scheme to simplify grammar and syntax, which he hoped to sell to the world. In the 1640s, Howes started his own free school in Poplar, in premises provided by the East India Company.

He also made a small but significant contribution towards solving New England's wolf problem. Acting on instructions from Emmanuel Downing, he supervised the shipping of four Irish wolfhounds 'and an Irish boy to tend them'.[14] Howes had some additional advice. 'I have learnt two devices to kill wolves,' he wrote to his friend Winthrop, 'one is with pieces of sponge laid covertly in such flesh or garbage they feed on; the other is . . . pieces of strong wire, twisted together . . . and the ends to be bowed and filed sharp and beards cut in them like fishhooks; and then put within their meat.' He then added cryptically, 'There is one also here in town that makes very good Shanlota prestheir waidtoh Vortimnoe agnud cloimnoan Ebafretah.'[15] This was not a message in Gaelic, but in rudimentary code. Removing every second letter yields the solution: 'Salt peter with Vrine and comon Earth'.

Howes was sending his friend a scientific recipe. The intended sense of the communication was: *There is a man here in town who makes very good saltpetre out of urine and common earth (and nothing else).* It was generally held at the time that the earth required to produce saltpetre, which is a key ingredient of gunpowder, needed enrichment with nutrients, usually supplied by adding bird droppings. The reason Howes employed a form of encryption in this letter was that the Crown held a monopoly in the manufacture of saltpetre; this meant that Howes's anonymous connection was risking imprisonment, or worse, for making his own. Gunpowder was a strategic resource and, when it was in short supply, saltpetre men would go from door to door demanding the king's subjects to hand over their urine – and sometimes their soil – for the war effort. As it turned out, Howes's thinly coded recipe became useful intelligence for the American colonists: Massachusetts took the hint and set up saltpetre sheds in each county.

As for the Irish boy sent to mind the wolfhounds, there is, sadly, no record of his fate. A young Catholic among the New England Puritans would have been like Daniel at the court of Darius the Mede. Howes complained to Winthrop that despite his best efforts to make a Protestant of him, the lad still refused to eat meat on Fridays and 'does not love to hear the Romish religion spoken against'. He challenged Winthrop to take the boy as his servant and, over a period of four years, try to convert him. In a work of fiction, Winthrop would have accepted the challenge and the wolfhound boy would have become George's first fast friend in New England. In real life, as it happened, he was never mentioned again.

### *From London to Salem, Massachusetts*

The Downing family moved to New England as part of the Great Migration, which saw 20,000 Puritans take ship for

America's northern seaboard. The migrants are frequently portrayed as refugees fleeing persecution. Yet the oppression and victimization they were escaping was comparatively mild for those troubled times when bloody religious conflict ran rife across Europe. Charles I did not massacre the Puritans; their property was not confiscated. A small number did suffer imprisonment, and a tiny few – the so-called Puritan martyrs – were barbarously mutilated: their ears cut off in public, as a lesson to the others. Unusually for martyrs, however, none of them lost their lives.[16]

A number of the Puritan clergy did, admittedly, lose their livelihoods – being expelled from their parishes after stern inspections by the Church of England authorities; but no more than a few score of those who sailed for New England had suffered such an experience. For the overwhelming majority of migrants, their 'persecution' took the form of a string of liturgical microaggressions meted out by the new Archbishop of Canterbury, William Laud. Altars were restored for the Eucharist, replacing the wooden tables favoured by the Puritans; images and stained glass began to reappear in churches that had previously been stripped bare. Ecclesiastical vestments were restored to service despite their papist heritage and fancy embroidery; prayers were once again given precedence over preaching, and free will over Calvinist predestination. This trend was bitterly offensive to Puritans, who saw it as tantamount to popery. The Puritans despised every aspect of the Catholic faith and pledged to expunge any lingering taint from the Church of England. Increasingly they were finding that England would not permit them to live as they wished; indeed, it threatened to force them into adopting forms of worship that were profoundly inimical to their beliefs. That said, William Laud did not actually become Archbishop of Canterbury until 1633, so his reforms cannot sufficiently explain the proleptic flight of the Winthrop fleet three years before.

There was a straightforwardly political dimension to the migration. The Puritans were strongly represented in Parliament, but had an uneasy relationship with the king. Strongly attached to ideas such as the Divine Right of Kings and the Royal Prerogative, Charles I could sometimes be somewhat high-handed with his Parliament, especially when he was short of money. In March 1629, Charles sent the MPs away and instituted an eleven-year period of personal rule. This allowed him to bring in new taxes that Parliament would have blocked, had they been given the choice, and that also allowed him to give Laud a free hand with the Church.

Yet, what chiefly led the Puritans to emigrate to New England was a belief that it was what God wanted of them. Each received the summons in a different way. For John Winthrop Senior, providence was theatrically emphatic. He made a careful note of it shortly afterwards: 'July 28 1629: My brother Downing and myself riding into Lincolnshire by Ely, my horse fell under me in a bog in the fens, so I was almost up to the waist in water; but the Lord preserved me from further danger.'[17]

When the incident occurred, Winthrop and Emmanuel Downing were on their way to Sempringham to meet Isaac Johnson and his wife, Lady Arbella, a daughter of the Earl of Lincoln, who were hosting a house party to discuss founding a new colony in Massachusetts. Winthrop became convinced that God had spared his life so that he would lead this adventure. He and Emmanuel Downing threw themselves into planning the colony, with much of the work being done in Downing's house in Fleet Street, with the six-year-old George playing nearby.

A fleet of eleven ships carrying the first wave of migrants set sail from the Isle of Wight just after Easter 1630 with Governor Winthrop aboard his flagship, which, of course, was called the *Arbella*. James Downing, George's half-brother, joined Winthrop on the twelve-week voyage, leaving the rest of the Downing family to follow later.

Everyone knew the expedition could be perilous. A decade earlier the *Mayflower* had landed 103 pilgrims at Plymouth Rock. Yet by the end of their first winter more than sixty of them were dead.

The manifests of the first wave of ships to cross to New England contained many names that that would one day feature in the honour roll of American letters: Pynchon, Lowell, Bradstreet, Stearns (Andrew Eliot of East Coker would join them later). The proportion of migrants who were literate was approximately twice that of the general population in England. Those aboard the ships of the Great Migration would contribute to the bloodline of America's Brahmin caste, its cultural and political elites. The new world was to be a small world: for instance, Hugh Peter's maidservant became the grandmother of Benjamin Franklin, and the descendants of Emmanuel Downing would include President John Quincy Adams, Vice President Aaron Burr and General William Tecumseh Sherman, no less.

Whereas three-quarters of Virginia's colonists belonged to the servant class, by contrast most of the Massachusetts Bay pioneers were gentry, professionals, merchants, artisans or farmers. But it was spiritual and moral elitism that occupied John Winthrop's thoughts as they set sail. He made a speech about how the Puritans' new colony would be 'as a city upon a hill. The eyes of all people . . . upon us.' The idea Winthrop elaborated of New England as a model moral community in a special covenant with God, and being morally superior to the old England they left behind, laid the basis of what would develop into the doctrine of American Exceptionalism; and Winthrop's city-on-a-hill trope, itself taken from Christ's sermon on the mount, has had continuing resonance in American political discourse down to the present day.[18]

Winthrop was not only a man of high moral rectitude; he was also a crafty political operator. He was careful to ensure that there was only one iteration of the patent or royal charter given to the Massachusetts Bay Company. He was also careful to take the original with him, so that there was no record back in London of the Massachusetts constitution, the limits of its independence or the powers of its governor. This broadly gave the colony freedom to make its own laws and determine its own affairs without reference to London. When a committee at Westminster did eventually demand that the document be sent back for scrutiny, Winthrop kept it locked in his office, judging that the twelve-week journey between London and Boston meant that only a couple of rounds of prevarication would be needed before the committee lost interest.

## *Salem, Massachusetts, 1638*

When the Downing family eventually reached Salem in 1638, after three arduous months at sea, they were soon reunited with the younger John Winthrop, who formally welcomed them into the town and later administered the oath when Emmanuel was sworn in as a freeman. Winthrop, at that time, was running a salt plant on the Bass River in the northern reaches of Salem. The enterprise was vital for the colony's economic development, as salt was so necessary for the preservation of meat and fish and had hitherto been in very short supply. Winthrop invested in large saltpans for slow and steady evaporation, yielding a product free of all impurities; but he also installed huge cauldrons for the rapid heating of seawater over log fires, producing quick salt for rush orders. A reliable supply of salt would make it possible for the colonists to store home-reared beef, reducing the need to import meat from old England; but the greatest beneficiaries would be fishermen, now able to harvest the abundant shoals of Atlantic cod between Cape Ann and Newfoundland. They would not only be able to feed Massachusetts, but also export to the Caribbean and even to England. To help start the fishing business, Emmanuel Downing brought in one of his brothers-in-law, Francis Kirby, a London skinner and fur trader already shipping beaver pelts. Kirby, in turn, persuaded one of his own cousins to supply venture capital. This was none other than Maurice Thomson, the merchant pirate of the Caribbean.

The fishing business was originally the brainchild of the pastor Hugh Peter. A Cornishman by birth, Peter invited experienced fishermen from his home village of Fowey (pronounced *Foy*) to emigrate to the Marblehead district of Salem to launch a brand-new Massachusetts fishing fleet. He sank some of his own money into a syndicate of local entrepreneurs to build (and operate) the town's first ship, the *Desire* – the same ship on which 'the Moor' would be trafficked to Boston. The relationship between the Protestant ethic and business success, so frequently remarked, doesn't simply inhere in Calvinist doctrine; money-making requires a Hugh Peter to chivvy fellow Puritans into economic action. Roaring his exhortations with the same passion as he preached his sermons, Peter drove the building of more ships; helped to establish a water mill; promoted glass-making; led the development of trade with the Caribbean islands; and even tried to market the services of Stephen Daye's new printing press to the governor of Bermuda. He was also the most assiduous champion of Harvard. Yet Hugh Peter was a fragile figure, oscillating between bouts of manic energy and prolonged withdrawal into silent, hypochondriac melancholy.[19]

Colonists arriving in Salem discovered that the area's indigenous people had already achieved an enormous amount before them. Large areas of land had been cleared for crops. The local tribe, the Naumkeag people, had refined a method of firing the underbrush in the woods without scorching the trees. Consequently the forests around Salem were not the impenetrable thicket common in New England, but rather contained a marvellous network of paths and bridleways.

John Winthrop Junior was just as energetic and industrious as Hugh Peter. In 1633, he took a dozen men in a small boat northwards up the coast to meet a sagamore – or tribal chief – at a spot that was then called Agawam and is now the town of Ipswich, Massachusetts. Winthrop cut a deal with the chief, purchasing all the land thereabouts for an unknown quantity of wampum and £20 in cash. He moved there, built himself a house, summoned more residents and founded a town. Of course Winthrop's interest very soon switched to another project.

The chief focus of Winthrop's attention was the Saybrook Colony. The name was a hat tip to two Puritan noblemen, Lord Saye and Sele and Lord Brooke, who were among the original investors in Providence Island and were now backing this new scheme, with Winthrop as its managing director. Their plan was to build a fortified condominium in America for the English Puritan elite. The Saybrook Company acquired some prime real estate at the mouth of the Connecticut River looking out over Long Island Sound. Plots were earmarked for a number of prominent Puritan politicians including, reportedly, John Pym, John Hampden, Arthur Hesilrige and Oliver Cromwell. Winthrop had shipped from England a massive portcullis and the winding mechanism for a drawbridge. Another of the investors, the Northumberland squire George Fenwick, travelled to New England to report on progress. A professional soldier with the magnificent name of Lion Gardiner, who had fought in Holland and was strongly recommended by Hugh Peter, was tapped to command the vast fort. Peter had originally come to New England under the auspices of the Saybrook Company and was due to be the community's minister, but found himself diverted to Salem. His travelling companion on the journey from England had been a talented young man called Henry Vane, who was also one of the Saybrook team; but Vane discovered a taste for politics and ran for office in Massachusetts instead. Both Vane and Peter returned to England to become significant figures in the Civil War.

Despite the best efforts of all involved, the Saybrook project was doomed. In 1636, Oliver Cromwell inherited from his maternal uncle, Sir Thomas Steward, a fine house in Ely along with an estate yielding a respectable income. If he had ever hankered after a new life in America, he lost the urge in that moment. Sir Arthur Hesilrige, for his part, had long since signalled an interest in moving to New England: at one time initiating due diligence for the purchase of an estate at Salem. Finding that several merchants had registered charges on the property, he finally chose not to proceed for fear of becoming embroiled in litigation. Hesilrige was also a director of the Saybrook Company, but found he could not readily dispose of his assets in England. One by one, the remaining Puritan grandees dropped out as the kingdom began to move towards civil war. Winthrop, Fenwick and Gardiner were left literally holding the fort.

*Henry Vane the Younger*

George Downing apparently spent the year during which Harvard remained closed dutifully practising his Latin and reading literature with Dr Fiske. Yet a future historian and mayor of the town of Salem later portrayed the young Downing as a roving outdoorsman more than a swot. 'The crack of his fowling-piece re-echoed through the wild woods beyond Proctor's Corner; he tended his father's duck decoys at Humphries' Pond,' Charles Upham wrote, 'and angled along the clear brooks.'[20]

Emmanuel Downing brought over from England all the nets, hoops and blinds required to construct a duck coy and set it up on a stretch of land with two ponds, lying to the south of the town, on the road from Salem to Marblehead. He also acquired the rights to fifty adjacent acres, enough space to ensure his coy was undisturbed by neighbouring farms.[21] He even managed to get a by-law passed forbidding anyone to fire a gun within half a mile of the place. Before long the nets were full of wild fowl and the first of Downing's commercial schemes was an unambiguous success. For Puritans, who lived in a permanent state of neurotic uncertainty about God – whether he was pleased or angry with them, whether they were predestined to be saved or damned – and who examined every incident and outcome for clues to their prospects in the afterlife, a profitable business venture brought an additional dividend: it confirmed divine favour, for the time being at least.

At some point, perhaps during his enforced gap year, George Downing must have learned to ride. In later life he became a man of such corpulence that the idea of him on a horse would have been absurd. But in his lithe years George would be required to travel long distances in a short time and to keep up with cavalry officers on the battlefield.

His mother was known to be a keen and accomplished horsewoman who rode out almost every day in Salem, and we know that Emmanuel Downing regularly made the seventeen-mile trip to Boston in the saddle. It is possible that George had already learned some basic equestrian skills on visits to Suffolk, but his childhood was mainly spent in Fleet Street and Lincoln's Inn Fields and it was only when he arrived in America that he had the chance to become a genuine countryman.

The Massachusetts genealogist Charles Pope counted the Downings as being among the colony's first true pioneers – 'first fellers of the primeval forests, first ploughers of the virgin soil, first makers of homes . . . first worshippers in the log meeting houses'.[22] Truth be told, Emmanuel Downing's family, as relative latecomers, avoided the hard-scrabble privations faced by the first wave of settlers in the Winthrop fleet. They did not, for instance, have to sleep in tents or wigwams while their clapboard house was being built. Instead they were put up as honoured guests by Hugh Peter in his conspicuously grand house in Salem, rising in three handsome storeys to a rooftop of decorative urns, its front door balanced on either side by twin lantern towers to light the garden by night, with fruit trees stretching away in the gated orchard behind. An old ink sketch shows eleven windows from the front perspective alone, so there were certainly enough rooms for Lucy and Emmanuel with all their children and servants.

Governor Winthrop indisputably brought the charismatic leadership to the Massachusetts Bay project that made it possible, while Emmanuel Downing was the workhorse that made it happen. He had manned the expedition's base camp in London for eight years, shipping out goods in response to Winthrop's requests. He therefore knew what to expect when it was his own time to light out for the territory. Some of the early migrants, noting that Boston lay on roughly the same parallel of latitude as Barcelona, had moved to Massachusetts expecting a Mediterranean climate. Emmanuel Downing knew that plenty of sheep's fleeces (dyed red, and not Puritan black) were required to survive the freezing American winter. As a reward for all the services he had performed for them from London – not only as logistics supremo, but also as general-counsel and lobbyist, arguing the colony's case before the Privy Council – the government of Massachusetts voted Downing more than 700 acres, upon which he set up a farm and built his own fine house, with stables attached. Lucy Downing named their homestead 'Groton' after the Winthrop estate in Suffolk where she was raised.

*Downing Mansion in Salem*

Growing up in London, young George had only ever known his father as a barrister, a respectable, professional man hurrying between his chambers in Inner Temple Lane and the Court of Wards next to Westminster Hall. Now, in a new context on another continent, the fifty-three-year-old Emmanuel was transforming himself into a farmer and commercial go-getter, with his fingers in furs, fisheries, mining and metals, timber, livestock and succulent ducks. Later he would diversify into strong waters, becoming one of America's first distillers of rye whiskey.[23]

This was not Emmanuel Downing's first experience of helping to create a new Puritan community and a new economy from scratch. After reading Law at Trinity Hall, Cambridge and completing his legal training at the Inner Temple, he had moved to Ireland to join his brother, Joshua, who at that time was a lawyer at the Court of Common Pleas in Dublin. The two brothers put together a consortium to acquire three estates near Mountrath, County Laois, on which they planned most discreetly to establish a Puritan plantation.

Emmanuel, by this time, had married his first wife, Anne Ware, a daughter of a member of the Irish parliament and the kingdom's Auditor General. Sir James Ware was enormously helpful in smoothing the way, obtaining privileges and exceptions for the plantation on the sly. Soon, having been spared many bureaucratic obstacles by Emmanuel's father-in-law, the Downing brothers had tripled their income from rents and had shipped in settlers from England. The restless Joshua soon left Ireland, going off to work first for the East India Company and later becoming a senior administrator of the navy. Emmanuel remained in Dublin, practising law at the King's Inns. Foremost among his clients was Sir Richard Boyle, later to become the Earl of Cork, whose son Roger, an infant at this time, would one day prove a generous patron of both George and Emmanuel Downing.

The Downings had a son, James, and two daughters, Susan and Mary, before Anne died suddenly in October 1621. It so happened that Emmanuel's old friend, John Winthrop, was visiting Dublin at this time. Six months later Emmanuel married John's sister, Lucy, sixteen years his junior; and in the autumn of 1623 she gave birth to George in Dublin. More children arrived in London, and a pair of twins would be born in the New World, so that by the time George returned to Harvard when it reopened, he had eleven siblings or half-siblings living in America.

Once the family was established in Salem, Emmanuel Downing stood for political office. He applied to become a member of the Court of Assistants, the most prestigious tier of government in the colony. The Assistants formed the political leadership, like a cabinet, but also sat as Massachusetts's most senior judges. Downing assumed that his long experience at the Bar naturally qualified him for the role. However, he did not win enough votes for election because, according to a contemporary report, 'jealousy was manifested, lest the governor should use influence enough to make his office perpetual'.[24] That is, people were worried that John Winthrop was trying to make himself governor for life by packing the court with members of his own family. Winthrop's endorsement turned out to be Downing's undoing. As a consolation prize, he was elected as deputy for the town of Salem to the General Court, the colony's legislature, and sat as a local magistrate. He gradually took on extra roles, establishing a land registry, organizing the fencing of cattle and the building of roads in Salem. His ubiquity in both business and politics steadily consolidated his power in the town.

Not a whisper of it was heard in the streets of Salem or Boston, but Emmanuel Downing had a dirty secret, presumably also unknown to young George. Much of Emmanuel's work at the London Bar involved acting as an attorney at the Court of Wards, a body that appointed legal guardians to supervise estates inherited by minors. The estates over which the court had jurisdiction were those where the deceased had been a tenant-in-chief of the Crown. Broadly, this meant a clientele drawn from the nobility, the gentry and others who had been beneficiaries of the distribution of confiscated church lands during the Reformation. Emmanuel Downing was in league with Sir Robert Naunton, the Master of the Court, spending men-only weekends at his manor house at Nelmes in Essex, plotting to appoint their cronies as guardians in order to embezzle the funds of naive young heirs. A market developed, with Downing and Naunton auctioning off guardianships, while also taking commission from the successful bidders. When the government eventually got wind of the court's dodgy dealings, Naunton announced his retirement. His signal that the game was up may have prompted Emmanuel Downing to go at last to New England. George's later life would show that he learned much from his father, but two things especially: to have an eye to the main chance, and the importance of being shameless.[25]

## *Cambridge, Massachusetts, 1642–5*

Harvard's first-ever commencement, or graduation ceremony, took place on Friday 23 September 1642. The venue was Old College, which had at last been brought into use thanks to the efforts of one of the Downings' neighbours, the Salem master carpenter John Friend, who had built the colossal fort at Saybrook.[26]

Both Emmanuel Downing and Hugh Peter were abroad on the big day and so missed George's graduation. Hugh Peter did, however, subsequently write about the occasion as if he had been there as an eyewitness. Peter was the co-author of a pamphlet entitled 'New England's First Fruits', published in London in 1643. The tract was partly a piece of brazen boosterism on behalf of the Massachusetts Bay experiment, and partly a rebuttal of the charge that the colony's Puritan ministers were not doing enough to save Native American souls. Missionary work was supposed to be one of the colony's top priorities – the official seal of the Massachusetts Bay Company depicted an Indian carrying a bow and arrow, saying 'Come over and help us.' The promise of evangelizing the indigenous population was a powerful fundraising tool for extracting donations from the merchants and liverymen in the City of London; but delivering on the pledge was a very slow business. For example, John Eliot, the minister at the town of Roxbury, translated the Bible into the Algonquian language, having first learned to speak himself from scratch. The whole process took him more than twenty years. So with little to announce in this area of endeavour, Hugh Peter and his colleagues placed Harvard College's first commencement centre stage in their upbeat account of the colony's progress.[27]

The students of the graduating class had been well rehearsed for this day when they would stand before a panel of grandees, including the colony's governor John Winthrop, to defend their theses and prove themselves as good as their counterparts at Oxford or Cambridge. The event began at about nine o'clock in the morning, with a procession led by a squad of halberdiers of the governor's ceremonial guard. Behind them filed the overseers with the governor and Harvard's president, Henry Dunster, in the lead. The VIP party took their seats on a platform. After prayers and an opening address, Dunster called forward each of the commencers in turn. George Downing and his fellow scholars displayed their mastery of languages, giving orations in Greek and Latin and a close reading of a psalm, providing a commentary on the grammatical, logical and rhetorical aspects of the Hebrew text.[28]

These excitements over, there followed a somewhat dismal lunch, where the overseers were served a selection of dishes the scholars typically ate. Presumably this was to confirm that the catering had improved since the departure of the deplorable Mrs Eaton and her goats'-dung puddings. Unbeknown to the commencers, the overseers held a secret meeting during the lunch break. There was only one item on the agenda. Mindful of the Nathaniel Eaton scandal, President Dunster wanted the trustees' prior consent to flog two freshers, both recent arrivals from England, who had been found guilty of 'swearing and ribaldry'. The board agreed and the sentence was carried out once the day's ceremonies were concluded and the guests gone.

After lunch, everyone returned to the hall for formal disputations, where George was able to play out his strongest suit: answering in Latin questions put to him by the examiners. George Downing and his fellow scholars clearly acquitted themselves to the examiners' satisfaction as every commencer was cleared to proceed to the climax of the day's ceremony.[29]

When the class of '42 stepped forward, one at a time, to receive their degrees, Benjamin Woodbridge was first up; George Downing, second in line. According to some authorities, the ranking order was based on a punctilious assessment of the social status of each graduand's family. The colonists were certainly acutely aware of class divisions, with only the quality referred to or addressed as Mister; those between the servant class and the gentry as Goodman and Goodwife (sometimes Goodie for short); and the servant class, frugally, by name alone. President Dunster's biographer claimed that the system was based on that used for establishing who sat where in church and a special committee would be convened 'to attend to this delicate service'.[30]

Yet for a number of reasons, the order of precedence in 1642 cannot be reconciled with the criterion of social standing. Benjamin Woodbridge, the son of a garden-variety Wiltshire vicar, by then dead, migrated to New England to join his elder brother, who had recently wed Mercy, a daughter of Thomas Dudley. It would have been perverse of Harvard's committee-of-delicate-service to place Benjamin Woodbridge ahead of George Downing, whose father, Emmanuel – an alumnus of Trinity Hall, Cambridge and a member of the Honourable Society of the Inner Temple – was by now well established among the social elite of Massachusetts. And although Thomas Dudley had also served as governor, George's uncle, John Winthrop, was the incumbent. It seems unlikely that Harvard would have wished to insult Winthrop, the guest of honour, by suggesting that his rival, Dudley, was more posh. In any case further down the list, in fifth position, came young Henry Saltonstall, whose father, Sir Richard, was a knight – an Esquire, if you please; and, prior to his return to England, indubitably the colony's top nob.

A radical challenge to the social-rank theory emerged from a paper read to the American Antiquarian Society in 1932 by the pre-eminent historian of Harvard, Samuel Eliot Morison. His research demonstrates that there is no consistency in the ranking of siblings or members of the same family over time; and quite frequently a goodman will be placed above classmates of quality lineage. Taking graduation records until the end of the century, Morison also rules out one after another common factor as the basis of class rankings. They do not correspond with the date of enrolment, or with when fees are first paid, or with the order of signing the register on arrival. They are found to be set during the freshman year, so cannot reflect a grade average of academic performance over time, nor the results of any test. They are certainly not in alphabetical order; yet neither are they entirely random.

Morison's conclusion was that in these early years, Harvard's ranking of students was essentially an exercise in predicting relative future prospects – the faculty's subjective assessment, largely on the basis of first impressions, to what degree each would shine in their future careers. The names at the top being, as modern college yearbooks put it, those deemed 'most likely to succeed'.[31]

Benjamin Woodbridge had spent one or two years reading for a bachelor's degree at Magdalen Hall, Oxford. The precise date of Woodbridge's arrival in New England is not known. His time at Oxford may have equipped him with enough academic charisma to propel him straight to the top of his Harvard class, displacing the college's original likely lad, George Downing. Harvard made the wrong call. Woodbridge went back to England, where he wound up as a worthy-but-dull vicar in Newbury.

There is no evidence, however, that the demotion rankled with George in any way. And there was no cause for Lucy Downing to doubt that George had been 'perfected in the Arts'. Shortly after graduating, Downing joined Harvard's faculty, becoming a fellow of the college, working as a tutor until late 1644. In collaboration with another fellow and one of his students, Sam Winthrop, the governor's youngest son, George Downing, in what was to be a rare display of generosity, purchased a parcel of land adjacent to the college and planted it with apple trees. They were quite possibly Roxbury Russets – the first colonial variety to emerge in New England. The orchard was given to the college and became a tranquil spot, exclusively reserved to the faculty, known as the Fellows' Orchard.

After Downing left Harvard to explore the wider world, young Sam Winthrop wrestled with existential anxieties, unable to fathom what God wished him to do. Just like his eldest brother, he dropped out of college without taking a degree. Fearing his father's ire, Sam ran away to Tenerife to become a merchant's clerk, which was as extreme as youthful rebellion could get in a seventeenth-century Puritan setting. As it happens, his father wrote eventually approving the move, but telling Sam he was in the wrong place. Following paternal steers, he moved first to Barbados, later to St Christopher (St Kitts) and finally to Antigua, where a wonder-working providence soon saw him established as a successful sugar planter with an estate full of African slaves. Sam Winthrop's itinerary has him almost exactly following in George Downing's footsteps.

George was in the Caribbean from February to July 1645 as a preacher, tasked with instructing the seamen aboard an island-hopping trading ship. 'I was twice at Barbados, thrice at Antigua, many times at Nevis, but most at St Christopher's; last at Santa Cruz.' 'If you go to Barbados you will see a flourishing island . . .' Downing reported excitedly to John Winthrop Junior. 'I believe they have bought this year no less than a thousand Negroes and the more they buy, the better they are to buy, for in a year and a half they will earn (with God's blessing) as much as they cost.'[32]

Downing was much struck by the importance of owning African slaves in making a fortune in the Caribbean. He called them 'the life of this place' and recommended a strategy of starting out by employing English indentured servants, who could be acquired for next to nothing up front, then putting the revenue they earned into buying African slaves.

It is striking quite how matter-of-fact he was about chattel slavery. Although Massachusetts was the first colony to pass a law making slavery legal, the colonists clearly perceived that there was some moral issue involved, as the statute specified that slaves could only be taken in the course of a just war. Slaves were also to be given legal rights, offered education and allowed to live in closer proximity with the families that owned them than was usual elsewhere.

In 1636, a conflict with the Native American Pequot tribe blew up, following the murder of a number of fur traders in Connecticut. The Saybrook commander, Lion

Gardiner, recorded a chilling conversation with a Pequot wearing 'an Englishman's coat'. The Pequot told him that he had killed colonists and could kill more 'like mosquitoes' and intended to go to Connecticut to do just that. He threatened to slaughter 'men, women and children' and to take away 'horses, cows and hogs'. He too was utterly matter-of-fact about his intentions.[33]

The response of the colonists was immediate and genocidal. Nearly 500 of the tribe – including women and children – burned to death within the palisade of one their fortified villages at Mystic in one of the early engagements of the war. The colonists' commander on the ground declared that the ease with which the conflagration had started was a sure sign that God was on their side. The Almighty had, John Mason said, 'laughed his enemies and the enemies of his people to scorn' by turning the village into a fiery oven. After a series of further easy victories, the colonists decided to extirpate the tribe. Their villages were destroyed and so was their social identity: the survivors were forbidden to use the Pequot appellation in perpetuity. Some were redistributed among other neighbouring tribes, but since it was deemed that the campaign qualified as a 'just war', the remainder were taken as slaves. A number of the new slave owners travelled down to Barbados or Virginia to exchange their Pequots for African slaves. The rules, it appears, were flexible enough to accommodate this arrangement.

By now some of the Boston merchants were pioneering a way to profit from the transatlantic slave trade without actually landing any slaves on Massachusetts soil. A ship went from Boston to Maio in the Cape Verde Islands and purchased Africans in the slave market there. The ship then dropped the Africans at Barbados, exchanging slaves for molasses, which travelled home to Boston to be processed into rum, which was in turn shipped to the Gambia to be exchanged for more slaves. And so the whole cycle would repeat itself indefinitely, vastly enriching the Boston ship owners, whose vessels never sailed empty.

The Civil War in England, however, was causing a severe servant shortage throughout the American colonies. Poor young men no longer went into service, they joined the army. The problem was exacerbated by the fact that the Massachusetts economy was changing rapidly. Both the Downing and Winthrop families, together with a group of London-based merchants, had invested in a new ironworks that would make the colony self-sufficient in a wide range of manufactures. The ironworks and the spin-off businesses it would stimulate would soon need a supply of cheap labour. And it was not just the younger generation of entrepreneurial Puritans, such as George Downing, who were proposing the deregulation of slavery. His father, Emmanuel Downing, was lobbying the governor with a scheme that was astonishing in its brazen cynicism. What if, Emmanuel Downing proposed, a 'just war' could be contrived against the Narragansetts, an Algonquian tribe who were plentiful in the area around Rhode Island, and the Lord should deliver into the hands of the colonists 'men, women and children enough to exchange for Africans'? This should not be treated as a pipe dream, he insisted. The problem had become urgent. 'I do not see how we can thrive,' he told the governor, 'unless we get a stock of slaves sufficient to do our business.'[34] George Downing took his father's words to heart and when he found himself, a few years later, in a position to help the ironworks resolve its labour crisis, he did so.

He clearly enjoyed his Caribbean adventure and, not being unduly modest, did not downplay how very much his hosts wished him to tarry longer in their island paradise. 'If you go to Antigua,' he told his cousin, 'you shall meet with a very understanding, courteous gentleman, Captain Ashton, the island's governor, with whom I am intimate. His love towards me was singular and I know that he will be wondrous glad to see you.' At Nevis, Governor Lake was 'likewise importunate for me to stay'.[35]

By 1645 the First Civil War in England was approaching its climax and the conflict had spilled over into the Americas. In broad terms, Virginia and Maryland were Royalist, while the north-eastern seaboard leaned towards Parliament. In the Caribbean the situation was complicated by the fact that islands had proprietors back in England whose loyalties did not always match those of the residents of the islands. Some of the Caribbean colonies changed sides during the war. And it was not simply a matter of allegiance. The war had made the seas perilous for everyone. The system of letters of marque to license piracy was now used by both sides, each commissioning privateers to attack the ships of the other. Even as George Downing went from island to island in his ship selling high-quality linen to the planters, not so very far away, aboard the armed tobacco ship *Reformation*, Richard Ingle, a Puritan pirate, was plundering the coast of Catholic Maryland in the name of Parliament. Meanwhile ships travelling to England from Boston had to take their chances with Royalist picaroons operating from Irish ports.[36]

George Downing's return to England appears to have been a spontaneous decision. In late August 1645, he told John Winthrop Junior that his ship was bound for England, but would soon return to the Caribbean on its way to New

England. He proposed that the pair should meet up in either Antigua or one of the other islands he had recommended. But the wanderer never returned. A few months later, Governor Winthrop recorded in his journal that George Downing 'continued in the ship to England and being a very able scholar and of a ready wit and fluent utterance was soon taken notice of' and had been appointed as a chaplain to Colonel Okey's regiment in Lord Fairfax's New Model Army.[37]

# CHAPTER 2

# Army versus Parliament

## *Old England, 1646–8*

BY THE TIME George Downing joined his regiment, the First Civil War was over, the conflict briefly paused. The unit to which he had been assigned, Colonel John Okey's regiment of dragoons, was created as part of the New Model Army in 1645 on the initiative of Lord Fairfax, the army's supreme commander or Lord General. It drew its officers and most of its men from a number of existing formations in the various regional association armies. Some came from the regiment previously commanded by John Lilburne, the future Leveller leader; others from a unit commanded by a Scottish officer, James Holborne; and yet others from Sir Arthur Hesilrige's regiment. Sir Arthur himself had laid aside his sword for a time to devote himself to politics. England's Puritans broadly divided into two groups: Presbyterians and Independents. Sir Arthur was one of the leaders of the Independents in Parliament.[1]

The New Model Army was itself only a little over a year old at this time. It was a highly disciplined, well trained, immaculately turned out and thoroughly professional force that was regarded as a huge improvement on the regionally based armies that it would largely replace. George Downing's position would most likely have been secured for him by Sir Arthur Hesilrige, who was a good friend of George's father. Emmanuel Downing had been visiting the politician to discuss various business ventures in the weeks leading up to George's arrival. Hugh Peter was also with the New Model Army at this time, serving as chaplain to the artillery train. Peter was particularly close to the army's second in command, Oliver Cromwell. The Lieutenant General, as Lord Fairfax's deputy was styled, was also one of the leaders of the Independent faction in the House of Commons.

*Colonel Okey*

George Downing was spotted only twice in 1646; once by a woman called Lydia Banks in Maidstone, Kent, who sent a message to Lucy and Emmanuel Downing via her sister, who lived in Salem. Lydia Banks wanted to say what an inspiring sermonizer George was. She had heard him preach the previous Sunday and wanted his family to know they could be proud of him.[2] The second sighting was in Hackney, where John Okey owned a large house, Barbour's Bern. Downing preached a highly political sermon attacking the Common Council of the City of London. Downing identified himself with the Independents, who were at odds with a conservative, Presbyterian establishment who wanted a negotiated settlement with the King. The Independent Puritans were similar in both theology and politics to the Puritans of New England and George fitted in effortlessly.

His performance on this occasion attracted hostile notices from a leading Presbyterian who remarked on the similarity in his preaching style with that of Hugh Peter. The Presbyterians particularly loathed Peter, whom they blamed for all kinds of radicalism in the army.[3]

The New Model Army had recruited a large assortment of political and religious dissenters. Some advanced a radical agenda. An emerging group, the Levellers, comprised egalitarians agitating for universal male suffrage and other constitutional reforms. The Nonconformist religious sects, such as Baptists, Anabaptists and even Catabaptists, demanded toleration and religious pluralism. The Independent MPs offered political protection to the Levellers and the various Nonconformists in exchange for their – and, by extension, the army's – support against the Presbyterian bloc in Parliament.

The politician who probably aroused the most antipathy among the Independents and the soldiery was the MP Denzil Holles. In 1645 Cromwell was warned that Holles and a group of his fellow Presbyterians were having secret contacts with the Royalists without Parliament's permission. The moment the First Civil War ended, Holles pressed to disband a large part of the army and to pack the rest off to Ireland.

This policy amounted to gross ingratitude: the army had, after all, just won the war; but Holles knew it was sound politics for a Presbyterian. The nation's merchants and landowners resented paying taxes to support the army; and local communities in districts where the troops were billeted were fed up with having to provide soldiers with board and lodging. Moreover, disbandment would leave the Independents disarmed and therefore impotent.

The soldiers, for their part, had good grounds for resentment. Their pay was in arrears and some were now facing irksome legal actions relating to horses or property they had requisitioned, or debts they had incurred, while on army business during the war. All ranks were calling for Parliament to indemnify them against these vexatious claims.

An important role of a regimental chaplain at this time was to elevate and maintain morale. During the First Civil War, Hugh Peter was known for going among the ranks before a battle with a Bible in one hand and a weapon in the other, preaching motivational sermons. Peter's signature histrionics, featuring soaring emotions and intense spirituality, quietened soldiers' fears and helped them brace themselves for the fight. George Downing arguably faced a different challenge in this brief interval of peace. He had to listen to the complaints of Colonel Okey's dragoons and respond sympathetically to them. Above all, he needed to reassure the soldiers that God and the Independents would ensure that Parliament did right by them. In a letter to his uncle, Governor Winthrop, he described this difficult time: 'We have since the sheathing of the sword sometimes enjoyed our lucid intervals, but then all hath quickly been o'erclouded, that no mortal eye could in the face of things see anything but ruin.'[4]

The root cause of the present divisions, Downing explained, was that different groups had such divergent motives for fighting in the first place. Some had fought against the King because they believed he was influenced by evil counsellors; others simply because he was a king; some fought for the installation of Presbyterian church government and the pulling down of episcopy; yet others had fought against oppression in general. For as long as the war lasted, these men of disparate motivation held together against a common enemy; once the fighting stopped, they simply fell apart.

Chaplains in the New Model Army tended not to remain with their regiments all the time and sometimes their service lasted only a few months.[5] There are no surviving records of precisely when and where Downing served with Colonel Okey's dragoons, but there are records of the dragoons' deployments in 1647 and evidence that Downing was familiar with the details of the dispute between Parliament and the army that dominated England's politics throughout that year.

Back in April 1646, Charles I rightly judged that he had lost the First Civil War. He was in Oxford at the time and knew that very soon the Roundhead army would surround the city and place it under siege. He calculated that he would fare better if he were to surrender to the Scottish Covenanter army rather than to the English Parliamentarians and asked a French diplomat to broker a deal. In early May, just before Oxford was fully invested, he slipped out of town on the sly. The King had trimmed his hair and beard and disguised himself in clerical weeds. He travelled incognito to Newark, where the Scottish Covenanter army, which was then in alliance with the English Parliament, was besieging a Royalist fortress. Charles I duly surrendered to the Scots, who took him to Newcastle, where they made him sign the Covenant – a solemn vow to uphold Presbyterianism.

Charles began the first in a long series of negotiations in which he tried to play off the Scots against the English, the Presbyterians against the Independents and Parliament against the army. He did not act in good faith and ended up serially exasperating each of his several interlocutors. At the beginning of January 1647, the Scots sold the King to the English Parliament. He was taken to Holdenby House in Northamptonshire, where two troops of Colonel Okey's dragoons were among the guard.

Even while under house arrest, Charles managed to keep in contact with his courtiers and advisers. He would ride out with his escort along the local lanes. On one occasion, at a narrow bridge, the King passed close to a countryman who was carrying a fishing rod. What happened next, it transpired, was a carefully executed brush pass, part of the repertoire of the secret agent down the ages. One of the guards became suspicious and the party halted. The rough-looking countryman turned out to be Humphrey Bosville, a Kentish squire of known Royalist allegiance. The King was found in possession of a packet of papers that he should not have had.[6]

Holles meanwhile had further antagonized the army. When the soldiers circulated a petition asking for their grievances to be redressed, he countered with a motion in the Commons called the Declaration of Dislike, which sought to suppress the petition and warned that any future ones would be regarded as mutiny. When some of the soldiers were called before Parliament to explain their actions, Holles toyed with the idea of hanging one of them as an example to the rest. Later, he sponsored a plot to hijack the artillery train that was then at Oxford. The plan was to take the guns to London and lock them in the Tower. Holles was aiming to set up a rival force to the New Model Army, built around the London Trained Bands, a formation largely recruited from the City of London and officered by reliable Presbyterian cronies.

As these plans developed, Oliver Cromwell hosted a modest lunch – reportedly of 'small beer and bread and butter' – in the garden of his home in London's Drury Lane. Intelligence was brought to the gathering indicating that Holles's design to confiscate the army's big guns had been frustrated. A young officer with Leveller sympathies, Cornet George Joyce, had seized the artillery train at Oxford. He then came to the lunch to confer about his next move. Holles was now believed to be preparing to snatch the King away from the army and bring him to London to do an exclusive deal with the Presbyterians. After a brief conversation with Cromwell, Joyce rode on towards Holdenby at the head of a scratch force of cavalry, where he took charge of the king's person on the night of 1 June; some days later scooping him up and taking him on in the direction of Newmarket, where Lord Fairfax was holding a rendezvous of his New Model Army.[7]

The King's party eventually put up at a remote manor house at Childerley, just north of the road from St Neots to Cambridge. Childerley Hall was the home of Lady Cutts, the widow of a recently deceased MP. Oliver Cromwell rode up to the house on 7 June to hold discreet talks with the King.

Between Childerley and Royston, where the army encamped a short time later, lie the villages of Gamlingay, East Hatley, Croydon and Clopton, which would all one day become the personal property of George Downing. It is not known when Downing first set eyes on these fair acres or conceived an ambition to make them his own, but Colonel Okey's dragoons, as well as being stationed at Holdenby, went on to take part in the long, slow and somewhat menacing movement of the army from Cambridgeshire to London during the summer of 1647.

The army resisted forced disbandment. It spelled out its grievances to Parliament in clear terms. It demanded that Denzil Holles and ten of his associates withdraw from the house, and for a period they did. When members of the London Trained Bands began intimidating Independent MPs, Sir Arthur Hesilrige organized their flight from Westminster to seek the protection of the army. Finally, on a day of extraordinary anticipation and tension, the New Model Army seized key points throughout the capital. Lord Fairfax marched his men through the City to Westminster, right up to the House of Commons. George Downing wrote to his uncle about 'Holles and his party's high endeavours against the army' and 'how near this brought us to blood'.[8]

By the end of the year the King, who had been installed by the army at Hampton Court, had removed himself to the Isle of Wight, where he became involved in fresh intrigues.

He encouraged a group of Scottish noblemen under the Duke of Hamilton to invade England – an adventure that became known as the Engagement. The invasion – in 1648 – was timed to coincide with Royalist uprisings in different parts of the country, and possibly with Presbyterian uprisings too.

This would be the Second Civil War – the first of George Downing's wars. In late 1647, Downing was tapped to become chaplain and private secretary to Sir Arthur Hesilrige, living at his house in Canonbury. It was likely for this reason that Downing did not accompany John Okey to the Putney Debates that autumn, where representatives of the soldiers from each regiment debated with grandees including Cromwell and Ireton. Hesilrige was appointed governor of Newcastle-upon-Tyne and George Downing went north with him in March of 1648.

## *Tynemouth, August 1648*

One afternoon in early August, between two and three o'clock, Lieutenant Colonel Henry Lilburne, governor of Tynemouth Castle, did something utterly unexpected and out of character. This officer had a long record of service to Parliament; was the brother of the Leveller leader, Freeborn John Lilburne; and had served under Sir Arthur Hesilrige for seven years. Yet quite suddenly, he turned his coat and declared for the King. He told his soldiers that they must now support the King too, and when a loyal corporal insisted that he was still for the Parliament, Lilburne ran him through with his sword. A substantial number of disaffected sailors, whether by coincidence or design or simply because they were drunk, came to join the revolt and were let into the castle. Lilburne then began taking potshots with his cannon at random targets in the vicinity.

*Sir Arthur Hesilrige*

News of Lilburne's defection was quickly brought to Sir Arthur Hesilrige at Newcastle. This was probably George Downing's first encounter of a military emergency of any moment. Hesilrige was decisive. He ordered a force of infantry to make their way to Tynemouth, supported by one hundred dragoons. He also sent a boat filled with ladders downriver.[9]

The plan was to attack by night. As the storming party approached the fortifications at half-past one in the morning, Lilburne began firing on them with his cannon.

Undeterred, the invaders swarmed up the walls on their ladders, only to find the ladders were too short. Still undeterred, they somehow scrambled over the parapet and took the castle. The whole affair was over in just half a day. Henry Lilburne's body was found among the dead.

The speed, brio and matter-of-factness with which the revolt was dealt with were characteristic of the Second Civil War, which was largely over within seven months. Lord Fairfax dealt briskly with Royalist uprisings in Kent and Essex, while Oliver Cromwell did the same in Wales, before racing up to Lancashire to trounce the main force of the invading Scots at the Battle of Preston. Hugh Peter had a cameo role in securing the Scottish commander's eventual surrender to Major General Lambert at Uttoxeter. By the time the news had crossed the Atlantic, his part had become somewhat inflated. 'My brother Peter took the Duke of Hamilton prisoner,' John Winthrop exulted in Boston.[10]

## *The Borders of Scotland, September 1648*

George Downing's initiation into the world of political intrigue occurred in the febrile aftermath of the Second Civil War. In his eight months as chaplain and secretary to Sir Arthur Hesilrige he had experienced politics only as a detached and callow observer. Now he was being drawn right into the most sensitive affairs of state, accompanying military leaders to secret talks in Scotland. He might even get a chance to prove himself directly to Oliver Cromwell himself. Like his mentor Hugh Peter, Downing was unusually adept at switching between the material and the spiritual, and it was well known that Cromwell liked his chaplains to be men of action and his officers to be spiritually assiduous.

Cromwell arrived in the Borders in mid-September. He set up his headquarters by the sea at the manor house of Cheswick, six miles south of Berwick-upon-Tweed. Even though he had only so recently beaten the Duke of Hamilton's Scottish army at Preston, Cromwell chose not to approach Scotland in the manner of a triumphalist victor coming to claim his spoils. He was studiedly unthreatening, even diplomatically emollient in his communications with the Marquis of Argyle, Scotland's new political leader. Cromwell wished to dispel any anxiety arising from his sudden appearance on Scotland's doorstep at the head of an army.

*Archibald Campbell, Marquis of Argyle*

Argyle was the leader of the Kirk party, or 'honest party' as Cromwell liked to call it, which had always opposed the Engagement – the Scots' deal with the King that led to their disastrous invasion of England. Cromwell asked Argyle to grant accreditation to three individuals sent ahead as an advance party. These were Colonel John Bright, Scoutmaster General Rowe and Mr Robert Stapylton.[11]

Colonel Bright – a bluff, practical soldier from Yorkshire – was there to supervise the withdrawal of Scottish garrisons from the border towns of Berwick and Carlisle and replace them with English troops. The recovery of these towns, captured during the recent hostilities, was the declared purpose of Cromwell's expedition. But there was another motive, clandestine and unspoken, which was why the head of military intelligence was among the delegation. William Rowe's secret mission was to form a political alliance with the most rigid Covenanters, who were trying to consolidate their control over Scotland's government. Rowe knew the territory. In 1643, he had helped negotiate the agreement that brought the Scottish Presbyterians in to fight on Parliament's side during the First Civil War. In the Borders, Cromwell's overarching aim was to lock the Royalists out of Scottish affairs altogether so that Scotland's army would not invade England again.

The third member of the team, Robert Stapylton, was one of Cromwell's chaplains. His job was to square influential ministers of the Kirk. Many clerics from the radical Covenanter tradition had a reputation for being obdurate, pernickety and impossible to deal with. Stapylton's task was to charm them out of their stubborn censoriousness and get them to approve Cromwell's schemes.

Stapylton may have had other designs in mind, perhaps

as covert as those of Rowe. For the chaplain was licensed to range far beyond religious affairs, operating as a political fixer behind the Arras. Like George Downing, he would later become involved in intelligence work and travel on diplomatic missions overseas and even be entrusted with a delicate and personal assignment, haggling with the fiancé's father over the details of a prenuptial agreement when Cromwell's son Richard became engaged to be married.[12]

Stapylton was already riding high in Cromwell's favour, whereas the twenty-five-year-old Downing was only now catching the Lieutenant General's talent-spotting eye. In Peter and Hesilrige, Downing had a pair of well-placed sponsors to vouch for his intelligence and industry, but the New Englander remained untested in an operational context. To progress in his career, Downing needed to carry out some act of service conspicuously well. This he achieved through silent and stealthy back-channel manoeuvres to further the relationship with Argyle and the Kirk party. Downing's involvement was clearly impressive, for Hesilrige's young amanuensis would soon have his own place in Cromwell's retinue and be singled out for a vital intelligence-gathering mission of the highest political complexity. Indeed, before long Cromwell would promote Downing to the position of Scoutmaster General, with the salary and bragging rights of a senior officer.

Before leading his party over the border into Scotland, Cromwell made another gesture of conciliation; one that was both morally sincere and politically theatrical. Some soldiers from a Durham regiment had gone across the Tweed near Norham Castle and stolen horses from farms on the Scottish bank. The Lieutenant General compelled the thieves to return the rustled horses straight away, cashiered their cornet on the spot and even suspended their colonel. Some of this, at least, may have been performative. The colonel, a chum of Hesilrige, was quietly reinstated some weeks later. But Cromwell was in earnest when he issued a dire warning to his soldiers that if any of them were ever caught stealing or looting they would face the death penalty. The Committee of Estates, which governed Scotland when its parliament was not in session, was sufficiently grateful for Cromwell's gesture that it declared itself ready to welcome the English expeditionary force on to Scottish soil.

In its own advance party the Scots had included the charismatic Archibald Strachan (pronounced *Strawn*). A man of intense and radical religiosity, Strachan was a famously fearless soldier who had served for several years in the English parliamentary army as an officer of dragoons. When the Engagement began, Strachan not only refused to have anything to do with it, but actually went so far as to ride into England to side with Cromwell, fighting under English parliamentary colours at the Battle of Preston. But now he had returned to serve Argyle's faction and had been appointed to carry secret letters back and forth between Argyle and Cromwell. This fact, along with his combination of righteous faith and martial energy, would have marked him out to a watchful Downing as an obvious contact to cultivate; and so might the elbow-gripping gossip that followed in the soldier's wake. Word had it that there was something 'very lewd' in Strachan's past. Knowledge like this could unpick a lock.[13]

Cromwell and his party forded the Tweed and set up headquarters two miles into Scotland at a tower house belonging to a local laird, Lord Mordington. The Marquis of Argyle and other leaders rode there to parley with the Lieutenant General. Their business was briskly executed. The Scots agreed to the handover of Berwick and Carlisle, though there was a brief hiatus as the commander of the Berwick garrison demanded further ratification of his orders to render the town to the English. The sign-off was eventually provided to settle his hash.

While waiting for this delayed resolution, a restive Cromwell had sent a squad of infantry under Colonel Thomas Pride to probe the garrison's defences. Pride's men drove all the sheep out of the fields beneath Berwick's bastioned walls, as if to signal to the Scots inside that if their occupation were to continue any longer, it must do so without the prospect of dinner. As a spectacular Parthian shot, Pride blew up the guardhouse on the town's bridge. At last Cromwell was able to report to London that, as of 30 September, Berwick-upon-Tweed was fully restored to Parliament's control and Sir Arthur Hesilrige had 'turned out the malignant mayor and put an honest man in his room'.[14]

Once an English garrison had been installed at Berwick, Sir Arthur appointed a governor for the town. His choice was a New England veteran well known to Downing: Colonel George Fenwick, lately governor of Saybrook, the fortified condominium on the Connecticut River. When Cromwell, Hesilrige, Hampden and Pym had all decided, for their different reasons, not to move to America after all, Fenwick, along with Downing's cousin John Winthrop Junior, had been left with a colony stripped of its *raison d'être* and a real-estate proposition without any customers. No other rich Englishmen could be found to take up the lots initially reserved for the Puritan grandees. So while Downing was away in the Caribbean, Fenwick and Winthrop decided to sell Saybrook and its fort to the nearby Connecticut Colony in 1644. Around this time, George Fenwick's wife died in childbirth and he had no heart to remain. Despite owning land in Connecticut and being elected as a magistrate, the native Northumbrian abandoned his colonial adventures and sailed home for good.

Within a few months of his return in 1645, Fenwick was selected as Member of Parliament for Morpeth at the age of forty-four. During the Second Civil War he led a regiment of local militia. Much of the land around Berwick belonged to old friends or relations and Fenwick was an ideal choice for the governorship of the garrison. He would have eyes and ears in every village. He would know where new recruits and fresh horses could be found; who might be hoarding food, and where.

While the Lieutenant General was hugger-mugger with the Marquis of Argyle at Mordington, part of his army had been racing northwards without him. Major General Lambert, with four regiments of cavalry and two troops of dragoons, set up camp at Seton House near Tranent in East Lothian, posting vedettes within ten miles of Edinburgh's city limits. Meanwhile, six regiments of infantry bivouacked around a tower overlooking a narrow defile at Cockburnspath, securing both the cavalry's rear and the road between Berwick and the port of Dunbar.

## *Edinburgh, October 1648*

Pausing only to hold a secret meeting with the Leveller, John Lilburne, Cromwell joined Lambert at Seton.[15] Sir Arthur Hesilrige and George Downing rode with him. The pace of events was about to pick up. Next day, Cromwell's party was welcomed into Edinburgh by the Scottish general James Holborne, who arrived at Seton with a coach for the visitors. As they entered the city, an escort supplied by Argyle's own regiment led them with great ceremony to Moray House in the Canongate, where they would remain for three nights.

*Moray House in the Canongate, Edinburgh*

On the first day, Wednesday 4 October, Cromwell received a stream of VIPs from the Scottish Parliament, the Committee of Estates and the Kirk. That evening, Argyle and his close ally Lord Wariston joined him for a working dinner. Argyle had led opposition to the Engagement in the Scottish Parliament, and after its ignominious defeat at Preston had managed to wrest control of Scotland's government from the Duke of Hamilton's party. His continuing dominance, though, was not at all assured. The marquis needed Cromwell's help to strengthen his political position.

The Scottish army that fought for the Engagement was now in the process of disbanding. Thousands of trained soldiers were being set loose on the streets of Glasgow, Stirling and Edinburgh. Many of them had received no pay for several months. Fortunately for Argyle, Cromwell had just received a message from London confirming that Parliament had voted to approve financial assistance to the Kirk party. He agreed to leave Lambert behind in Scotland with a force sufficient to keep the peace until Argyle's government was secure. On Thursday, however, he added a stipulation to the deal: anyone who had taken part in the Engagement was not merely to be barred from military service, they must also be disqualified from every public office and position of trust.

Later that day, three ministers of the Kirk visited Cromwell in the Canongate. Robert Blair, a former moderator of the General Assembly, led the delegation. Downing would already have met him years before, in New England, had it not been for some catastrophic Atlantic weather. Back in 1636, Blair was one of a group of Presbyterian clergymen who decided to join the Puritan migration to Massachusetts. They had a ship specially built for them in Belfast after striking up a correspondence with Downing's cousin, John Winthrop Junior. A party of 140 migrants duly set sail on the *Eagle Wing* that autumn.[16]

They were not alone. Also on board was a consignment of children who had been procured for the Bay Colony by Sir John Clotworthy, an associate of Emmanuel Downing in County Antrim. Very little is known about the trafficking of these children because Clotworthy was in the habit of encrypting his letters such that they could only be read with a casement. This was a sheet of paper into which an irregular sequence of rectangles had been cut. When superimposed on a text, a secret message appeared in its windows. The children were probably intended to work as indentured servants.[17]

A hurricane blew up off the coast of Newfoundland, tearing into the ship's rigging and fracturing her rudder. While the sailors were trying to repair the damage, Blair and John Livingstone, a fellow minister, addressed an urgent enquiry to their fellow passengers: was it truly God's will that they should be travelling to Massachusetts after all? The clergy deemed it best to let God answer this question himself. If he sent them better weather, they would persevere. If not, they would apologize for their presumption and turn back home. As it happened, the Almighty sent them a storm even worse than the first. So it was that the *Eagle Wing* returned in early November to Carrickfergus Bay, where her ill-fated voyage had begun. Although the expedition was an utter failure, it nonetheless inflated the reputations of Blair and Livingstone as men of reliably keen judgement in discerning the intimations of providence – something that would have profound implications for Scotland's political future. The children were presumably returned to Clotworthy's clutches. There appears to be no further word about them.

A dozen years later, emerging from Moray House, Robert Blair now delivered his judgement on Oliver Cromwell's character. The three Presbyterian ministers had interrogated the English general about his views on church government, religious tolerance and the monarchy. He had assured them that he was in favour of the monarchy and pledged his continuing support for the Stuart dynasty; and asserted that he was against religious toleration. But he refused to be drawn on church government, telling them only that he was still giving the matter careful consideration.

'I am very pleased to hear this man speak as he does,' gushed David Dickson as the trio spilled out onto the Canongate after the meeting. 'And do you believe him?' countered Blair. 'If you knew him as well as I do, you would not believe one word he says. He is an egregious dissembler.'[18]

Cromwell was indeed disingenuous in his responses that day. On the question of church government, Cromwell, as an Independent, was decidedly in favour of local congregations retaining autonomy over their own affairs. He repudiated both the bishops in the traditional model of Anglican church government, and the worthy elders of the Presbyterian alternative. Insofar as Cromwell gave Presbyterianism any consideration at this time, it was with a view to frustrating it. While he was away in Scotland, the English Parliament, where the Presbyterians held sway, had been negotiating with the King on the Isle of Wight. According to the latest news to reach the Canongate, a deal was imminent that would likely provide for Presbyterianism to be introduced throughout England for a trial period of three years. This would likely require the destruction of the New Model Army so that religious uniformity could be imposed without fear of armed resistance from the many Nonconformists in its ranks.

Cromwell could hardly discuss such issues with the three Scottish ministers who descended on him that day. He was not free to write his own ticket in Edinburgh. He had come as a military commander, but was only the Lieutenant

General, not Lord General; it remained Thomas Fairfax's army. On political matters, Cromwell was answerable to the English Parliament, where many of his colleagues were rivals, not allies. He knew that anything he said to the representatives of the Kirk would certainly be reported straight back to the Presbyterian leadership in London.

When addressing the question of religious toleration, Cromwell avoided telling Robert Blair a direct lie only through sophistry. Strictly speaking, complete religious toleration would include Catholicism. Since he genuinely was not considering any concessions to popery in England, Cromwell felt able to claim, with a deadpan expression and a muted conscience, that he 'altogether opposed toleration'. This formulation allowed him to sidestep the very issue about which Robert Blair most wished to confront him: the presence of heretical sectaries among the soldiery.

The Independents had an informal alliance with Baptists, Separatists and members of an emergent Millennialist group styling themselves 'the Fifth Monarchy Men'. These minorities were disproportionately well represented in the army, as they were among the Levellers, whose political voice was growing louder. The Independents offered broad religious tolerance in exchange for political and military cooperation against the Presbyterians. Argyle's Covenanters, rigid Presbyterians to a man, looked upon these groupuscules with vehement contempt. Robert Blair made clear to Cromwell early on in their meeting that he and his Kirk colleagues regarded the sect-infested English army as the last remaining obstacle to completing the work of the Reformation. They wanted England brought into line with Scotland, with total uniformity of doctrine and the Presbyterian system of church government legally enforced in both kingdoms. Cromwell was uneasily aware that many in the English Parliament felt the same way and at this very moment might well be finalizing an agreement with the King to bring such schemes to fruition.

The vexed issue of toleration (sometimes termed 'liberty of conscience') had long divided Puritans on both sides of the Atlantic. In New England, the elder John Winthrop had set his face like flint against it. The governor's obduracy had led to a rupture with his friend Roger Williams, one of the early colonial pioneers, who, pushed out of his post as pastor of the church at Salem, went off to found his own colony at Providence, Rhode Island. For those who did not see eye to eye with the Massachusetts leadership, Williams's community became a place of sanctuary, particularly for New England's Baptists. But Williams was well connected with the Independent leadership in London. He had served as chaplain to one of Oliver Cromwell's cousins and was a close friend of Sir Henry Vane, with whom he stayed on a long visit to England in 1643 while preparing the publication of a book championing toleration.

During his tour of the Caribbean, George Downing had noticed how the colony's religious intolerance damaged Massachusetts's reputation. 'The law of banishment for conscience,' he warned John Winthrop Junior, '. . . makes us stink everywhere.'[19]

Meanwhile, Hugh Peter, who had replaced Williams at Salem, was now an enthusiast for toleration too, having spotted its potential for advancing the Independent cause in England. Peter promoted a rainbow alliance of the rest of the godly versus the Presbyterians.

Cromwell himself favoured toleration; and not only because it suited him politically to do so. It was not the principle of religious freedom that swung him in favour of a policy that did not extend beyond godly Protestants, but rather, it appears, the feeling that persecuting or killing a person simply for following the dictates of their conscience was an action unbecoming in a saint. For his part, Robert Blair found any such toleration utterly repugnant.[20]

The twenty-five-year-old Downing, absorbed in these talks, witnessed a masterclass in the art of evasion, learning how political expediency may require even the godly to tell fibs. Oliver Cromwell was not yet the statesman he would one day become, but in the Canongate he showed himself already adept in performing the ethical acrobatics that statecraft demands.

But there was a starker untruth. Cromwell's unqualified pledge of allegiance both to the institution of monarchy and to the royal house of Stuart now seems a shockingly brazen deceit. Four months later, the King will be tried and beheaded and Cromwell and his party will institute a new republican government in London. As he sits with the Covenanters in Edinburgh that day, is Cromwell knowingly working towards this outcome, the script already written, Charles I's end irrevocably sealed? There have been suggestions that Cromwell entered into a conspiracy with the Covenanters in October 1648. 'What passed among them came not to be known infallibly,' recalled the Scottish clergyman Henry Guthry, in his memoirs, 'but it was talked very loud that he did communicate to them his design in reference to the King and had their assent thereto.'[21]

Guthry, though, was hardly an impartial or reliable witness. At the time of the Canongate talks, he was minister at the Church of the Holy Rude in Stirling; but just a month later, he was ejected from his position as the Kirk rid itself of anyone who had supported the Engagement. Being summarily deprived of his living may well have influenced Guthry's recollection of what was 'talked very loud' at that time. Besides, there was no good reason for Oliver Cromwell to share such a momentous secret with outsiders, particular those as temperamentally volatile as the Kirk party. The Covenanters, as it transpired, were furious when the King was convicted and lobbied hard against his execution, insisting that the Covenant itself imposed an obligation upon them to support him.

Radical elements in the English army had for some time insisted that the King must be called to account for the bloodletting of the Civil War. Indeed, the notion of 'blood guilt' had been part of anti-Royalist rhetoric since the early days of the conflict. The death of innocents cried out for vengeance, the soldiers insisted to one another and to their officers: the King must answer for it. And the longer the soldiers' other grievances went unaddressed – particularly in relation to pay and indemnity – and their calls for political and constitutional reform went unheeded, the more they thirsted for a reckoning. This was partly a gnawing urge for expiation, rooted in religion and superstitious anxieties. Whenever God was displeased, and providence cast a cold eye upon their projects, the soldiers would remind themselves that the blood of the righteous dead remained, to their shame, yet unavenged.

At an army prayer meeting in Windsor in April 1648, Cromwell had invited his officers to interrogate all their latest actions so thoroughly as to identify what might have so vexed their heavenly father that once again He had let chaos loose upon the land. With a nudge from Cromwell, they settled on an answer: Parliament's negotiations with the King were the source and fountainhead of the nation's sorrows.

During the Second Civil War, even men of meek temperament began to join the clamour for justice. The fresh bloodletting was unjustifiable. And the fact that Charles I had invited a foreign army to invade England meant that talk of Treason was no longer intemperate rhetoric, but a plausible legal indictment. Cromwell, his son-in-law Henry Ireton and other grandees were now inclining in a more radical direction, exasperated both by the King's slippery scheming with the Presbyterians, and by the Presbyterians' slippery scheming with the King.[22]

But was there anything so well developed in the minds of the Independent party leadership, at this juncture, as a 'design' to submit to the Scots for approval? If Cromwell really did broach the topic in Edinburgh, he could surely only have done so privately with the Marquis of Argyle, and perhaps only in terms of a forced abdication and exile, rather than the beheading of a king. Such an ambition, of course, would have been entirely consistent with the answer Cromwell gave Robert Blair.

Oliver Cromwell's own account of the Edinburgh visit was sent to the Speaker from Dalhousie on 9 October 1648 and read to Parliament one week later. Unusually, a second letter covering much the same ground was also read to the House on that same day, presented as a letter from the Lieutenant General's quarters at Carlisle. A filleted, toned-down version of this letter can be found in John Rushworth's *Proceedings in Parliament*, but the unexpurgated – full-throated – version was the one prepared as a pamphlet for general sale at the sign of the Black Spread Eagle. This radical publishing house in St Paul's churchyard belonged to Giles Calvert, whose clientele included the Levellers John Lilburne and William Walwyn, the Digger Gerard Winstanley and a clutch of emergent Ranters.

*A True Account of the Great Expressions of Love from the Noblemen, Ministers & Commons of the Kingdom of Scotland unto Lieutenant General Cromwell & the Officers and Soldiers under his command – Declared in a Letter to a Friend* is a decidedly upbeat tract. It reads as if someone had passed Cromwell's letter to the Speaker on to an ambitious young aide, with orders to accentuate the positive. Cromwell's visit to Scotland is presented as a vast diplomatic triumph. *Great Expressions of Love* was published anonymously. But the text contains a number of clues, perhaps even giveaways, as to its authorship.[23]

Crafted propaganda of this kind would generally be the work of more than one hand. It is easy to imagine Scoutmaster Rowe (and perhaps Mr Stapylton) putting in their twopenn'orth on the document's scope on the road to Carlisle; and some basic drafting may have been undertaken by Cromwell's secretary Robert Spavin. But since the Lieutenant General liked to have his successes announced with much flourish by Hugh Peter, it would have been odd had he not made use of the sorcerer's apprentice, then so conveniently to hand.

The pamphlet is written in the first person, with a consistent and distinctive narrative voice, from the viewpoint of someone who has been at Seton immediately prior to Edinburgh, and who is lodging at Moray House for the duration of the visit. The narrator is either present at the sequence of meetings between Cromwell and his many visitors or very thoroughly briefed on them afterwards.

Whereas Oliver Cromwell makes no mention of his

encounter with the three ministers of the Kirk in his own report, perhaps intuiting that things have not gone so well as he had hoped, his rapporteur is certain that the meeting has successfully resolved all friction. 'They spent four or five hours together in discourse, in which both parties dealt clearly and nakedly with each other so that mistakes might not grow through misunderstandings,' he recalls. 'Much prejudice and many jealousies were then removed and more satisfaction given and received than I could rationally imagine.'

His enthusiasm is perhaps most intense when God is invoked. 'I have seen so much of God in this business of disposing by his providence of our affairs,' he whoops, 'that my heart is much induced to believe that he hath a very glorious work to bring forth in that kingdom [Scotland]. When I consider,' he continues,' the great work of God this last summer [victory in the Second Civil War], methinks . . . every deliverance says clearly God only was here. They are the Lord's doings and they are marvellous in our eyes.' With God Himself so complicit in Cromwell's military and diplomatic successes, how could the Presbyterians in the House of Commons gainsay the Lieutenant General now?

Occasionally we glimpse, between the lines, brief flashes of a young innocent abroad – a Massachusetts Yankee at the court of Oliver Cromwell. Witness our narrator's open-mouthed wonderment at the pomp and flummery; his unfeigned gratitude to the Committee of Estates for picking up the tab; his unselfconscious appreciation of a posh lunch at Edinburgh Castle, anticipating Charles Pooter by nearly 250 years: '. . . a banquet of more sumptuousness and variety and plenty than I expected on that side of the

Tweed'. The text suggests a different kind of innocence as well. Were the Covenanters really genuine in their 'many expressions of love' towards the Lieutenant General, or would they prove to be false friends? Cromwell would not have to wait long to discover the answer. And as it turned out, George Downing would be the one to tell him.

## *The North of England, autumn 1648*

Cromwell left Scotland and went first towards Carlisle, where the party was quartered at Naworth Castle, the home of Charles Howard, a local nobleman, who was soon to become fast friends with George Downing. Howard was away at his second home at Henderskelfe in Yorkshire (now Castle Howard) when his unexpected guests turned up at Naworth. His steward sent out to a local merchant for chickens and wine, and Downing once again found himself treated to a fine feast.[24] Then to Newcastle, for a grand dinner hosted by the mayor, then Durham, York and on to Barnard Castle, all in eleven days. A conference was held at Barnard Castle bringing together the leading families of the northern counties with a view to increasing security and dealing with the threat posed by moss-troopers and brigands. Orders were given for the slighting of castles and the raising of militias. The plan was to secure the North not only against banditry and another invasion from Scotland, but also against any surprise Royalist uprising.

All of this was sensible and necessary, yet why was Cromwell not hurrying to London as fast as his horse would carry him? After all, the Lieutenant General had received news at Edinburgh of an urgent political crisis. A deal between Parliament and the King – the outcome of the Treaty of Newport – was expected any day and such an agreement might well lead to Fairfax's army being disbanded. Stopping that, one would think, must surely be Cromwell's top priority? But that raised a larger question: what to do about Charles I? If the decision had not been already taken, it would have to be taken soon.

The business was, of course, in hand. Cromwell was working in lockstep with his son-in-law, Commissary General Henry Ireton. While the Lieutenant General tested the mood of the army in the north, Ireton was doing the same in the south. In talks brokered by Hugh Peter, Ireton sat down with the Leveller leader John Lilburne to discuss plans for a new dispensation. The army was close to bursting with impatience. Regiments and garrisons were drafting petitions demanding that the King be put on trial without further delay. One of the earliest petitions was drafted in Newcastle by the Leveller Paul Hobson, who was Sir Arthur Hesilrige's deputy. Messengers travelled between Ireton and Cromwell bearing top-secret letters. George Joyce, the young officer who had abducted the King from Holdenby and made him a prisoner of the army, carried some of the most sensitive correspondence from one to the other.

Cromwell, who had been marching south, stopped to attend to the siege of Pontefract Castle, where one of history's wild cards had just been played. On 2 November Cromwell's secretary, Robert Spavin, in a private letter from Knottingley, suggested that Cromwell and Ireton had by then settled on a political direction, expressing the hope that the country would soon be rid of 'that old jog-trot form of government of King, Lords and Commons'. It would not have been entirely out of character for the secretary to have sneaked a look at papers that he had no business reading. In the summer of 1649, Spavin would be sacked for forging Cromwell's signature to fabricate a laissez-passer.[25]

*John Lilburne*

What the Lieutenant General found at Pontefract would delay his return to London by some weeks. Pontefract Castle had been in the hands of Royalists since July. The Parliamentarian commander charged with besieging the castle, Sir Henry Cholmley, had made little progress turning the occupants out. Indeed, the supposedly besieged garrison appeared to be free to come and go from the castle at will. A party had recently sallied out to snatch a local bigwig from his house and had taken him back to the castle before demanding a cash ransom. Lord Fairfax sent Colonel Thomas Rainborowe to take over command of the siege. Rainborowe had successfully taken Colchester Castle only a few weeks before.

Rainborowe was a prominent Leveller. He had made the famous speech at the Putney Debates putting the case for a universal male franchise: 'I think that the poorest he that is in England hath a life to live, as the greatest he; and therefore truly, Sir, I think it's clear, that every man that is to live under a government ought first by his own consent to put himself under that government; and I do think that the poorest man in England is not bound in a strict sense to that government that he hath not had a voice to put himself under.'[26]

The thirty-eight-year-old Rainborowe was also, as it happened, related to George Downing; in fact, doubly so. At least three of Rainborowe's siblings had migrated to Massachusetts. His sister Judith married one of Downing's cousins, while his sister Martha had recently become Downing's aunt.[27]

The Royalists in the castle had sent a spy to Doncaster, where Rainborowe had put up at an inn on the market square. The agent undertook a thorough target reconnaissance, noting the strength and disposition of the sentries at night. At around midnight, twenty-two horsemen slipped out of the castle gates and, if their own account is to be believed, made their way silently past the besiegers' pickets and rode eighteen miles south to Mexborough. They rested there until around noon on the Saturday before crossing the River Don and disappearing into the woods beyond the tiny settlement of Butterbusk. Early the next morning, after checking for the prearranged safety signal from their agent in the town, the horsemen emerged onto the Sheffield Road, approaching Doncaster from the west.

They were expecting only one sentry at St Sepulchre's Gate and that is what they found. Their commander told the guard that they were from Colonel White's regiment and bringing urgent letters from Lieutenant General Cromwell. This was plausible as Colonel White was at that time encamped only twelve miles back along the road from which they had just emerged. Once safely through the gate, the horsemen divided into three parties – one securing their lines of escape, another making ready to engage the town's guards if the alarm were sounded, and the third heading straight for Rainborowe's lodgings, where they announced themselves as messengers sent by Cromwell. They had brought with them a package stuffed with blank paper, but elaborately wrapped and sealed, to occupy the attention of Rainborowe and his lieutenant while the snatch party quickly moved through the doorway and took them prisoner. His abductors assured the colonel that were he to cooperate, he would not be harmed. It was their purpose, they said, to exchange him for the Royalist general Sir Marmaduke Langdale. In fact, though they could not have known it, Langdale had already made his own escape from Nottingham Castle.

Until this moment, the plan had worked perfectly. It was all too good to last. One of the kidnappers dropped his sword. Rainborowe barrelled past him and picked it up. The colonel's lieutenant then grabbed the hapless abductor's pistol. The Cavalier swordsmen went into action, piercing Rainborowe's throat and running the lieutenant right through as he struggled to prepare the pistol for firing. Spurting blood, Rainborowe continued to stagger towards his attackers, sword in hand. An officer cut open his abdomen and, according to one account, Rainborowe fell to the ground and died. According to another, he was stabbed a further seven times. Yet the alarm had not been sounded. There was no bang from the pistol. The captain of the guard was in any case a drunkard, who was still sleeping it off after a particularly heavy night. The raiding party rode out through the town's gate unchallenged and returned to Pontefract Castle.

Within days, the Independents and the Levellers were in uproar. Thomas Rainborowe was declared a martyr. His body was brought to London and his coffin, draped in rosemary branches, was escorted from Tottenham High Cross to St John's churchyard at Wapping by fifty coaches and close to 1,500 horsemen. The Levellers adopted Rainborowe's sea-green colours for their own ribbons.

Talk of blood guilt and the need for expiation was now reaching a crescendo. Yet the day after Thomas Rainborowe's funeral the Commons voted, subject to the Treaty of Newport being agreed, to allow the King to return to London and to restore to him 'all his Houses, Honours, Manors and Lands, with the growing Rents and Profits thereof . . .'

A few days afterwards, the army countered with its Remonstrance, drafted by Henry Ireton, which demanded 'That the capital and grand Author of our Troubles, the Person of the King . . . may be speedily brought to justice.'

The King's fate was now more or less settled. Nevertheless, Oliver Cromwell would continue to signal that some kind of deal might yet be possible; indeed, he did so right until the end. Cromwell was not a binary politician. He could ride two horses at once, while advancing three agendas. This risked making him appear insincere at times, a hypocrite or a double-dealer; or, alternatively, an irresolute ditherer. Yet these moments of seeming indecision can be seen as manifestations of deference to a higher power. A godly leader might choose to keep his options open simply out of spiritual good manners: to give the Holy Spirit room to point the way. In a letter written from Knottingley on 25 November to Colonel Robert Hammond, Cromwell discusses a way of discerning what is the best course of action to take. He cites the study of 'outward dispensations' and seeking 'to know the mind of God in all that chain of providence'. Cromwell is trying to persuade his friend to overcome his own qualms about acting against the King, inviting him to 'seek that spirit to teach thee; which is the spirit of knowledge and understanding, the spirit of counsel and might' and to allow the Lord to be 'free to speak and command in thy heart'. He is at the same time explaining how he himself was coming to his own decision in the matter.

It is clear that Cromwell had interpreted the army's military successes in the Second Civil War, culminating in his own victory at Preston, as signs from heaven. It was as if he had made the same bargain with the radicals as Robert Blair and John Livingstone made with their fellow passengers aboard the *Eagle Wing* when they found themselves in peril on the sea: let God himself decide. If things go well, then onwards! If not, abort. For Cromwell's army, things had gone supremely well. 'My dear friend, let us look into providences,' he wrote excitedly to Hammond, 'surely they mean somewhat. They hang so together; have been so constant, so clear, unclouded.' In short, God had given the signal that the King should be put on trial. In Massachusetts they would have recognized this method of moral reasoning – it was the way Governor Winthrop decided every issue. Hugh Peter would have understood and espoused it too. For George Downing it was second nature, the New England way.

## *London, December 1648–February 1649*

Parliament chose not to bother debating the army's remonstrance, and gave short shrift to a request for the settlement of arrears of army pay; instead it persisted with discussing the Treaty of Newport. For its part, the army considered this behaviour arrogant and insulting and duly marched on London. For the soldiers, the only question was whether to dissolve Parliament altogether or purge it of the Presbyterians who were championing the treaty. The Levellers opposed a forced dissolution, fearing that without a parliament, military dictatorship would become inevitable, threatening those ancient and somewhat mystical English liberties that underpinned Leveller ideology. The Independent MPs were opposed to dissolution too, for without a parliament they themselves would have no authority, no legitimacy, no standing. Ireton began by favouring dissolution as a prelude to more thoroughgoing reform. A purged Parliament would be bogus and absurd, he thought, 'a mock-power, a mock-parliament'.[28] Cromwell might perhaps have agreed with him, but was not there when the decision had to be finalized. He was still on his way south. Ireton compromised. For the time being, a mock parliament would have to do.

The action that came to be known as 'Pride's Purge' began at dawn on 6 December 1648. Parliament's regular guards were intercepted on their way to work and stood down. In their stead, soldiers from Colonel Thomas Pride's regiment secured the parliamentary estate. The colonel himself stood on the steps outside St Stephen's Chapel alongside Lord Grey of Groby, one of the Independents, checking each arriving Member of Parliament against lists that had been drawn up the previous night.[29]

Once an MP had been identified, he was either let in, informed he was excluded, or politely told he was under arrest. All did not go perfectly to plan. A small number of members got in who should not have done and were dragged out screaming in protest, somewhat subverting the studied courtesy that Colonel Pride had managed to maintain until that point. Forty-five MPs were arrested, and many more were excluded or walked out in protest against the purge. Those who had most determinedly supported coming to a negotiated agreement with the King were now barred. This left two hundred or so members still sitting in what became known as the Rump Parliament. A month later, they voted to establish a court to try King Charles I for High Treason.

Neither George Downing nor Sir Arthur Hesilrige attended or took any part in the trial or execution of Charles I. Hesilrige was asked to be one of the judges, but declined. There does not appear to have been any political or principled objection to the regicide advanced by either of them. Their friends and allies – notably Cromwell and Hugh Peter, Sir Henry Vane, even Colonel Okey – were behind the action. The governor of Newcastle and his chaplain were simply not in London at the time. The Leveller leader John Lilburne also declined the offer of being a judge at the trial and went to Newcastle, where he had at least one meeting with Hesilrige. The most likely reason for Hesilrige and Downing's absence was the need to maintain security in the North. John Lambert also missed the trial and execution for the same reason.

Downing's silence at this time had, as it were, an echo in New England, where the King's execution went almost unremarked. With the King dead, a republican form of government – the Commonwealth – was established in England with a unicameral Parliament governing through a Council of State, of which Cromwell, Hesilrige and Henry Vane were members.

## CHAPTER 3

# The Breda Mission

### *Edinburgh, autumn 1649–July 1650*

'One downeham or Downing, chaplain to Sir Arthur Hesilrige is now taken notice of both as an intelligencer and a seducer. He has occasioned one gentlewoman not to come to church, and it is thought he has seduced my Lord Craighall and his lady.' This brief report, contained in a letter written from Edinburgh in the icy January of 1650, represents the first recorded sighting of George Downing as a spy. Nobody knows who wrote it, nor indeed the identity of its recipient. But it is one of three letters discovered among miscellaneous state papers, all of which relate to the very heart of Downing's secret mission.[1]

His new role had begun, officially, when Oliver Cromwell put him on the payroll of military intelligence at the beginning of November 1649; although an intelligence report from Edinburgh in fact suggests that he had started work at least three months earlier.[2]

Downing had 'seduced' some of the most elevated members of the Edinburgh establishment. John Hope, Lord Craighall, was one of Scotland's leading judges, along with his younger brother James Hope, of Hopetoun, who was also a member of the Scottish Parliament. Lady Craighall belonged to a family of rich, merchant burgesses in Edinburgh. She and her husband lived in somewhat chilly grandeur at their two principal residences: Granton Castle, perched above the briny shores of the Firth of Forth, three miles north-west of the city centre; and their town house, a mansion in the Cowgate, two minutes' walk from the Parliament. That George Downing should have managed to penetrate this exclusive milieu in barely a few months of receiving his commission testifies either to a calculating charm or an irrepressibly unctuous manner; and quite possibly both.

The overall head of England's intelligence and security apparatus at this time was Thomas Scot, Member of Parliament for Aylesbury and zealous Republican and regicide. Scot was also a member of the Council of State, in whose offices in Whitehall Palace the spymaster established his base. His remit spanned both foreign and domestic intelligence. The Council's secretary, Gualter Frost, supervised the management of operations and was responsible for integrating the gathering of intelligence with the state's propaganda campaigns, frequently slipping copies of agents' reports to the approved writers of news. Frost had long been a denizen of the secret world, serving his apprenticeship carrying sensitive messages between a group of Puritan opponents of Charles I, including Sir Arthur Hesilrige, John Pym and Lord Brooke, who were engaged in illegal contacts with the Scottish Covenanters in 1639–40. Frost later served as an intelligence officer for the Committee of Safety, before going on to coordinate secret work for a succession of Whitehall committees, culminating in the Council of State.[3]

*Thomas Scot*

One of Scot and Frost's closest collaborators was the experienced agent-runner William Rowe, the Scoutmaster General, who had been present at the talks at Moray House in the Canongate in 1648. As the most senior intelligence officer of the army, Scoutmaster Rowe served two clients: the military chain of command and the Council of State. Working from rooms at the back of the Bull's Head tavern at Charing Cross, Rowe was in constant and direct communication with Cromwell, who was in Ireland at this time, while also maintaining a cordial and collegiate relationship with Scot, whose daughter he later married. Rowe was a subtle and intelligent man who would own to anxieties about the moral and physical perils of the espionage trade. 'I have not a few times sighed that men set to work by me have necessarily sinned,' Rowe confided to Cromwell. 'And of late, the sufferings, maims and injuries of some I have employed have had their impression more than perhaps needed . . . I have, in both these respects a melancholy soul.'[4]

Downing had been instructed to send reports on the progress of negotiations between the Scots and their new king, Charles II. The execution of Charles I had horrified Scotland; the Scottish Parliament had tried many times to make representations on his behalf and to save his life, but Oliver Cromwell had been too busy, or too determined, to pay them any heed. The Scots regarded the killing of the King as a breach of their Covenant and as a betrayal of everything they understood to have been agreed in the Canongate. To the English, their outrage would have seemed absurdly inflexible and ungrateful. After all, Argyle's Kirk party owed its position of primacy to Cromwell's support and the presence of Lambert's cavalry at a key moment in the autumn of 1648.

At the beginning of Downing's mission, Charles II was still in Jersey, where he had been publicly proclaimed king in the Royal Square of St Helier in February 1649, twelve years before he would eventually be crowned King of England in London. Charles left Jersey soon afterwards via Paris for the city of Breda in the southern Netherlands, which in those days belonged to the Prince of Orange, husband of Charles's sister, Mary. The Princess of Orange travelled to Breda from her home in The Hague to spend time with her wandering exile brother. Another visitor from The Hague was Elizabeth, Queen of Bohemia, Charles I's only surviving sister and mother of his cavalry commander, Prince Rupert of the Rhine. Before long a bustling court had come into being at Breda, crowded with the nineteen-year-old Charles's usual retinue of aristocratic exiles, guns-for-hire, beautiful young women, desperate chancers and an uncertain number of Commonwealth spies.

Through the summer and autumn of 1649, Charles had been contemplating three possible strategies. The first was to voyage to Ireland, where he would meet up with the Marquis of Ormond's Royalist army and, hopefully, secure the island kingdom as a base from which to launch invasions of Scotland and England. This plan was scuppered in mid-August when Oliver Cromwell, with Hugh Peter at his side and 12,000 men behind them, landed near Dublin and swept on to seize the coastal stronghold of Drogheda, with its garrison of Irish Catholics and Royalist forces. On Cromwell's direct order, the defenders were shown no mercy. 'Drogheda is taken,' Hugh Peter communicated tersely to the Commons. 'Three thousand five hundred and fifty-two of the enemy slain and 64 of ours . . . Aston, the governor killed. None spared.' Nobody knows how many civilians were slaughtered during the atrocity. The unfortunate Aston, commander of the Royalist troops, was beaten to death with his own wooden leg, which his killers believed – wrongly, and astonishingly – to contain a trove of golden coins.[5]

The news of the fall of Drogheda effectively ended the King's first tactic. Option two was the Marquis of Montrose. A romantic hero among the Royalists, painted in black armour and silken curls by Van Dyck, Montrose actually began his military career fighting against Charles I as one of the most ardent Covenanters. But at the onset of the Civil War he changed allegiance and formed a Royalist army to lead an uprising against them through the whole of Scotland, even turning in with a raiding party at the gates of Argyle's estate. The Covenanters loathed Montrose as the very epitome of a malignant turncoat; and he disdained them in return. Intent on restoring the King,

Montrose toured the courts and chancelleries of northern Europe winning pledges of arms, money and troops. Every crowned head of Europe must surely have been shocked at the beheading of Charles I, so that one might expect kings and princelings, Catholic or Protestant, to be equally eager to see England's republican experiment fail. Montrose certainly encouraged such thoughts, inviting monarchs and monarchists everywhere to invest in an expedition to restore to Charles all three of his kingdoms.

The response was less generous than hoped for. The Duke of Friesland offered board and lodging for Montrose's troops while they prepared to take ship for Scotland, but no arms or money. The King of Denmark offered kind words, but nothing else. The Queen of Sweden approved the scheme in principle, but refused to be the first to commit. If Montrose could return with an established coalition of princes, then she would deign to join it. At last Montrose had a windfall in Gothenburg. Not a crowned head, but a merchant prince of sorts – an expatriate Scottish businessman – gave him enough money to hire soldiers and ship them across to Scotland. This good fortune generated further luck. The Duke of Courland, from western Latvia, stood him two shiploads of rations; while the King of Poland offered 4,000 extra soldiers. News of Montrose's bonanza reached Scotland and rattled Argyle's gates once again.

Charles II's third option was to throw in his lot with the Presbyterian Covenanters. They had taken the initiative, approaching him at The Hague soon after his father's death. In Charles's view, their manners had been presumptuous and their demands oppressive. But now that Ireland was out of the question, he had to reconsider. The King decided to keep options two and three simultaneously in play for the time being. He therefore agreed to receive a representation from the Scots' go-between, George Winram, Lord Liberton, while he was still on Jersey in early 1650. Some members of the King's circle were implacably hostile towards any kind of deal with the Scots and joked about throwing Winram over a wall and cracking his skull.

As it turned out, Winram not only departed with his skull intact, he took home an invitation from the King for the Scots to send commissioners to Breda for further talks. But as soon as the Covenanter's back was turned, Charles sent a secret letter to Montrose telling him to ignore any reports he might hear of a deal with Argyle; nothing would be agreed, he assured his friend, to undermine Montrose's own position in the royal affections. This communication could be construed as a pledge to Montrose that the King had no intention of keeping any promises that the Covenanters might extract from him. It arrived too late for Montrose to read it before leaving Gothenburg. He had already set out for Scotland, but was now stuck in sea ice off the Swedish coast. Later, the letter would fetch up in George Downing's hands.

When the King's party quit Jersey for the Netherlands shortly afterwards, in rather too much of a rush, a trunk full of top-secret papers was accidentally left behind by his secretary, Robert Long. No one at court appears to have missed the trunk at the time, and Long saw no benefit in drawing attention to his own negligence. The trunk subsequently found its way to the intelligence office in Whitehall. The Royalist spymasters became worried that Scot would be able to construct an almost complete record of Charles's most sensitive dealings at this time.[6]

Scoutmaster Rowe was also receiving intelligence of very high quality from George Downing in Edinburgh, as well as from intercepted letters from the city of uncertain provenance. 'Will the King come or will he not?' According to a dispatch from the middle of January, that was 'every man's discourse' in the city and the preponderance of opinion was that he would.[7] However, another report suggested a measure of ambivalence on the issue among the nation's political leaders, perhaps even second thoughts; certainly an ebbing and flowing of enthusiasm, 'as you see water in the heart of the channel at the first turning of the tide set one way, when on each side towards the banks it runs still another way, so methinks I see here a tide against the tide, a stream against the stream . . .'[8] Argyle himself was clearly in favour of bringing the King to Scotland; but only on terms that would leave him in control of Scotland's government. John and James Hope – Lords Craighall and Hopetoun – represented a more radical strand, favouring a close alliance with Cromwell and open to rejecting a deal made at Breda.

For the undecided, there were two distinct concerns. First, the Covenanters were adamant that the King must himself sign the Covenant and do so with absolute sincerity. 'It were better the King not come at all than that he come not as a changed man' was a commonly expressed view.[9] The test would be that he should behave henceforth with a strict moral probity, which would require him to swap his louche, malignant friends for the old Sobersides from the Kirk. Second, the Scots were profoundly unsettled by the prospect of Montrose's imminent arrival.

Had George Downing been sending nothing more than titbits of table talk *chez* Lord and Lady Craighall, that high-end political gossip would itself have justified the costs of the operation. But William Rowe was receiving far more for his money. A synopsis of Winram's letter reporting on his encounter with the King was sent by express to London within a day of its arrival in Edinburgh. Rowe and Thomas Scot also received details of Argyle's contacts with the King's mother, Queen Henrietta Maria in Paris, and of his correspondence with the Prince of Orange at The Hague.

No sooner had the Committee of Estates chosen whom to send from Scotland as commissioners to treat with Charles at Breda than their names, budget and terms of engagement went swiftly to William Rowe's desk and subsequently to Cromwell himself. This included the news that one of the Kirk's choices was John Livingstone, Robert Blair's travelling companion on the abortive voyage of the *Eagle Wing*. These dispatches contain the occasional disclosure confirming that the mission George Downing and his colleagues were embarked upon was not restricted to intelligence-gathering. Scoutmaster Rowe's office was a department of dirty tricks as well.

The King's letter to Montrose, for instance, was deliberately leaked to the Scottish government just when they were considering whether to come to a deal with the King at Breda. 'I had sent me a copy of the King's Letter to Montrose,' an agent who was almost certainly Downing confided to Rowe, 'which I put into such hands as it was then produced in the Committee of Estates.'[10] In Downing, Rowe had an agent sufficiently adroit, astute and well placed to insinuate such a letter into the system at this crucial juncture.

The intelligence charts a shifting disposition over an interval of only a few months as the Scots' early vacillation resolves into enthusiasm. 'Never greater longings and workings to get the King hither, never greater zeal and vehemence against the sectaries.'[11] By April 1650 this fervour had, remarkably, settled into a wilful determination on the part of the Scots to repeat the catastrophic error of the Second Civil War: 'Only this rest assured of, that not a people alive can be more desperately and unanimously bent upon invading England.'[12]

Spies at this time had to protect both their own identities and the vital contents of their reports from potential snoopers. A huge proportion of letters sent from major cities through the postal system were routinely intercepted and examined by government agents. Sometimes a spy would write his dispatch entirely or partly in numerical code, the text becoming a string of numbers that only someone with a key to the cipher could decode. Such communications were frequently forwarded to Oliver Cromwell with interlined deciphering in William Rowe's hand. Obviously any document composed in a numerical cipher immediately announced itself as an item of secret intelligence and would command the immediate attention of government spy-catchers.

Another commonly used device, which seems to have been especially favoured by George Downing, was the word-substitution cipher, where significant names and terms relating to a mission were given individual code-words. This allowed the spy to adopt a cover identity and, like an actor, remain in character as he crafted his reports. Someone posing as a grain merchant, for instance, who had been tasked with reporting on military dispositions, might use words like 'wheat', 'rye' and 'barley' to stand for cavalry, infantry and artillery, and so forth. He could then improvise other plausible gossip and news that tended to strengthen the impression that his missive was simply what it purported to be: correspondence between two cereal traders. The advantage of this method was that, if composed with flair, a letter thus encrypted might get past the scrutineers even if intercepted, and continue on its way with full clearance.

Rowe's agents employed subtle deceptions to misdirect the Scots' counter-espionage officers. Spies might, for example, sprinkle their reports with false clues concerning their nationality or religion. This could have the authorities hunting for a Scottish Presbyterian rather than, say, a New England Independent. But the smallest careless slip could blow their cover. Rowe received more than one dispatch containing a dutiful misdirection suggesting that the writer was a Scot, but bearing an English, and not a Scottish, date. At this time, New Year's Day in England (and in the New England colonies, as it happened) fell on 25 March. By contrast, the Scots had begun their year on 1 January ever since 1600. Accordingly, a genuine Scotsman would have dated his letter, say, 10 February 1650; while an Englishman (or New Englander) would have written 10 February 1649.

It appears that George Downing would sometimes evade the Scottish mail censors in the most reliably effective way, by slipping across the border into England and posting his letters from Carlisle. He had also managed to acquire a friend there who agreed to act as a *poste restante*, passing on the instructions that arrived in return from Thomas Scot and William Rowe in London.

One possible candidate for Downing's Carlisle contact is Charles Howard of Naworth, who was the scion of a cadet branch of one of England's grandest families. His kinsmen included the Dukes of Norfolk, the Earls of Arundel, Suffolk and Berkshire, Barons Howard de Walden and Howard of Effingham. Some generations back, the Howards had married into the Dacre family, whose male line became extinct, and from whom they inherited a string of castles, including Naworth, Charles's home, lying thirteen miles north-west of Carlisle, close to the border with Scotland.

Like many members of his vast extended family, Charles Howard was brought up as a Catholic and as a Royalist. In 1645, as parliamentary soldiers closed in on Naworth during the First Civil War, the seventeen-year-old Howard was smuggled out of the castle by his guardian and put on board a ship. That same night, when the ship suddenly foundered on treacherous rocks, the young Charles was rescued from the water by passing Royalist troops. They had barely hauled him to safety when a force of Roundheads fell upon them out of the dark. For the first time in his life Charles Howard found himself fighting hand-to-hand against the parliamentary army.

This was a criminal offence, for which Howard could be classed as a 'delinquent' and suitably charged. The punishment could involve anything from substantial fines to the confiscation of his houses or estates. He was sent as a prisoner to London and there summonsed to appear before the committee that would determine the extent of his fate.

Was it providence, romance or subterfuge that saved him this time? Charles Howard married the daughter of the MP for Carlisle (who was, inevitably, a Howard cousin) and converted to his new wife's Presbyterianism. The authorities were persuaded to strike out his delinquency and settle for a one-off payment of £4,000 – a sum he could comfortably afford.

Expediency, doubtless disguised as necessity, persuaded Howard to switch his political allegiance as well as his religious denomination and he became a committed Parliamentarian. During the Second Civil War, he levied his own troop of horse and gallantly charged a Royalist band outside Carlisle. When Cromwell's party, including George Downing, arrived in this city in October 1648, Howard entertained them to dinner. Soon afterwards, he would be continuing a long family tradition.

Generations of Charles Howard's Dacre forebears had been Lords of the Western Marches, charged with maintaining law and order on a feral frontier. The border between England and Scotland was bandit country, terrorized by local gangs known as moss-troopers, who had rustled and smuggled and extorted back and forth across this landscape for centuries. Other families had tried and failed to tame them. However, it was rumoured that the Dacres and, subsequently, the Howards had a singular advantage in policing the marches: many of the moss-troopers were their tenants. The aristocrats knew them only too well, could even sit down and bargain with them. They did not want the gangs to be jailed, still less hanged, or to give up their nefarious enterprises altogether; the landlords wanted their rent. For their part, the moss-troopers were happy to accommodate these overlords, who understood the subtlety and nuance of the border lands' economy; but they were defiant of outsiders and the rule of law.

For all the talk of revolution and turning the world upside down, the Commonwealth understood that the old traditional ways were sometimes the most effective. So the

Council of State appointed Charles Howard as High Sheriff of Cumberland in 1650 with a commission to keep a lid on crime and Royalist unrest. Howard entered into the role as to the manner born. When Charles I's lands came up for sale, he bought Carlisle Castle with his own money and put a garrison in it. Increasingly drawn into Oliver Cromwell's circle, Howard modified his religious posture once more, declaring himself an Independent.

For George Downing, slipping down to Carlisle on the sly to file his latest intelligence from Breda, the world of the Howards, with its turreted castles and Cavalier dash, offered at the very least a respite from those dreich and dismal Edinburgh afternoons among the Covenanters in the Cowgate. The man now rumoured to be a seducer might himself have been seduced by the discreet charm of the aristocracy. For now, Downing could refer to Charles Howard as his friend; but the day was not far off when he would call him brother.

### *Breda, Southern Netherlands, spring 1650*

At Breda the King was coming to a decision, although, in truth, it was more a matter of accepting necessity than exercising free choice. He was flat broke and the royal courts of Europe were not inclined to provide him with any more than the barest subsistence. The plan to launch an Irish invasion had not survived Drogheda and all he had in play now was Montrose, of whose Scottish expedition too little was at this point known. England's Presbyterians were pressing Charles to agree terms with Scotland's Covenanters. Some even planned coordinated uprisings across England to coincide with his arrival in the kingdom at the head of a Scottish army. Even some of the Levellers, who had begun to turn against the army and the government, were recommending a deal with Argyle. Among the old Royalists, the preference was for Montrose, as it was in Charles's own heart; his reason, though, forced him to incline increasingly towards the Covenanters.

If one coalition was beginning to cohere, another would have to be brutally torn apart. The old Cavaliers, many of them traditional Anglicans or Catholics, were reviled by the Covenanters as 'malignants'. They could have no place in Argyle's array. Charles understood that he would have to hold many loyal companions at arms' length and perhaps even shamefully repudiate some of his truest friends. The scaly truth was that it might be impossible to conclude such a treaty without lowering himself in his own moral estimation. Some of Charles's closest counsellors, aware of his predicament, suggested that he should feign sincerity as he submitted to each of the Covenanters' conditions. They could make him say it, the argument ran, but they could not make him mean it. According to philosophers down the centuries, a man might render an outward oath invalid by clinging tightly to a mental reservation. In any case, once formally crowned king in Scotland and positioned at the head of an army, with or without Montrose at his side, Carolus Rex would be free to turn his back on Argyle and exercise the age-old royal prerogative of changing his mind.

While George Downing was stealthily reporting on how developments at Breda were received in the salons of Edinburgh's political establishment, Thomas Scot had insinuated another spy into Charles's entourage to find out what was going on within the Royalist camp. Major Richard

Fauconer had fought in the parliamentary cavalry during the First Civil War. He descended from an old Hampshire family with land in and around the Meon Valley. 'By birth and education,' he proudly declared, 'I claim a parity with the better sort of gentlemen.'[13] Once the fighting was done, however, things began to go badly for him. He lost his patrimony and took to drink, though perhaps not in that order.

The circumstances in which Fauconer was recruited as a spy are not known for certain. But the case officer to whom he initially reported was none other than George Joyce, who had climbed the ranks from cornet to lieutenant colonel in just three years. In a recent posting, Joyce had been put in command of Southsea Castle, only eight miles from Fauconer's home at Westbury. Joyce would later say that it was a simple Hampshire social connection that led to the penurious officer's induction into the secret world.[14]

Fauconer himself preferred to imply a seamless transition from military service to the world of espionage. There is evidence, however, that the major's debts and heavy drinking led him to become a highwayman and that he had actually been awaiting trial in Aylesbury jail when he was offered – *Dirty Dozen*-style – the choice between a long stretch in prison or the opportunity to redeem himself by volunteering for a perilous assignment. The Member of Parliament for Aylesbury at that time was Thomas Scot. Spymaster Scot could well have had a turnkey on the payroll to tip him the wink about any out-of-the-ordinary prisoners, such as this gentleman desperado, Richard Fauconer.

As it turned out, the major made a natural fit with the soldiers of fortune who tramped around Europe in Charles's train. Many had fought for the King's father and gone freelance on the continent after the debacle, only to be discharged again on some foreign field a thousand miles from home. To describe these men as mercenaries would suggest a degree of military expertise that in most cases had long-since been washed away by Rhenish wine. Like Fauconer, they were timeworn, shady and decrepit, with many a tale of past glory but without prospects. After leaving the shores of Jersey, they staggered through France and into the Spanish Netherlands; and Fauconer – stranger, interloper, spy – journeyed alongside them proposing toasts and charging bumpers, until, in a blur of camaraderie, he was accepted as one of the squad.

Fauconer was a good listener and many chose to confide in him. Thus he was soon able to amass details of plans for uprisings in almost every county of England. Some were well-developed designs, others pitifully inchoate; some were ingenious, and others hare-brained. But when set alongside the King's inclination towards a deal with the Scottish Covenanters, Fauconer's reports helped his London spymasters to chart a credible threat of synchronized nationwide uprisings timed to coincide with another invasion from Scotland – all in furtherance of the Presbyterian interest. Fauconer gave these reports to Colonel Joyce, who later sent him to be debriefed by Captain George Bishop, the secretary to the close committee of the Council of State, the very man whom Thomas Scot had put in charge of frustrating Royalist plots. Arrests would surely follow.

The Prince of Orange's base at Breda was a proper castle with its own bowling facilities and plenty of room for Charles's ramshackle court. It was here that the King received the Scottish commissioners in his bedchamber with maximum flummery, countering their moral condescension with his own social punctilio. The best way to preserve his dignity in the face of their reproachful expressions was to force the Covenanters to observe all the courtly formalities. He would send the Kirk ministers to the brink of apoplexy by threatening to receive Holy Communion on his knees, which proved an even more enjoyable provocation than flaunting his mistress, Lucy Walter, along with their illegitimate child.[15]

Charles was still hoping for news from Montrose in Scotland, but nothing came. As it turned out, on 27 April 1650 the marquis had been defeated at the Battle of Carbisdale in Sutherland by Colonel Archibald Strachan and his forces. Montrose escaped from the field and went on the run, but was hunted down, captured and taken to Edinburgh, where he was hanged in fine silks and fancy lace at the Mercat Cross. His corpse was dismembered and the quarters distributed between Aberdeen, Stirling, Glasgow and Perth. His head was impaled on a spike above the Edinburgh Tolbooth, where it remained, come rain, wind and snow, for many months.

In Breda the King was in any case set to yield. At the beginning of May, to the surprise of almost everyone involved, he signed an agreement. Charles pledged to take the Covenant. But John Livingstone and other strict Covenanter commissioners did not believe he was in earnest and began to plan elaborate tests of his sincerity.

To complement the intelligence Fauconer was gleaning from the bottom levels of the Breda court, the English could look to a higher source. This was John Pell, graduate of Trinity College, Cambridge and a former professor of mathematics at the University of Amsterdam, who now occupied the same position at the Orange College of Breda. Pell, a correspondent of Descartes, gave his name to a celebrated equation that some experts today regard as so advanced that it should more properly have been attributed to Fermat. Pell was not just an extremely senior wrangler, he was also a friend of intelligence officers and code-breakers. He had a brother, Thomas Pell, who had emigrated to New England to become the surgeon at the Saybrook Fort, working for George Fenwick.

Pell's superior, the rector of the Orange College of Breda, was a Huguenot theologian named André Rivet, who had been tutor to the Prince of Orange in the 1630s. Rivet was consulted by the Scottish commissioners during the Treaty of Breda and – probably at the request of the prince – helped to mediate between the King and three ministers of the Kirk, who were becoming known among the court as the 'bigot clergy'.[16] Rivet was reportedly present when Charles signed the outline agreement on 1 May and appears to have disclosed the details to Pell, who duly reported them to London.[17] Pell had been recruited through his friends Samuel Hartlib and Theodore Haak, who were working for Gualter Frost. Hartlib and Haak were of an altogether superior class of intelligencer. They were accomplished scholars, in touch with everyone who mattered in the Republic of Letters and Sciences. Their correspondence with intellectuals throughout Europe brought to the Whitehall intelligence office sophistication and reach. A few months after the treaty concluded, the Council of State instructed that 'That 50 pounds be paid by Mr FROST to Mr THEODORE HAAK and so much also to Mr SAMUEL HARTLIB in regard of the many good services by them done by their correspondency in parts beyond the seas, and to enable them to continue it.'[18]

As soon as the King had indicated his consent to the proposed terms, the Scottish commissioners sent the text of the agreement back to Scotland for approval or revision by the Committee of Estates. Meanwhile a news blackout was imposed, so severe that even the smallest gossip dried up, leaving spies and newsbook correspondents (some wearing both hats at once) only able to report their frustration to London. 'Things are kept under such secrecy as I know not what to affirm for the truth,' one admitted. 'The very favourites differ in their reports – whether to abuse us that are of the tribe of club intelligencers, or because they know not, I cannot determine. But the business is [closely held] among a few and a supper or a pottle of Rhenish can do little now . . .'[19]

The truth was that it mattered little to London how the articles of the agreement stood at this point. George Downing would be making his report once the draft reached the Committee of Estates, and that would reveal all. As it turned out, the treaty was still very much up in the air. Edinburgh would insist on changes to the text and pile on yet further conditions in the future.

The Scottish Parliament's messenger, Edward Gillespie, delivered the latest demands at the beginning of June, just after the King had surprised everyone by announcing that he was taking ship for Scotland straight away. The letter insisted that unless all its conditions were accepted, the Treaty of Breda would be deemed null and void. Prominent among the fresh stipulations was that the King's closest and most 'malignant' friends, among them the new Duke of Hamilton and the Earl of Lauderdale, were forbidden to land on Scottish soil. But they were due to travel on Charles's ship the very next day. This crisis prompted a frantic dash by the ministers of the Kirk to catch up with the royal party and their fellow commissioners. However, when their boat reached the little port of Ter Heijde, where the modest squadron of three men-of-war lent to the King by the Prince of Orange lay at anchor, the winds were too strong for them to attempt a landing; perhaps reminding John Livingstone of tempest-tossed nights aboard the *Eagle Wing*.

Eventually the clergymen were put ashore at Scheveningen and rode to the Prince of Orange's country house at Honselaarsdijk, south of The Hague. Livingstone did not record what he thought of the palace, whose architecture owed a good deal to the Palais de Luxembourg in Paris. It seems unlikely that any house built for amusement and pleasure – let alone one with a fancy papist aesthetic – would hold much charm for Livingstone, who, only a short time before, had descried Charles's habit of 'balling and dancing 'til late'.[20]

In any case, by the time he got there, the King and his party were gone. A further mad dash to Ter Heijde ensued, followed by a hurried debate on the beach about whether to sail or stay. It appeared that the lay commissioners were content to put to sea, hoping to resolve any outstanding business in the course of the voyage. However, the three Kirk zealots – James Wood, George Hutcheson and Livingstone himself – still had doubts about what the King was up to and what precisely their duty required of them.

At one point Livingstone tried to persuade the other commissioners to disembark from the King's ship and confer with him in a small dinghy alongside. Only when sharply rebuked by the Earl of Cassilis that this would be 'unseemly', did he finally agree to go on board and attend a meeting in the gunnery room. The fastidious minister nonetheless took the precaution of arranging for a servant to hold the dinghy ready so that he could quit the negotiations at any time and be rowed back to shore, voiding the treaty, should any of Edinburgh's terms not be agreed upon to his full satisfaction. Someone – likely Lord Liberton, who had been working towards this moment ever since braving the Royalist bloods in Jersey – got the better of him by quietly sending the boat away. The King's ship, together with its two escorts, had set sail for Scotland and the port of Ter Heijde was fast vanishing from sight before John Livingstone realized that, for better or worse, they were all at sea.

So began a voyage of proliferating perils. Just before the captain gave the order to weigh anchor, the King received a visit from John Webster, an English merchant living in Amsterdam and a staunch ally of the house of Stuart, who had ridden hell for leather to warn his majesty that the English Parliament had sent no fewer than twenty-two ships into the North Sea to arrest him. There was a plan in place to mitigate this danger. The Prince of Orange had given secret orders to a squadron of warships currently guarding the Dutch herring fleet off Shetland to break away and escort Charles's party safely into a Scottish port.

The journey between southern Holland and the mouth of the Spey was only 500 miles as the crow flies, but on this occasion it took more than three weeks to complete. Adverse winds drove the royal ships way off-course to the estuary of the Elbe, near Hamburg. Eventually their captains decided to take shelter in the tiny archipelago of Heligoland (which translates as 'Holy land'), where negotiations between the Scottish commissioners and Charles resumed.

Once again the King held out for a long time, before abruptly throwing in his hand and agreeing to everything asked of him; which again struck some of his interlocutors as downright suspicious. On 11 June, Charles signed the Treaty of Heligoland.

By the time the King's ships reached Shetland, the herring fleet had departed and, with it, their escort. On 24 June, four English vessels hunting for the King entered the estuary of the Spey and began checking the bays. Satisfied that all was clear, they eventually sailed away in a southerly direction. Approaching from the north and shielded from view by a sea haar, the royal party slipped into the bay at Garmouth, where the King swore both the National Covenant and the Solemn League and Covenant, before going ashore to be greeted by jubilant subjects.[21]

Some days later he visited Aberdeen. But lest Charles forget that Argyle was really the master now, the King was lodged at a merchant's house where, from his bedroom window, he could contemplate the severed arm of the Marquis of Montrose, hung upon the Justice Port across the street. Charles had opportunistically disowned Montrose as soon as he had committed to the Breda agreement, so the putrefying limb was not just a political warning; it was also a moral reproach.

## *Edinburgh, June–July 1650*

While Charles had been at Honselaarsdijk at the end of May, preparing for his voyage to Scotland, George Downing was recovering from a brutal beating. He had been paying a visit to Leith, probably on espionage business, and was walking back to Edinburgh's city centre when two men set upon him. Downing appears to have been able to identify his assailants or, at the very least, provide sufficient information to allow the authorities to do so. The Lord Advocate, Scotland's leading law officer, responsible for supervising the investigation and prosecution of crime, was instructed by the Parliament to have the perpetrators arrested and brought in for questioning. The city's magistrates were notified of the offence and instructed to assist in its resolution. Meanwhile the Lord Provost, essentially Edinburgh's mayor, was required to liaise with Downing, providing assurances to the victim that the crime would be properly dealt with by all the appropriate authorities.

It would not be surprising if the ambassador of some major European power were to receive such prompt and courteous service from the criminal justice system, but George Downing was neither extraordinary nor plenipotentiary; not even a person of any eminence at all. Or so it seemed. To the ordinary Scot in Edinburgh, Downing was merely the twenty-seven-year-old chaplain to an English provincial governor remotely based at Newcastle. Of course some people were aware that under this modest clerical cover, he was also an intelligencer; but the plying of that trade would more normally lead to an arrest than to the levels of privilege and access immediately offered to Downing. When he was mugged on the way home from Leith he did not file his complaint to the local constable, but directly to the Marquis of Argyle, the *de facto* head of Scotland's government. When Downing asked him to act, the marquis obliged.[22]

Those who were so solicitously attending to Downing's injured dignity were, ironically, the prime targets of his espionage. The English, as we shall see, had penetrated Argyle's own household. Whether he knew it or not, the Lord Provost would turn out to be the source of so much of Downing's intelligence on Scottish military powers.

By this time Oliver Cromwell had returned in triumph from Ireland to London. On 20 June, the Council of State would vote to send an army to invade Scotland. Downing's original mission – to report on the Scottish end of the Treaty of Breda – was almost done. For the rest of his time in Edinburgh the spy's focus would be on the King's arrival and reception; on the relationship between the factions in Scotland's government and at the King's court; and on the granular details of Scottish preparations for war.

Thomas Scot, in an account of his time in charge of the Commonwealth's intelligence-gathering organization, would later name the spies who worked for him in various countries across Europe. He identified only two associated with operations in Scotland during this period; and only one of them, George Downing, was resident in Edinburgh. There may have been others supplying London with intelligence from the Scottish capital who were not on the official payroll – but it is a reasonable assumption that any piece of prime intelligence bearing the stamp of Thomas Scot's organization, together with an Edinburgh 1650 dateline, was the work of George Downing.

The question of provenance arises in connection with a letter found among the papers of the poet John Milton, who had been appointed as one of the secretaries to the Council of State in 1649. The identity of its author has not yet been established, but he was indubitably a secret agent. The document, which was encrypted using word substitution, was sent by express messenger from William

Rowe to Oliver Cromwell in late July 1650, shortly after the Lieutenant General and his invading army had crossed the border into Scotland. Scoutmaster Rowe attached a brief, introductory note: 'I herewith send your Excellency a letter from the same hand that was so abused in Canny Gate as your spy. For collusions sake he writes thus, with the privity of Argyle's Mr Household, but useth to write another of occurrences and news . . . By this, your Excellency may discern some things considerable . . .'

The mention of 'Canny Gate' points to Downing, since we know that on the only previous occasion when Oliver Cromwell and William Rowe had visited the Canongate together, in October 1648, George Downing was with them. Although the letter's signature reads 'Ralph Pudsey', we can be sure that this person had no hand in composing it. The real Ralph Pudsey was a papist and a Royalist, and more to the point, he was already dead – slaughtered in the massacre at Drogheda. Pudsey's widow was even at this very moment seeking to prevent her assets being seized by George Fenwick and Sir Arthur Hesilrige, who were developing saltpans and collieries on the River Wear and snapping up the land of local recusants and delinquents – an enterprise that Downing, so recently Hesilrige's amanuensis, would have known all about.

Rowe added translations of the encrypted text between the lines for Cromwell's benefit (rendered here parenthetically and italicized). To do this, he must have had a copy of the codebook himself – further corroboration that the letter's author was employed by the Commonwealth's intelligence department. In fact, as Rowe explained to Cromwell in his covering note, the letter had not originally been sent to him; but rather was 'intended to another', probably a fellow member of the magic circle, maybe Thomas Scot himself. Just as Cromwell was able to discern 'things considerable' about how matters stood in Scotland on the threshold of hostilities, so we can discover from a close reading of the raw intelligence a good deal about the world upon which George Downing had been spying:

Edinburgh, 23 July 1650

Sir,

Yours I have received yesterday by the post, but not being dated, as many of yours happen now and then to be, it makes me suspect interception here or there.

As for any letters to Herbert [*Sir James Montgomery*], my weekly and constant enquiries have been fruitless, and I shall desire, seeing there is no hope of his recovery of fortune (far less of honesty or esteem here) that you rather stand to the hazard of payment of what you are engaged for him, than any way to have to do with such a bankrupt.

I have not as yet met with the merchant who William Smith charged with the payment of the 10 l, but I understand he is very honest, and a great dealer here for the Londoners; yet I shall earnestly entreat, that seeing the factors, especially John Dickenson [*the Committee of Estates*], have been so careful in buying and shipping [*providing & raising*] those two commodities, that Mr Lemon [*England*] (or those of his partners who intend the Rochelle voyage [*the Presbyterians*]) would either advance their proportion of the money [*army*], and let Dickenson know what they resolve; or not expect the benefit of the adventure; for (truly) seeing the times are so troublesome, and wars so threatening betwixt the nations, they have no reason to expect either thanks or benefit of the bargain, unless they run an equal hazard.

I confess the seas are troubled, but that will not hinder us to put to sea, for a water at the worst will do our turn. I fear we shall not enjoy long correspondence, and seeing the Goods are both bought and shipped [*raised*] (and demurridge, you know, is costly) I would entreat in case the merchant packet fail, that you rather hire an express to let us know what the Rochelle merchants intend, than that we stay here upon unnecessary expense, and lose the benefit of the season.

The ship's name is the Blessing of Leith, her master one Captain Crispe [*David Leslie*], who is very resolute and pressing to put to sea [*march*], and I am confident will do what becomes him. His freight per mensem is very reasonable, only he has for his own adventure of the last year's crop about three quarters of wheat [*three thousand foot*] long since shipped [*raised*], and fifteen quarters [*thousand foot since*], which (with much ado) he has gotten licence to export, and skins of several years and kinds [*numbers of horse*], about seven or eight thousand; but for wool [*horsemen*] it is needless to expect it, for it always goes along upon the skins [*horses*].

I much fear the fishing this year, in regard of the troubles, no herrings are as yet taken in the West Country, nor is the fishing of the Isles very promising, therefore, and because such commodities very scarce, and bills of exchange not so current as formerly, I would advise you to stay you please, there, and not to send anything, unless it be Virginia tobacco; as for sacks we have enough, and very cheap.

Sir, I pray you write to Mr Welch [*himself*], as he wrote to you long since from Charlem [*Carlisle*], and direct it as you were wont to do to his friend and mine (not meddling with the condition of affairs in either kingdom) for all letters were opened in several parts. Your cousin Thomas Johnson [*Mr Archibald Campbell, Argyle's Mr Household*] desires you to be mindful of his business, not forgetting his love to his friends in the fields or elsewhere; and if you can do any good in it, and that it be needful, he be acquainted that you use means to advertise him by any means. As for news, if I find it safe to adventure any, you shall have it from my friend; but I am unwilling (in the place where I am) to meddle.

I pray you, if you receive that 50 pounds of my brother, pay it not to Mr Smith, till I give direction, for in that I conceive it best to do as I find his bills acceptable and answered here. I pray you fail not to write to your cousin or Thom. Johnston [*sic*] effectually about the business so often pressed (especially about the pieces of Taffeta) and let them know what they cost you there, and then they will understand how reasonably I used them.

I pray you let me know when you hear from my brother, and in what condition he and my mother there are in; we have not heard from them this long time; but this I can assure you, that Robinson [*the King*] is well, and may have upon his word (such is his fair carriage) what he pleases. I will not trouble you further, than with the tender of my humblest service, to subscribe myself

Your faithful and most humblest servant,
Ralph Pudsey

Mrs Wisdom [*Cromwell*], by her carriage, has lost her expected friends; I fear she finds them real enemies, and it is my very opinion, although I be sorry for it.

For his very loving friend Mr Samuel Smith, merchant, at Mr Kirk, linen draper, his house in King-Street, Westminster, London.[23]

*

Let us examine the key sections one by one:

*As for any letters to Herbert* [Sir James Montgomery], *my weekly and constant enquiries have been fruitless, and I shall desire, seeing there is no hope of his recovery of fortune (far less of honesty or esteem here) that you rather stand to the hazard of payment of what you are engaged for him, than any way to have to do with such a bankrupt.*

Agent 'Herbert' is portrayed in the letter as a reprobate; there is a discernible tone of moral reproof. He is dismissed as a 'bankrupt', who has lost all esteem in Edinburgh and will never get it back; the reader is led to infer that Herbert has welched on some agreement and has now absconded. The scenario that is strongly suggested by the letter sees him recruited by Commonwealth spymasters for an intelligence mission, being given a down-payment in advance, but later failing to deliver the promised information and now proving unresponsive to all endeavours to establish contact. Best to simply write off the loss and have no further commerce with the wretch: that is the agent's advice to headquarters.

While some of this may have been true, Sir James Montgomery did not deserve such opprobrium. He was no sleazy cozener, but rather a gentleman of honour and integrity, a Cavalier in the best chivalric sense of the word. An erstwhile courtier to Charles I, Montgomery had returned to Ulster, where his family had been among the earliest Scottish settlers, migrating on their own initiative from Ayrshire to County Down some years ahead of the Protestant Plantation.

Sir James lived at Rosemount on the Ards Peninsula, adjacent to the ruined Cistercian priory at Greyabbey. It was a home of tremendous beauty and charm, with spectacular views out across Strangford Loch. His kinsmen owned most of the land in the peninsula. Sir James was a second son; his elder brother had been styled Viscount Montgomery of the Great Ards, as had been their father in his day. Now Sir James's young nephew, who was roughly the same age as George Downing, had succeeded to that grand title and, by virtue of some astute soldiering and derring-do, was promoted in 1649 to be commander-in-chief of the Royalist army in Ulster. This third Viscount of the Great Ards was remarkable in a further respect. A fall from a horse had left him with a unique thoracic aperture – crafted, in fact, by the King's physician William Maxwell, in which his heart could be clearly observed beating behind a diaphanous membrane when its metal cover was removed. Charles I himself had asked for a sighting and his royal wish was, of course, granted. Another who shared this privileged glimpse into the workings of the human heart was William Harvey, who found it gratifying as it visibly confirmed his theory about the ceaseless circulation of blood.

The viscount was reputedly an adept swordsman, dancer and player of the lute; but as a general he was, it turned out, no match for Cromwell's army. After a rout in the fields at Lisnastrean in the first week of December 1649, the viscount slunk away. He was lucky to make his escape from the field. His seneschal's son, who had been by his side on the battlefield, was taken prisoner by English soldiers with his hands still bloody from the slaughter at Drogheda. 'He was, contrary to laws of war,' recorded a Montgomery family account, 'shot by order and thrown into a sawing pit.' This was corroborated by the Attorney General for Ireland, William Basil, who reported to the Council of State that at least 1,400 had been killed at Lisnastrean and the army had given 'no quarter to any Irish'.[24]

Sir James Montgomery, a colonel with eight years' experience in fighting the Irish rebels, who had previously dispensed both military and avuncular advice to his commander-in-chief, missed the engagement at Lisnastrean as he already felt compelled to bid farewell to his beloved Rosemount and flee across the sea to Scotland. That the blood of the noble houses of Eglinton and Glencairn ran in his veins brought Sir James no advantage under the captious eye of Argyle. The Ulsterman had remained an Episcopalian and had refused to defer to the judgement of the Presbytery in Belfast in political matters; worse, he had shown himself prepared to consort with an uncovenanted king. The Committee of Estates declared Montgomery a 'malignant', and *persona non grata* in Scotland. He had no option but to travel to Holland and place himself at Charles's service there.[25]

If Sir James really had been recruited as an agent by the Commonwealth intelligencers, it would have been either in Scotland or the Netherlands that the pitch was made. Montgomery was by this time landless and penniless. Thomas Scot had it in his power to solve both problems. The spymaster could sanction a sizeable cash sum to see Sir James get through his current crisis; but more importantly, he could promise to restore Rosemount and the other Ards estates seized by the Commonwealth.

Aside from this letter from Edinburgh, which implies that Sir James was in some measure beholden to the intelligence department – 'stand to the hazard of payment of what you are engaged for him' – one of the three mysterious letters among the state papers held at the British Museum also suggests that Montgomery may have been employed as an agent of influence. That letter of intelligence, dispatched from Carlisle in January 1650, listed the parties then minded to persuade Charles to throw in his lot with Argyle. 'The Prince of Orange is of the same endeavour and opinion [as Queen Henrietta Maria],' the writer avers, 'as is Lauderdale and the rest of the Scottish lords at the Hague . . . and Sir James Montgomery, I am confident, has his instructions of negotiation in this particular.'[26] This letter was dated 22 January 1650, less than a month after Montgomery had left Scotland and probably too soon for news of his activities on the continent to have been brought from Holland, suggesting that any bargain with Mephistopheles had been struck in Edinburgh before he left.

And to crown it all, there was the money: more than one hundred gold pieces entrusted by Sir James to Alexander

Petrie, the minister of the Scottish church in Delft. Sir James's instructions were that the funds should be used to pay for his son William to attend the university at Leiden, where he would study under the Scottish philosopher Adam Stewart. Sir James, who was himself an alumnus of the university of St Andrews, understood the value of education. If he could not leave the boy his Rosemount estate, then at least he could ensure the lad would have something to say about substance dualism. The Academy in the Netherlands at this time was noisily and furiously divided between supporters and opponents of René Descartes. At Utrecht, students ran riot in the streets and the French philosopher himself narrowly avoided prosecution for insulting the university's rector, Guysbertus Voetius, whom he had called a 'stupid pedant' as well as 'absurd, coarse, impertinent and impudent'.[27] The disputations were more civil at Leiden, but the philosophers no less partisan, with Adriaan Heereboord, the professor of logic, championing Cartesianism, while Adam Stewart argued for Aristotelian orthodoxy.

Having left his gold at Delft, Montgomery slipped from view. As a young man, his father had served as a captain in the army of William I of Orange against the Spanish and consequently Sir James may well have had contacts in The Hague, where there was, in any case, a lively exile community, including many Scots and Irish noblemen. Besides, he did not have to linger in that location for long. The King and his court left Jersey in February 1650, travelling via France to Breda. Sir James almost certainly joined them there for the treaty and was among the Royalists gathered at Honselaarsdijk in early June. He travelled back to Scotland with the King, despite being one of the malignants that the

Committee of Estates had explicitly declared unwelcome on Scottish soil.

Banished from court on Argyle's orders and forbidden even to approach the king's person, Sir James nevertheless managed to make clandestine visits to the royal household and have 'secret speech with his Majesty' on more than one occasion.[28] While making his way south from Garmouth to his own palace in Fife, the King stopped at St Andrews to visit Robert Blair, the minister who had so vehemently denounced Cromwell as a liar in the Canongate. One might think that after Breda and Heligoland, the King would have heard quite enough from Kirk zealots and would not have freely chosen to suffer yet another, but Blair's wife just happened to be Sir James Montgomery's sister, Katherine.[29]

At the end of July 1650, Sir James was at Leith when Charles reviewed his army on the links, and was later at Dundee, where he entrusted his son William to a merchant, who took the boy across the North Sea from Inverness to Holland. At some point Montgomery must have spent time in Edinburgh, for when a couple of years later young William Montgomery finished his philosophy studies at Leiden, he would be rewarded with another bag of gold, to be collected from Lord Tweeddale's house on the High Street.

Sir James certainly would have been a prize catch for the Commonwealth intelligencers. He had access to a class of persons that were hard to reach: the leading Royalist noblemen that Charles regarded as his true friends, and in whom he confided; first among them, the Duke of Hamilton. Without an agent in place, Thomas Scot and his team would be reliant upon intercepted communications between the King's entourage in Scotland and the government in exile on the continent, which were frequently too stale to provide actionable information. One such letter obtained at about this time was from the Scottish Royalist John Ayton, writing with minimal disguise as 'Jonsonius' to Sir Edward Nicholas, a former Secretary of State and a member of Charles's Privy Council, a man with a thirst for intelligence and gossip that was impossible to quench. Ayton's letter brought news of attempts by some of the nobles who had been branded 'malignant' to ease the terms of their exclusion. 'Hamilton and Lauderdale have sent a petition . . . offering all satisfaction, provided they may be permitted to live privately in their own houses in the country,' Ayton reported. 'Some write that Lauderdale will be admitted, and Hamilton confined for a time to the Isle of Arran, which is in the West, near Dumbarton, where he may live like a prince.' The Marquis of Argyle, Ayton noted, had slyly convinced the King that he too thought the rigour of the sanction was excessive, 'though he be the only author of it'. John Ayton himself had been on an earlier Argyle blacklist and was one of the favourites whom Charles had reluctantly agreed to leave behind in Holland.[30]

Meanwhile, according to Ayton's account, an elaborately whiskered old Cavalier, Patrick Ruthven (pronounced *Riven*), Earl of Brentford, 'is at Edinburgh, drinking as fast as ever, until he sees what [the Scottish] Parliament will do with him'. In the Swedish army during the Thirty Years War, Ruthven had been the hero of countless battles from Latvia to the Rhine. Knighted by Gustavus Adolphus, he was appointed governor of Ulm, a city on the Danube eighty miles north-west of Munich. In the First Civil War, Ruthven held the rank of field marshal and commanded the Royalist army at the battles of Edgehill and Brentford.

During his long military career he had been shot twice in the head as well as in both arms, one leg and a shoulder. He had also pioneered a chilling psy-ops technique using flares and fireworks to inscribe a message in the night sky above a town he was besieging, summoning its surrender. Yet, as with Sir James Montgomery, none of this counted for much before the rigid Covenanters. 'After much scoffing at his titles', a fellow excluded malignant reported, Ruthven was peremptorily informed that there was no place for him in Scotland's army; and again, just like Sir James, he retired to Dundee.[31]

That Ayton's missive to Sir Edward Nicholas was acquired so readily is testimony to the already octopus-like reach of the Commonwealth espionage network, little more than a year after it came into being. Ayton's letter had never passed through any British postal or courier system. It had been sent from Middelburg, the capital of Zeeland, to Nicholas, who was at that time in Utrecht, another city in the Dutch Republic. Nevertheless, within a few weeks it (or a copy) was being passed around the table of the Council of State in Whitehall and may well have been provided to George Downing.

Yet in Scotland it just may have remained possible for 'Herbert' successfully to evade Thomas Scot's tentacles. Given Sir James Montgomery's potential value as an asset, George Downing's indignation at his absence without leave is understandable, even if most of Downing's sneers were unwarranted.

What Herbert did next is a matter of conjecture. Though there is a *prima facie* case that Montgomery entered into some kind of arrangement with the intelligencers, it is by no means certain that he ever fulfilled his end of the bargain.

Sir James could well have scooped up his down-payment and absconded without compunction. Cromwell's army had, after all, deprived him of his land and livelihood when they marched into County Down. It would not tax a man's conscience to relieve Cromwell's spies of a few bags of gold.

On the other hand, in the following months Sir James's nephew, Viscount Montgomery of the Ards, did receive markedly lenient treatment from the Parliament in London. In the Ards the spoils of war appear to have been left largely in the hands of the loser. The viscount was able to negotiate a deal preserving the greater part of his estate on condition that he simply withdraw from Ireland until political unrest abated. He received a pass authorizing his journey to Holland, where he visited his young cousin, William Montgomery, at the University of Leiden and the Princess Royal at Honselaarsdijk.

If the indulgence of the Commonwealth government towards the lord of the Ards had required some *quid pro quo* from Sir James in Scotland, then that has remained a well-kept secret among all parties to the bargain. What Sir James was up to remains opaque. He may have been in Perth the following year when his friend, Lord Duffus – his companion aboard the ship that ferried the King's party from Holland – surrendered the town to Oliver Cromwell after only a few hours defiance. If Montgomery really did facilitate the surrender, then his recruitment would have been a top-grade intelligence coup. The quick capitulation of Perth was a key element in Cromwell's strategic design in the run-up to the Battle of Worcester in 1651, which ended the war.

Thereafter, it appears, Montgomery withdrew to

Duffus's castle, which lay some seventy miles north-west of Aberdeen. It was in this remote corner of the Highlands, between the Cairngorms and the sea, that the leading Royalists gathered to plot their next moves, believing themselves well out of earshot of Cromwell's spies. Many of them stayed at the Earl of Dunfermline's castle at Fyvie, which, as it turned out, was not really a safe house at all.

At a time when the fighting appeared to be over, though it was only paused, Sir James quit Scotland, travelling incognito as a merchant. He chose the pseudonym 'James Huson' on account – his son would later aver – of his unshakeable attachment to the truth: Montgomery's father was christened Hugh, so his chosen moniker allowed him to avoid telling a lie when challenged at a checkpoint. Sir James likewise instructed his servant, whose father's name was Thomas, to go by 'Thomson'. At Newcastle the pair embarked on a coal boat bound for London, but during their first night at sea a storm blew up, separating their barque from the rest of the convoy. On the following morning, alone upon the swell, the coaler caught the attention of a pirate ship from Dunkirk.

Sir James Montgomery, an expert gunner, took charge of the coaler's cannons and fought a gallant maritime duel off the hulking chalk cliffs of Flamborough Head. The action ended when a chance-in-a-million shot from the privateer sent a ball through one of the coaler's portholes to bounce off the deck and spin diagonally upwards, ripping into Sir James's throat. It killed him. But chance was not done yet. When the pirates boarded, their leader became overwhelmed with remorse on discovering their victim's true identity. For the young picaroon was himself an Irishman from the Ards and his family knew the Montgomeries well.

Courtesy of this gentleman, Sir James was buried at sea with full pirate obsequies.

On the face of it, it would seem inherently unlikely that someone like Sir James Montgomery, with his over-scrupulous attachment to truth and a record of gallantry, would have entered into a squalid collaboration with Commonwealth spies to betray his king; but the Civil War had a way of making double-dealers out of even the most honest men and women.

> *Your cousin Thomas Johnson* [Mr Archibald Campbell, Argyle's Mr Household] *desires you to be mindful of his business, not forgetting his love to his friends in the fields or elsewhere; and if you can do any good in it, and that it be needful, he be acquainted that you use means to advertise him by any means. As for news, if I find it safe to adventure any, you shall have it from my friend; but I am unwilling (in the place where I am) to meddle.*
>
> *I pray you, if you receive that 50 pounds of my brother, pay it not to Mr Smith, till I give direction, for in that I conceive it best to do as I find his bills acceptable and answered here. I pray you fail not to write to your cousin or Thom. Johnston effectually about the business so often pressed (especially about the pieces of Taffeta) and let them know what they cost you there, and then they will understand how reasonably I used them.*

The agent referred to in the Pudsey letter as 'Thomas Johnson' was, according to Scoutmaster Rowe's invaluable crib, Mr Archibald Campbell, described as master of the Marquis of Argyle's household. It appears that the marquis did not run to a 'master of the household' as such, but had long employed an Archibald Campbell as his 'confidential agent' and man of affairs. By the end of 1649, however, this Archibald Campbell was in his grave. It is most likely that Downing's agent was his son, another Archibald Campbell.

This Campbell would certainly have qualified as a prize intelligence catch. Aside from his position in Argyle's retinue, which placed him close to the centre of political decision-making, Archibald Campbell of Kinpunt had married into one of Scotland's wealthiest merchant families, the Grays of Pittendrum. His in-laws' Edinburgh home, off the Lawnmarket, later known as Lady Stair's House, was one of the finest in the city at that time. Campbell's brother-in-law, the Master of Gray, would later that year command a regiment of foot in Scotland's army and, thanks to a special Patent of Honour supplied by the late King, was the heir apparent of Lord Gray, a officer in the *gens d'armes* of the King of France, who had been given leave to spend the last years of Charles I's reign helping to organize Royalist plots in Edinburgh.[32] Campbell himself was a kinsman of Lord Loudoun, the Lord Chancellor. Between his own family and his in-laws, he had connections with every faction from Montrose's former circle to the Covenanters, and encompassing both the highest nobility and Edinburgh's mercantile elite. The Grays, however, had previously been made acutely aware of the danger of being too well connected when their late paterfamilias, Sir William Gray of Pittendrum, was imprisoned in Edinburgh Castle after his secret correspondence with Montrose was exposed. Gray had the wherewithal to buy his way out of trouble and eventually did so, but the experience took a toll on his health, his reputation and his treasure chest. This time, it appears, his son-in-law, Archibald Campbell, was keen to suppress any risks on behalf of his wife's family and, courtesy of George Downing, apparently took out insurance with Oliver Cromwell. Should the English emerge triumphant, then the Royalist Grays would not lose their influence or fortune.

> *he has for his own adventure of the last year's crop about three quarters of wheat* [three thousand foot] *long since shipped* [raised], *and fifteen quarters* [thousand foot since], *which (with much ado) he has gotten licence to export, and skins of several years and kinds* [numbers of horse], *about seven or eight thousand; but for wool* [horsemen] *it is needless to expect it, for it always goes along upon the skins* [horses] . . .
>
> *this I can assure you, that Robinson* [the King] *is well, and may have upon his word (such is his fair carriage) what he pleases.*

The 23 July letter provides very detailed intelligence about the numbers of troops raised in the levy and the current standing of the King. Such information can only have been obtained from members of the Committee of Estates. George Downing's access to senior political figures appears to have come courtesy of Lady Craighall, whose husband John Hope, brother-in-law James Hope of Hopetoun and friend James Stewart of Kirkfield all sat on the committee. The last-named, in his role as Commissary General, actually controlled the army's finances and would probably have had the latest data on unit strengths brought to him every week. All three found themselves in a conflicting position: they were preparing to go to war against the English despite strongly disapproving of Argyle's alliance with the

King and were tempted to come to an accommodation with Oliver Cromwell instead. Indeed, one possibility up for consideration involved selling the King to the English.

Lady Craighall was born Rachel Speir. Her father and uncles were successful Edinburgh merchants trading mostly with Campvere and Middelburg in Holland and – like George Downing's cover persona, Ralph Pudsey – dealing in linen, silks, Naples satin and fancy buttons. As a teenager, Rachel was abducted and raped by a young man of her own class, a family friend.[33] A society that burned witches and believed that people generally got what they deserved in life might be expected to have been chilly in its response to such a serious sexual assault. As it turned out, it was the most rigid and strait-laced Calvinists of them all – intensely religious men, such as Wariston and the Hopes – who seem to have shown the most tenderness and sympathy. For the rest, the ravishing of Rachel Speir, like so many Edinburgh scandals, became something that everyone in the city's mercantile milieu would have known all about, but no one openly acknowledged.

Rachel went on to marry John Skene, the son of a judge, and in 1636, on the death of her father-in-law, became Lady Curriehill. The couple had a child, who died in infancy, after which Lord Curriehill sold his estates, raised a regiment, went to Germany and died there in battle. On 7 December 1643 Rachel Speir married John Hope, becoming Lady Craighall.

Effective intelligencers are alert to psychic pain, and some can ruthlessly exploit it. The mysterious WJ, author of the letter accusing Downing of being Lady Craighall's 'seducer', should not, however, be taken too literally. The seduction he mentions surely means recruitment for the purposes of espionage, rather than for sexual pleasure; although the selection of such a charged word might betoken shared knowledge between writer and reader of Lady Craighall's atrocious assault – a casually misogynistic allusion betraying a sensibility coarsened by intrigue, but having no further significance.

The Hope brothers would have been the most likely sources for the upbeat news concerning 'Robinson' (Charles's codename in the Pudsey letter), as only a few days earlier, on 18 July, they had visited the King at Falkland.[34] The Hopes were significant figures in the Kirk party, as well as elevated judges. Moreover, James led a parallel life as an industrialist. He owned lead mines, from which he hauled ore to Leith to be shipped on to Holland. He even bought his own gold mine at the unlikely El Dorado of Crawford Muir in Lanarkshire and had presented the King with a shiny sample of its product.

Charles himself was fascinated by science and technology. He talked to the Hopes at length about mining and metals, going on to tell a story about finding amber in an English cave. In this way he charmed and disarmed two of his severest critics. Indeed, James Hope was so strongly opposed that he had only the previous month voted against the levy to provide Charles with an army. Yet after the King's visit, Downing could say of 'Robinson' that 'such is his fair carriage' he could have 'what he pleases'.

Now it was time for Oliver Cromwell's spy to pack his bags and steal out of the city. Downing's lodgings were in the Sciennes (pronounced *Sheens*), formerly the Convent of St Catherine of Sienna, a Dominican nunnery founded by Scottish noblewomen widowed at the Battle of Flodden in 1513. The Reformation had swept away all traces of Catholic iconography, and the buildings eventually passed into the ownership of kinsmen of Lord Wariston. They allowed the cloisters to be used as a hostel for Protestant clergy visiting Edinburgh. As chaplain to Sir Arthur Hesilrige, Downing qualified for a room. After nine months and more in residence, he would probably have been stretching the indulgence of his hosts, were it not for Wariston's interest in keeping him under some sort of rudimentary surveillance. Wariston's suspicions of the chaplain were confirmed when his source at the Sciennes told him that in all the time Downing was there, he had never once been seen to pray.[35]

# CHAPTER 4

# Mr Downing Goes to War

## *East Lothian, July and August 1650*

WITHIN SIX WEEKS of his landing at Garmouth, an English army had arrived in Scotland to fight the King. Thomas Fairfax, whose wife was a Presbyterian and had for some time been pressing her husband to retire, had at last been persuaded to stand down. Oliver Cromwell succeeded him as commander-in-chief of the Commonwealth army and marched north. Crossing into Scotland from Berwick on 22 July 1650, he established his headquarters in the familiar policies of Mordington House.

The invaders found Berwickshire and East Lothian entirely desolate. The countryside had been systematically emptied, horses and livestock driven away. It was as if there had already been a massacre without any shot being fired. Nearly every adult Scottish male under the age of sixty had received a summons to the muster, or an order to move out. Only the wraithlike women, 'pitiful, sorry creatures, clothed in white flannel', were to be seen in the abandoned streets.[1] Yet, wherever the English soldiers went, a Scottish scout would be lurking in the treeline, observing their movements through a perspective glass, poised to carry intelligence to Edinburgh at a gallop.

Thus Lord Wariston, who was in the city, knew within hours when Cromwell moved his base to Sir James Nicholson's house at Cockburnspath and when he strode out from there to Dunbar to pick up supplies from the ships sheltering in Belhaven Bay.[2] News was also travelling in the opposite direction. One of Cromwell's staff officers reported to London that he had seen intelligence from Edinburgh that on the previous Monday most of the inhabitants of the city had shut up their shops and carried away their goods towards Stirling.

Sometimes, out on patrol, Cromwell's cavalry would have a fleeting encounter with their spectral enemy, perceiving perhaps the scent or squeak of leather, a whispered command carried on the night air or a glimpse of a horseman in the gloaming. On one occasion there was a more palpable contact, when the tip of a Scottish lance, as if out of nowhere, ran smack into English armour; but the Scot lost his balance, tumbling from his saddle down into a gorge, leaving his horse as a prize for a startled English trooper.

Oliver Cromwell had a knack of requisitioning the most well-appointed manor house in any district he visited. Yet even he was forced to endure privations in Scotland. By the time the army arrived there, Mordington House had been stripped of everything, right down to its cooking utensils. The headquarters staff had to repurpose a helmet as a pan for their porridge and roast their meat in a sheet of chain mail. The regimental officers too were miserable in their billets. 'In those quarters where we came between Berwick and Edinburgh,' one later recalled, 'we found not sheets in any house, and those beds that were left, were most nasty, greasy, full of fleas and lice.'[3] Nor, with the exception of Lady Winton at Seaton, did the Scots make an effort to extend the most basic courtesies. 'There was not any one of them that made officer or soldier of this army eat or drink, of their own accords,' the same officer recalled, 'so churlish and crabbed are they . . .'[4]

On Friday 26 July the army reached the town of Haddington, three and a half hours' march inland from the port of Dunbar and sixteen miles east of Edinburgh. When they arrived, Cromwell's staff received intelligence that the Scots were planning to march out to engage his army at Gladsmuir, a short distance from the town. This proposed battleground had a charmed association for the Scottish general David Leslie. It was here that his force had mustered, back in September 1645, ahead of their surprise attack on the Marquis of Montrose's army at Philiphaugh. Leslie's Covenanters, materializing out of the morning mist, had caught their Royalist enemies off-guard. The officers, including Montrose himself, were away in the nearby town of Selkirk, eating breakfast. On this occasion, by contrast, Leslie found that Oliver Cromwell had his men standing-to bright and early, so as to select the more advantageous ground for themselves. Observing this, the Scots drew off and there was no fight at Gladsmuir that day.

It was at about this time that George Downing appears to have linked up with the invaders. His time as a secret agent in Edinburgh was now over. According to the spymaster Thomas Scot, Downing's espionage mission ended 'when the army marched in'.[5] From now on, Downing would serve on Cromwell's staff as an intelligence officer in the field. On 24 July, the Council of State gave Scot instructions to write to both William Rowe and George Downing ordering them to ensure the Council was sent daily intelligence reports from the theatre of operations. Edmund Prideaux, the Postmaster, was charged with establishing a dedicated team of messengers, with horses ready at stages along the way, to express these dispatches directly to the Council.

As it happened, Scoutmaster Rowe had not come into Scotland with the army, but had remained at Newcastle to organize logistics. Some weeks later, Rowe found himself seconded to Sir Henry Vane's staff and then promoted to secretary to the committees dealing with Scottish and Irish affairs.[6] This meant that Downing had to take on the full range of Scoutmaster General responsibilities rather sooner than he, or anyone, had perhaps envisaged.

The English followed the Scots almost as far as Edinburgh before setting up camp at Musselburgh, some five miles or so to the east. The Scots, for their part, were sheltering behind a line of fortifications stretching from the end of the Canongate to the port of Leith, two miles to the north. Comprising a deep ditch with trenches, parapets and gun positions behind, the earthworks ruled out any attack by cavalry on the northern end of the line. The Scots had also placed artillery on nearby hills and put out a screen of infantry on the high ground at Salisbury Crags and Arthur's Seat to give notice of any English movements. To the south, their position was protected by the city walls and by the great gun-platform of Edinburgh Castle. George Downing, who had so recently lived in the city, was able to contribute up-to-date intelligence on the enemy's dispositions.[7]

Cromwell decided to draw out his entire army of 10,000 infantry and 5,000 cavalry and stand them nose to nose with the enemy – 'to see if they would fight'. He installed artillery on St Leonard's Hill, 'hoping to annoy them' by peppering their dugouts with shot; but David Leslie refused to be provoked into quitting his prepared positions, preferring to use the shelter they afforded against the heavy rain, which began that afternoon and continued throughout the night. All the while, the English soldiers lay drenched and shivering in the open. Meanwhile, four ships of the Commonwealth navy had sailed up the Firth of Forth and begun firing their big guns into Leith, while the army's field artillery pounded the Scots as they huddled in their trenches. The cannonade roared into the early hours.[8]

The next day, Cromwell, no longer in the mood for battle, began to march his soaked and by now ravenous army back to Musselburgh with the promise of a meal and the chance to dry out by a crackling fire. David Leslie chose this moment to send a large force of cavalry to attack the rearguard of the departing English column. Major Generals Lambert and Whalley pivoted, then charged the harassing Scots, driving them back behind their own lines. At one point in this 'hot dispute' a Scottish lance pierced Lambert's arm and thigh. Then, almost immediately, his horse was shot through the neck, causing him to fall to the ground, where he was taken prisoner by the enemy and dragged away. Fortunately for the major general, Lieutenant Empson, a gallant officer from Cromwell's own regiment, raced through the Scottish lines after them and succeeded in rescuing Lambert, escorting him safely back to base. All this time, as the actors in this drama would subsequently discover, the young king had been watching them from a place high on the castle's rampart.

Lord Wariston had also been a spectator, from a neighbouring vantage point. He was disappointed to see the Scots worsted by the English army. Although neither side performed as well as they would have liked, and could plausibly claim that providence had sent an ambiguous signal, Wariston and his fellow zealots had confidently assured everyone beforehand that it would take only a small number of godly Scots to defeat the despised sectaries without difficulty. To the chagrin of the professional soldier David Leslie, Wariston and his group of civilian commissioners, most of them ministers of the Kirk, were now interfering in the fine detail of military operations. Leslie might have hoped that their first engagements going awry might lead the civilians to back off and leave warfare to the military; but these initial reversals had the opposite effect. Perhaps seeking to justify his and the ministers' meddling, Wariston reached for an occult explanation for the failure of Scottish arms to win the day. He blamed a regiment of evil spirits that he claimed had been summoned by the Devil himself to reinforce the Commonwealth army. Wariston had obtained this critical intelligence, he said, from the confession of a witch. Besides, he noted, the English general was known to consult the astrologer William Lilly.[9]

The Lord General did not need a soothsayer to tell him that the Scots, having failed once, would try again that very night. 'We came to Musselburgh . . . so tired and wearied for want of sleep and so dirty by reason of the wetness of the weather,' Cromwell recalled, 'that we expected that the enemy would make an infall upon us, which accordingly they did between three and four o'clock . . .'[10] The anticipated attack came, however, from a wholly unexpected direction. A force of more than 800 cavalry had ridden sixteen miles during the night, taking a great loop to the south of the English camp and then pressing on as far as Prestonpans – a town further down the coast to the east of Musselburgh – before coming at the English from the opposite direction from their base at Edinburgh. No one had foreseen that.

On encountering a picket post on the edge of Musselburgh, two Cavaliers stepped forward to speak to the Roundhead guards, calculating that their English accents would prove disarming. But the sentries were not fooled. They sounded the alarm and the Scottish horde had to rush the checkpoint, killing the cornet in charge, before thundering across the fields towards the English lines.

Amid shouts and trumpet blasts, Lieutenant General Fleetwood's cavalry quickly pulled on their breeches and boots, leaped into their saddles and began to pursue the Scots through the streets of the town. Meanwhile the infantry opened up, discharging volley after volley at the raiders as they swept by. The resolve of the pot-valiant Scots soon broke and they fled back to Edinburgh in disarray, chased much of the way by the cavalry and sniped at by Colonel Okey's dragoons, who had been posted along the highway against just this eventuality. The English took scores of prisoners and brought the important ones to George Downing for interrogation.

The captured officers revealed that the King himself had commissioned the attack and that Colonel Strachan had pledged to bring Oliver Cromwell back to Edinburgh, dead or alive. Strachan, who was Musselburgh born, had, by some accounts, volunteered to lead the expedition, but had been denied the honour. The cavalry commander, Robert Montgomerie (a kinsman of the gallant and mysterious Sir James), had been placed in charge instead. This decision reflected the ambivalence with which the Scottish leadership viewed Archibald Strachan. He was, on the one hand, the dashing hero who had defeated the hated Montrose; but, on the other, a long-standing crony of the English sectaries. Could he be trusted? No, not entirely, it appeared. For this mission Strachan was given command of the second wave. Downing also informed London that he had been told that Wariston himself, together with two of the commissioners from the Treaty of Breda, had originally intended to lead the charge, but had eventually thought better of it.

George Downing also learned from his prisoners that the attacking horsemen had been specially selected for their skill and experience. Some were battle-scarred Cavaliers, veterans of the First and Second Civil Wars. A number of these were heard shouting, 'Remember Pontefract!' as they charged, signalling perhaps that they had been associated with that equally daring nocturnal sally that had resulted in the killing of Thomas Rainborowe two years previously; or, at the very least, that they had been up against Oliver Cromwell before; and yet here they were, still defiantly in the saddle.

The King, according to some of the prisoners, had given each horseman two shillings for his supper. Inevitably quite a number got drunk before they rode out. This reckless generosity on Charles's part went some way towards explaining why, despite having the advantage of surprise, the Scottish raiders returned to base in the early hours of the following morning with little to show for their boldness. As the attack went in, Oliver Cromwell was at nearby Inveresk House, comfortably out of reach; while George Downing and the headquarters staff, together with the artillery train and magazine, were secure behind the sturdy walls of the Stoneyhill garrison, on the further bank of the Esk. The night-riders had displayed considerable daring and cunning, yet in the end they had failed to redeem the military disappointments of the previous day.

The reports sent back to London from Musselburgh, informed by George Downing's questioning of the prisoners, contained some totally duff intelligence: accounts of the deaths in action of Colonel Strachan and Major General Robert Montgomerie. Downing himself wrote:

> Strachan, by all probability is killed, not only by the description of his person which they that killed him gave, but also of his clothes, and by his pistol and sword which are taken; by all which, both we and our prisoners do conclude him to be Strachan. After he was dismounted, he refused quarter, struck at one with his sword, and discharged his pistol; whereupon they killed him. But he being one of the last men that was killed and close by their line, they [the enemy] recovered his body.[11]

In respect of Strachan's fate, it is clear from his report that Downing has not simply passed on some scraps of gossip or given undue credence to battlefield rumour. He makes a show of having been painstaking in assembling his evidence. He has collected witness statements from the soldiers who claimed the kill. He has examined the pistol and sword brought back from the scene and has obtained verification from Major Brice Cockram and Cornet Joseph Shet (two of Strachan's officers, now Downing's prisoners) that the weapons had indeed belonged to their colonel.

By contrast, no evidence whatsoever was cited to support the claims about Major General Montgomerie. These were tacitly acknowledged to be mere hearsay. For sure, inaccuracy was common enough in the reporting of military engagements at this time. Indeed, gross exaggeration was the norm on both the Royalist and the Commonwealth sides. The claim that an enemy grandee had been killed could equally have been an example of the natural boastfulness of soldiers, or a routine piece of propagandizing, calculated to damage the enemy's morale. Indeed, at the very same time that the rumours of Montgomerie and Strachan's deaths first went into circulation, the Scottish side were putting it about that their raiding party had seized no fewer than eighteen sets of English colours and that the captains of all the English ships in the Firth of Forth had defected to the King; not a word of which was true.[12]

Nevertheless, there was something particularly suspicious about the manner in which Cromwell's headquarters handled the Strachan and Montgomerie stories. The issuing of the false reports appears orchestrated. A series of officers writing from Scotland repeated the same facts in the same order, as if they had been passed out as lines to take. For good measure, Oliver Cromwell recycled them himself, ensuring the erroneous narratives were read at the highest levels of government and entered the official record. Moreover they were sent off to newsbook publishers and pamphleteers, even though, by the time the accounts could be printed and circulated, everyone would know the stories of the Scottish officers' deaths were untrue.

Yet if this were a calculated misdirection, it cannot have been one intended to deceive the Scots – they had only to look out of their windows to see Montgomerie and Strachan, in the pink of condition, strutting about outside David Leslie's lodgings at Broughton. Nor could the Strachan narrative have been a Scottish ploy to gull the English. For that to be the case, we would have to believe that the resourceful Scots had found a body double for Archibald Strachan, dressed him in the colonel's clothes, equipped him with his distinctive weapons and then persuaded the gallant lookalike to lay down his life for the Covenant by picking a fight with some English cavalry at a place where he could be sure that his corpse would be retrieved by his fellow countrymen and not taken away as a trophy by the sectaries. Fat chance of that.

Once it is established that Strachan did not die on the night of the Musselburgh attack, then George Downing's dispatch to London can only plausibly be construed as putting up smoke. The army in Scotland was deceiving the politicians at Westminster. Scoutmaster General William Rowe and Oliver Cromwell had already agreed to keep from the Council of State the baleful news contained in the Ralph Pudsey letter – that Mrs Wisdom had lost all her friends. They had kept mum about this for two good reasons. First, they feared that any loss of confidence in the prospect of detaching the Covenanters from the King could lead London to withhold the reinforcements and supplies that the Lord General urgently needed. Second, they believed the news might encourage Presbyterians in England to coordinate an uprising in the shires along the lines that had been so frequently discussed by Fauconer's sources at Breda. Now it fell to George Downing to keep the awkward truth from London for a while longer. Strachan was among the Scots that Cromwell and Downing had long been cultivating. No doubt they had led their English associates to expect early and sensational defections from the Scottish to the English camp. By removing two pieces temporarily from the chessboard, declaring them missing in action, Downing helped his boss dodge any demands from the Council of State for an explanation of why the Covenanters had not yet broken with the King. Certainly such questions were already being asked at the army's headquarters in Scotland. 'We very much wonder,' one of Cromwell's staff officers wrote shortly after the Musselburgh attack, 'that none of the honest party amongst them do fall off yet to us. If they would appear, our work might receive a more speedy result.'[13]

During the first week of August the English army paused its campaign. In place of martial manoeuvres, Cromwell attempted a rhetorical sortie, writing to the leaders of the Kirk and beseeching them, 'in the bowels of Christ', to consider that they might be mistaken in making common cause with Charles. His letter followed others that had been sent to the Scots in the name of the officers and soldiers of the army. But while the English could discern godliness in the Covenanters and entertained a genuine hope that they might once again be brothers-in-arms, the Scots were no longer prepared even to pretend to reciprocate, instead denouncing the religious practices of the sectaries as blasphemous. Cromwell's forbearance was all the more remarkable given some information revealed by Downing's interrogation of the prisoners: that among the riders that night at Musselburgh were at least two ministers of the Kirk, and that they had incited the others to give the English no quarter.[14]

One of the reasons for the sudden military standstill was that it had become apparent to the English commanders that their logistics plan was not working well enough. They had been trying to land supplies at Fisherrow, close to the mouth of the Esk near Musselburgh. The tiny harbour there had existed since ancient times, but was unsuitable for vessels of heavy draught, such as those now arriving from Newcastle and London. The ships had to stand off in the deeper channels of the Firth of Forth while their freight was landed piecemeal by a flotilla of lighters, tugged at all the while by unusually strong rip currents.

Cromwell solved this problem by marching his entire army twenty-three miles east to Dunbar, on the North Sea coast, where his ships could discharge their freight in the natural harbour of Belhaven Bay. This provided the additional advantage of removing the English troops beyond reach of further raids from Edinburgh while they loaded themselves up with biscuit, tents and fresh powder for their guns. Once provisioned and rested, the Commonwealth army duly marched back to Musselburgh and reoccupied their old camp.

Then began an extraordinary *pas de deux* across the hills to the south and west of the Scottish capital as David Leslie and Oliver Cromwell's two armies, as though intertwined, manoeuvred in search of a battlefield. Each army would accuse the other of dodging the fight, but the truth was that both generals were expert at reading the ground and were equally determined to avoid doing battle where the topography favoured their opponent. Other factors were in play too, not least Cromwell's reluctance to keep his men out on manoeuvres for more than a few days in succession. From time to time the English would abruptly shrug off their dancing partner and slip back to Musselburgh for a meal, for the Scots had removed every horse-drawn vehicle in the Lothians. The Commonwealth army could not obtain any kind of cart, not even for ready money. Unable to bring up fresh water and rations in the field, they had to keep returning to base.

By now Cromwell and his senior officers had agreed that they could not mount a successful assault on Edinburgh from the east and had begun to explore other options. These would call for diligent intelligence-gathering. From a secure position in the Braid Hills, to the south of the city, they edged their way along the Scottish defensive line, testing the prospects of a drive up through Ravelston Dykes, on the west side of the city, to meet up with their ships at the fishing village of Cramond. If this ruse worked, Cromwell would have the choice of either attacking the fortified line running between Edinburgh and Leith from its relatively unprotected rear; or, alternatively, interdicting Leslie's supply shipments from Stirling and starving the Scots out of their fastness. There was intelligence suggesting such an outcome could be achieved quite quickly. A patrol report had already passed across George Downing's desk at Stoneyhill recounting an encounter between English scouts and a group of desperate, famished women who had made a risky, night-time escape from Leith to scavenge for food.

Leslie quickly worked out what the English were up to on the western side of the city and stationed heavy guns on the high ground at Murrayfield to thwart their stratagem. Cromwell countered by preparing to move his army in a wider westwards arc, aiming this time to rendezvous with his navy in the bays beyond Dundas Castle, near Queensferry. Writing from the front in late August, the Scottish Chancellor, the Earl of Loudoun, acknowledged the effectiveness of English espionage. 'The enemy has sure intelligence amongst us of all our resolutions,' he warned Argyle, 'and knows our difficulties.'[15] Just ten days previously, however, Downing had suffered a setback when two merchants, Patrick Crichton, a resident of the Canongate, and Robert Robeson, were arrested by the Scottish authorities and charged with having communication with the enemy.[16]

At this time, Downing and the English commanders were busy analyzing the implications of a declaration signed by the King at Dunfermline on 16 August, a copy of which David Leslie had delivered to Cromwell by a trumpeter. Drafted by the rigid Covenanters who had accurately divined that Charles's concessions to them at Breda and Heligoland, together with his swearing the Covenant at Garmouth, were all less than wholeheartedly meant, the document threatened to strip Charles of all self-respect. When Wariston and Argyle had first presented it to him, the young king flat-out declined to sign. Thereafter, every Polonius among the Scottish nobility was sent in to bully, badger, bluster and persuade. For a week the King held out. In the end, however, Charles understood that if he wanted to continue with the war and regain his three kingdoms, he really had no choice but to sign. The situational ethics that had been employed at Breda were given another whirl. With pretended pieties and sham surrender, while making all the mental reservations required to invalidate an oath, Charles swallowed the indignity and made a show of accepting the unacceptable. The London newsbook *Mercurius Politicus* sealed his humiliation with a succinct and painfully accurate account of his submission:

> The Scots King has been in the penitential chair. He has acknowledged his father's sin and his own wickedness in opposing the work of Reformation

> according to the Covenant; and his [Catholic] mother's idolatry; and promises to become a good boy for the future, and to own the Kirk as his oracle in church matters and the Committee of Estates in civil; and to do as they would have him.[17]

For George Downing the important question was whether there remained any prospect of the Covenanters transferring their support to Cromwell now that the king had signed the declaration. The English strategists had hoped that Charles would remain obdurate, and that the creaking alliance between the Kirk party and the Crown would collapse. At this key moment a group of Scottish officers, including Colonel Strachan, held a parley in the field with an English delegation. Downing alerted London to what seemed a significant exchange during this secret colloquy. 'Strachan . . . being asked seriously . . . what he thought of their King, and whether he conceived him any whit the better since his signing the late Declaration, replied that he thought him as wicked as ever, and designing both their [the hardline Covenanters'] and our destruction, and that of the two, he thought his hatred towards them was the more implacable.'[18]

As it turned out, by consenting to the declaration, Charles had, for the time being at least, stilled dissension among the Scots and kept Argyle's faction fastened to his cause. To the English, a bloody contest with Leslie now looked inevitable. The Scottish army, meanwhile, was once more being wrung dry. The declaration had licensed a fresh round of purges, which saw thousands of experienced soldiers excluded from service as morally and ideologically suspect. The royal household was also scrubbed clean. Many of the king's favourites, who had originally been excluded shortly after his arrival at Garmouth, had somehow crept back into Charles's retinue. Now they were to be driven out once again, this time with prejudice. It was at this point that the government issued a warrant for the arrest of Sir James Montgomery, who went on the lam.

Wariston records in his diary how he had spent the whole day of 16 August 1650 going through all the regiments of horse and foot and 'purging out and placing in officers'.[19] He was busy creating an army of saints to rival Cromwell's own. God, in time, would judge between them. No one, of course, knew the day or the hour, but the English were doing their best to press for a reckoning sooner rather than later. In the final week of August, Colonel Monck led an attack on a Scottish position at Redhall, a fortified house that commanded a crossing over the Water of Leith. Once again the two armies were drawn up facing one another. Following some adroit artillery preparation and the placement of satchel bombs, Colonel Monck and his men stormed in. Before long the Scots were hanging white sheets from the windows in surrender. Meanwhile the rest of the Scottish army looked on shamefaced at their own impotence, unable to break ranks to relieve their comrades for fear that the English would swarm in and overrun their positions.

The storming of Redhall was George Downing's first opportunity to observe Colonel Monck in action. This officer would become a close ally of Downing, a collaborator in many a murky scheme, someone who would help secure the young American's long-term political future. The two had little in common by way of education and background, but they formed an almost immediate bond and their fortunes would remain yoked together for many years to come.

George Monck came from a family of distressed gentlefolk in deepest Devon. By 1608, the year of his birth, no fewer than seventeen generations of Moncks had grown up in the manor house at Potheridge. There was said to be a touch of royal blood, a Plantagenet or maybe even two, somewhere higher up the family tree; but there was no longer any money. The family had dissipated their fortune. Yet thanks to a wealth of cousins and a prosperous grandfather, Monck enjoyed a happy enough childhood, dividing his time between Potheridge and the nearby city of Exeter. His family's social milieu was extraordinarily broad for provincial gentry, spiced with interesting and unusual people, such as Sir Walter Raleigh, executed when George was ten, and little Thomas Rolfe, the infant son of Pocahontas, who came to live nearby with his guardian when his mother died during a visit to England.

When he was sixteen years old, George Monck and his brother Thomas were drinking beer at an inn in Exeter when they encountered Nicholas Battyn, a minor official who had gulled their father out of the last of his money and then, out of malice, had him arrested for debt. The indignant brothers confronted him and began to thrash him with cudgels. While Thomas was wrestling with the innkeeper, who had intervened, George followed the already badly battered Battyn into the street and stabbed him with a sword in front of witnesses.[20]

George Monck had been contemplating a military career for some time; now he could delay embarking upon it no longer. To avoid prosecution, he ran away to war, enlisting as a soldier of fortune on the continent, fighting for Protestant causes. He helped out the Huguenots at La Rochelle and the Île de Ré and ended up in the service of the States General of the Dutch Republic, against the Spanish in the Netherlands. At the siege of Breda in 1636, Monck was the first man into the breach when the mines were sprung.[21] Thus he became Storming George, an expert in close-quarter infantry fighting, combining the pike press with judicious use of musketry. He would later add artillery to his repertoire, as he assaulted the bastions of the rebellious Irish Catholics in County Kildare.

This battle-etched veteran had an invaluable lesson for young Downing: one can swap sides and yet prosper. Monck had served in the Royalist army, until captured by Sir Thomas Fairfax's men at the Battle of Nantwich in 1644. After two years in the Tower, Monck was back on the battlefield, in Parliament's service. Now here he was outside Edinburgh as one of Oliver Cromwell's trusted colonels. Not that there had been no resistance to his rehabilitation. Monck had initially been allotted Colonel Bright's old regiment, but the soldiers refused to serve under him on the grounds that Monck had personally fought against them at Nantwich. Oliver Cromwell, however, trusted this professional soldier, whom he judged to be a man of honour. The general's solution to these awkward circumstances was to give Bright's regiment to Lambert and conjure an entirely new one for Monck, drafting equal numbers from Arthur Hesilrige's and George Fenwick's regiments, which were serving at that time as the garrisons of Newcastle and Berwick respectively. Now those soldiers were already showering themselves in glory at Redhall. Monck's scratch unit would go on to win great renown for its service in Scotland, and later for its part in securing the Restoration.

The regiment would subsequently be given a new designation: the Coldstream Guards.

Once Redhall was cleared, Cromwell led his men down from the hills and across the river, heading north-west towards the coast. Meanwhile his secretary, John Rushworth, had packed several ships with supplies and was racing from Musselburgh up the Firth of Forth, aiming to rendezvous with the army at Queensferry. The Scots too were on the march, travelling in the same direction on a parallel track, until the two armies came face to face once again at Gogar Burn.

According to George Downing's account, the English were keen to fight that day, but the ground would not allow it – there being bogs on both flanks that were impassable to cavalry. With a conventional battle out of the question, Cromwell decided on an artillery exchange instead. 'We drew up our cannon,' he later recalled, 'and did that day discharge two or three hundred great shot upon them; a considerable number they likewise returned to us . . .' The English were fortunate to be protected from the incoming fire by the hand of providence. 'There was several strange shots,' Downing recorded, 'one was at Major Hobson's troop which was drawn close together to prayer, and just as the Amen was said, there came in a great shot among them, and touched neither horse nor man.'[22]

Such uncanny workings of the supernatural did not spring solely from the excitable imagination of a chaplain-turned-spy; Charles Fleetwood, Cromwell's second in command, corroborated Downing's interpretation, testifying himself to 'very strange and remarkable deliverances'; and Captain John Hodgson, an officer of Lambert's regiment of foot, also averred that God was covering his head that day. Hodgson recalled only one shot flying among his pikemen, while 'all that were aimed at us flew over or short'.[23] General Cromwell's own report of the engagement pointed up the differential body count: fewer than twenty killed or wounded on the English side; around eighty killed among the Scots. Downing's tally was broadly similar, but he added the detail that only four of the twenty or so English casualties were actually fatalities.

Judging that he would neither be able fully to engage the enemy, nor to slip past them to join Rushworth and his ships at Queensferry, Cromwell began to withdraw towards Musselburgh. The army spent 'a tempestuous night and a wet morning' just a mile from Edinburgh, with many men falling sick. The Lammas rains had started to fall as the English army came into Scotland and had barely ceased since. Typhus and dysentery were by now rife. The Scots, meanwhile, had sneaked away after dark, moving eastwards, and were threatening to interpose themselves, according to George Downing's account, 'between us and our bread and cheese'. Out came the artillery pieces once again to do 'notable execution' upon the Scots, who, Downing sarcastically observed, 'very gallantly drew away'.

Once safely back within their base, Cromwell and his senior officers held a council of war. It was agreed that it would be fruitless to continue pursuing Leslie's army across the countryside. A change of strategy was proposed whereby a large military stronghold would be established at Dunbar, with a number of subsidiary garrisons in key towns and, in Downing's words, 'spoiling what of their country we cannot get under our power'.[24]

'It is thought here that you are too soft towards Scotland,' William Rowe was almost at this very moment writing to Cromwell, communicating London's desire for a tougher approach towards the enemy, calling specifically for the expropriation of all the corn and cattle in the hands of the Scottish gentry and laying waste anything of value that could not be confiscated.[25]

News of the king's declaration hardened attitudes against the Scottish Presbyterians within Cromwell's headquarters, bringing the officers into line with John Milton, one of the secretaries to the Council of State, who had expressed his exasperation at opposition to the execution of Charles I. In 'The Tenure of Kings and Magistrates', a pamphlet defending the execution, Milton attacked the hypocrisy of the Presbyterians who had 'born arms against their king, divested him, disanointed him, nay cursed him all over in their pulpits and their pamphlets', only to turn 'revolters to those principles' and denounce the regicide. They had 'juggled and paltered'.[26] When Milton's personal copy of Shakespeare's First Folio – heavily annotated – was discovered in a library in Philadelphia in 2019, scholars spotted many allusions and influences, including the similarity between Milton's phrases about the Scottish Presbyterians and a passage in *Macbeth* concerning the deceitful witches:

> And be these Juggling Fiends no more believ'd,
> That palter with us in a double sense,
> That keep the word of promise to our eare
> And breake it to our hope.[27]

Members of Cromwell's inner circle who had so earnestly anticipated the defection of the Kirk party before being disabused by the declaration expressed similar feelings of disappointment and resentment. The lines from *Macbeth* perhaps even find an echo in George Downing's own lament that 'if ever there was an unworthy juggling, which the Lord will witness against, it's among those with whom we have to do'.[28]

# CHAPTER 5

# The Dunbar Fight

*Dunbar, September 1650*

AFTER LOADING HUNDREDS of feverish infantrymen onto ships bound for Berwick and pausing at Prestonpans to burn down the house of a local laird, as punishment for helping the Scottish night-raiders in their attack on Musselburgh, Cromwell's army marched to the sound of beating drums towards Dunbar to establish a fastness. The Scots, misreading the situation, believed they at last had the accursed English sectaries on the run and followed closely, scratching and clawing at Cromwell's rearguard.

Outside Haddington the two armies appeared briefly to square up to one another in anticipation of battle, only to slump yet again into bathos. At about this time the Scots snatched an English trooper, treating him to a boastful tour of their ranks, pointing out their massively superior numbers, before inviting him to defect. When the loyal soldier refused the temptation, they cheerily returned him to his unit, presumably imagining that the account he took back with him would depress English morale.

As he was learning to perform the role of a Scoutmaster General in the field, George Downing would have been keen to garner any information he could about Leslie's dispositions and intentions. The trooper's story provided useful intelligence not only about Scottish strengths and ordnance, but also about the arrogance of their officers. A second abduction would reveal, from the horse's very mouth, what the Scottish general David Leslie was thinking.

A squad of enemy lancers launched a surprise attack on a cottage that housed the most forward observation post along the English line, carrying away a soldier who was missing an arm; but not before, despite the man's disability, he had got off three shots at his attackers. When this sturdy hero was dragged before Leslie, the one-armed warrior was in no mood to display deference to the Scottish general. Rather, he was in a froth of righteous indignation at the lancers for stealing twenty shillings from his pocket during his abduction. Nevertheless the old sweat had the presence of mind to remember precisely what the Scottish commander asked him and took the details back to his own superiors.[1]

Leslie had asked how could the English fight if they had shipped half of their men and all their great guns. Hearing this, Oliver Cromwell immediately realized that Leslie had misinterpreted the loading of the sick onto ships at Musselburgh as the first part of a phased withdrawal of his entire force. In Leslie's mind, Cromwell correctly divined, the English were pulling out of Scotland altogether and were using Dunbar merely as a staging post on the way to Berwick. Consequently the Scots had sent men ahead to squeeze the pinch point at Cockburnspath and had brought their 27,000-strong army up onto Doon Hill – the blasted, windswept edge of Lammermoor that glowered over the coastal plain, with the Berwick road running beneath.

The English army, still 12,000 strong despite the flux and camp fever, now took up positions in battalia along the left bank of a rocky stream that began as the Spott Burn and became the Broxburn as it ran dimpling past Broxmouth, the Earl of Roxburgh's house; this, with its deer park and walled garden and view out to Doon Hill, was commandeered by Cromwell for his forward base. The burn ran for the greater part of its length through a glen, forty feet wide and fifty deep. The sides in most places were almost sheer and where they were not, they had steeply sloping grassy banks that provided each of the opposing forces with a natural fortification and a minatory prospect. The burn could, however, be crossed more easily in three locations: first, along the Berwick road; second, at a ford immediately adjacent to what had been the one-armed soldier's observation post; and third, at a point beyond Broxmouth House near where the bubbling burn finally debouched into the sea. The Scots on Doon Hill had stationed most of their infantry on a narrow shelf along the right bank of the burn. Thus once again the warring parties were arrayed in battalia, facing one another across a ravine. The English infantry wore Venetian red; the Scots, hodden grey.

On Monday 2 September, Cromwell and a group of his senior officers met in the garden of Broxmouth House to observe the goings-on over at Doon Hill through a perspective glass. David Leslie had brought his cavalry down from the heights onto the flat land between Meikle Pinkerton farm and the sea. As the English commanders watched, Leslie also began 'shogging', as Cromwell later put it, the infantry units at the right-hand end of the Scottish line down the slope and onto the plain, along with eight or nine field guns.

It is possible that Leslie did this believing that Cromwell was planning a sudden break for Berwick, punching his way past the light defences along the road, leaving Leslie and his army to pick their way unsteadily off the hill while the English sped away to Cockburnspath. This new manoeuvre did indeed block the road, but threw away the advantage of the high ground. As Cromwell, Lambert and Monck agreed, by abandoning their impregnable positions on the hill, the Scots made themselves vulnerable to attack, and if Cromwell could bottle up the main force of Scottish infantry on their shelf, he could effectively keep them out of the battle while he destroyed the rest.

That night the English army did some shogging of its own, dividing imperceptibly into three groups. The first, formed up like a spear with six regiments of cavalry at its tip, was led by Lambert, Fleetwood and Whalley; behind them came Monck's infantry brigade. The second group, made up of some of Colonel Overton's musketeers and Colonel Okey's dragoons, took up positions along the edge of the burn alongside the artillery, who had been moved up from their hiding place in a nearby farm and were now distributed along the bank with a good number of guns concentrated within a pair of salients, formed by bends in the burn, affording direct lines of fire into the enemy's positions on Doon Hill. Meanwhile the third group, comprising Colonel Pride's brigade and the Lord General's own regiment of foot under Colonel Goffe, as well as Lambert's new regiment of foot (formerly Colonel Bright's), together with Colonel Packer's cavalrymen, forded the burn close to the coast, before swinging to their right, such that they would have their backs to the sea when they engaged the Scots drawn up on the plain.

The preparations went on quietly through the night, punctuated by prayer. Henry Hudson, who worked for Sir Arthur Hesilrige, later remembered how Cromwell had ridden by torchlight among the various regiments 'biting his lip until the blood ran down his chin without his perceiving it, his thoughts being busily employed to be ready for the action now at hand'.[2]

Yet despite their careful plans and preparations, when the hour came for battle to commence, John Lambert was late. A frisson of anxiety rustled through the English ranks as a trumpet sounded in the Scottish camp. Did it mean that the enemy was already up and alert and might even fall-on first? As it turned out, the Scots were anything but prepared for action. Many of their officers had chosen to dine and sleep at a farmhouse some distance from their men, whom they left shivering in the rain that lashed Doon Hill during the night. The infantry had been ordered to extinguish the matches they needed to ignite their powder and would spend the first crucial minutes of the action struggling to get their weapons ready to fire.

Finally Lambert led the English vanguard across the burn and charged the Scottish horse. But the Scots had put their lancers at the front, and the first English charge was repelled. The English kept coming in wave after wave, and eventually the Scottish cavalry formations grew fragmented and the battle became one in which small groups of horsemen fought hand-to-hand in different parts of the field for almost forty-five minutes without let-up. Numbers came to matter less and less; skill-at-arms and stamina would decide it.

Colonel Monck's pikemen were also repulsed at the first press, but displaying dogged resolve, they thrust themselves back into the melee. It was not recorded quite where on the field George Downing was that day. What is certain is that he was in the thick of the fighting at Dunbar, emerging with 'three great wounds in his arm, besides others'.[3]

As the flanking force wheeled right and prepared to join the action, the hanging haar suddenly dissipated and the battlefield was flooded with golden light. The Scots, looking out towards the sea, beheld the numinous sight of their attackers coming at them, silhouetted against the rising sun. Dunbar was where God was due to make his choices – between Cromwell and Leslie; between the English Parliament and Charles Stuart; between the Presbytery and tolerance; and between the rival battle cries of 'the Covenant' and 'the Lord of Hosts'.

For every minute the fighting raged on the plain, the guns and dragoons along the brink of the ravine had blasted at the infantry on Doon Hill until they could bear no more and quit the field. Just as the English commanders had predicted, confined to their cramped plateau with no room to turn, the main body of Leslie's army was simply unable to take part in the fighting at all.

On the other side of the battlefield, their forty-five minutes now almost up, the intense, but scrappy cavalry contest was reaching its denouement as the surviving Scots began to disengage and bolt for the hills. Most made for Haddington, while others fled to Edinburgh, some even as far as Stirling. The rout of the Scottish horse on the plain led their infantry on the lower slopes to lose heart in turn. Thousands threw down their weapons and surrendered; but not Lawers's sturdy Highlanders, who stolidly stood their ground, and every single man died on his spot.

Magnificent, yet to no avail. The Almighty had decided for the sectaries. Cromwell's elation was boundless, a beatific intoxication. 'Oliver was carried on as with a divine impulse,' an eyewitness recorded. 'He did laugh so excessively as if he had been drunk, and his eyes sparkled with spirits.'[4] Cromwell bade his cavalry briefly halt and gather round to sing together the 117th Psalm. Then they resumed the chase of the fleeing Scots.

On the following day, George Fenwick sent an urgent dispatch to the Council of State from Berwick:

> Last night I had some intelligence of a defeat our army had given the Scots but durst not venture to write of it, it being only from Scots themselves. This morning I sent out a party to gain further intelligence and they bring me in word that our army on Tuesday morning fell into the Scots' quarters, have slain 4,000, taken 10,000 prisoners, 180 colours, and 9 pieces of cannon . . . with all their baggage. Though there may be some error in these particulars, the substance is certain. David Leslie, I hear, and 4,000 horse are fled to the West.[5]

## *The hospital at Kinross*

Once the bloody gashes on his arm had been dressed, George Downing set about counting and sorting the prisoners. Oliver Cromwell ordered some 5,000 of them to be set free at once to take a long and painful walk home. These were the wounded that were judged unlikely to return to the colours. There was no food for them, and anyway it was better that they should be sent back behind the Scottish lines as a cautionary lesson in the hazards of war. One band of walking wounded, twenty-two strong, having crossed the Firth of Forth and trekked across Fife, turned up at the Countess of Dunfermline's lodgings at Kinross, where the countess's companion, Anne Murray, had established a rudimentary hospital. Some of their injuries were extremely serious: one soldier had been shot in the arm, another run through with a rapier from beneath the right shoulder to the left breast, and a third had a gash so deep in his skull that his brains were exposed. Mistress Murray's balsam soothed them all.

Murray had an extraordinary backstory. Her father, who was Provost of Eton, died when she was very young and Anne was brought up at court, where her mother held a junior position in the household of Queen Henrietta Maria. In 1648, at the age of twenty-five, Murray, together with her lover, Colonel Joseph Bampfield, arranged the escape of the Duke of York (the future King James II) from Parliament's custody. The young prince sneaked out of St James's Palace during a game of hide-and-seek so that his absence would not quickly give rise to alarm. Wearing women's clothing provided by Murray, he boarded a ship to Holland. Bampfield was a secret agent of inconsistent allegiance. As an avowed Royalist, he had undertaken clandestine assignments for Charles I himself. However, some years later Thomas Scot would name Bampfield as his only Commonwealth spy in Scotland other than George Downing.

Murray's visit to Scotland had been made at the instigation of Bampfield, who had met the Earl of Dunfermline at Breda and arranged an invitation. She had received the summons while with her friends Sir Charles and Lady Howard, whose guest she had been at Naworth since the autumn of 1649. The Commonwealth authorities, meanwhile, had arrested Bampfield for his part in rescuing the Duke of York and locked him up in the Gatehouse jail, which stood next door to Westminster Abbey. On the night before the colonel was due to be put on trial for his life, he escaped. Or so he claimed. Bampfield's story was that he had managed to procure a bottle of *aqua fortis* and used it to burn through the bars of his cell window, before lowering himself to the street on a rope made from his bed sheets. Although nitric acid can dissolve iron, the ease with which Bampfield acquired the acid and the unfeasibly speedy removal of the bars seem suspicious. Besides, cutting through prison bars with *aqua fortis* had become a widely circulating meme in Royalist conspiracy circles since the acid featured in an abortive attempt to rescue Charles I from Carisbrooke Castle in 1648, a plan masterminded by one of Charles's notably proficient female spies, Jane Whorwood, together – according to his own unreliable account – with the astrologer William Lilly.

Anne Murray attributed her lover's lucky escape to God finally heeding her own fervent entreaties on the colonel's behalf. Even in a godless age, this is a more plausible explanation than Bampfield's own story; but there were circumstances suggesting that quite other mysterious forces might have been at work. The Gatehouse was conveniently placed for the headquarters of Thomas Scot's espionage operation at Whitehall. It would have been remiss of the intelligencer not to have at least tried to recruit someone with the colonel's skills and experience. In the event that Bampfield was indeed given the chance to purchase his own life, a staged escape offered a way of placing him back into circulation. Although there is no evidence that he did actually perform any services for Scot until at least two years later, the period in between remains one of the murkiest in his very murky career. Bampfield's next move was to travel to Breda for the treaty, but the king refused to receive him. He found himself banished from court and compelled to seek new patrons and fresh employment in a pitiless profession. Much later, Bampfield would turn up at Fyvie Castle, where Anne Murray was still tending some of the wounded.[6]

## *The Durham death march*

Despite their fractures and gashes, those Scottish soldiers from Dunbar who ended up in the care of Mistress Murray were the fortunate ones. Once Downing had completed his reckoning, the remainder were sent south on what for many would become a death march. Major Hobson commanded an escort as far as Berwick, and along the way he or his officers shot about thirty prisoners who claimed to be too sick or exhausted to take another step. The rest – between 3,000 and 4,000 in number – were handed over to George Fenwick, who sent them on towards Newcastle. At Morpeth the by now ravenously hungry prisoners were detained for a while in a walled vegetable garden, where they found cabbages and various root vegetables, which they dug up with their fingernails and ate raw. This proved to be a terrible mistake. When they resumed their journey, many prisoners began to collapse by the wayside with painful stomach cramps, vomiting and bloody diarrhoea – symptoms of a condition known as the flux.

At Newcastle, three prisoners died and 140 became too sick to continue the journey. Yet more collapsed and died on the way to Durham, where the castle and the cathedral had been turned into a POW camp to receive them. According to Sir Arthur Hesilrige, it was not only the flux that was responsible for the continuing attrition of prisoner numbers. 'They were exceedingly cruel, one toward another,' Sir Arthur reported. 'If a man was perceived to have any money, it was two to one that he was killed before morning and robbed; and if he had any good clothes, he that wanted [them], if he was able, would strangle him and put on his clothes . . .' They were, Sir Arthur judged, 'rather like beasts than men . . . so unruly, sluttish and nasty that it is not to be believed'.[7]

Nevertheless, Hesilrige assured the Committee on Irish and Scottish Affairs that he had swallowed his distaste and exceeded the bounds of duty in promoting the prisoners' welfare. 'They had potage made with oatmeal and beef and cabbages – a full quart at a meal for every prisoner. They also had coals daily brought to them – as many as made about one hundred fires both day and night; and straw to lie upon . . .' Lest his virtuous conduct not be fully appreciated, Sir Arthur piled on the detail and the hyperbole: 'Those that were sick had very good mutton broth and sometimes veal broth and beef and mutton boiled together and old women appointed to look to them in the several rooms. There was also a physician, which let [their] blood and . . . gave the sick physic. And I dare confidently say there was never the like care taken for any such number of prisoners that ever were in England.'[8]

Hesilrige's defensive boasting may have been down to the provisional accounting the governor provided to the committee. This showed a further 1,600 fatalities and the tally was increasing every day. 'We perceive that divers that are seemingly healthy and have not been at all sick suddenly die; and we cannot give any reason of it,' Hesilrige confessed. 'Only, we apprehend they are all infected and the strength of some holds it out until it seizes upon their very hearts.'

London's interest in the Dunbar prisoners was not rooted in humanitarian concern. Within a week of the English victory on the battlefield, Scottish prisoners had become a commodity. The Council of State met to consider a proposal for making use of the captives on 10 September, and a little over a week later orders were speeding their way to Sir Arthur Hesilrige instructing him to earmark 1,150 prime Scotsmen to be sold into forced labour in the American colonies. The Scots were taken to London, where some were housed in an improvised prison camp on Tothill Fields in Westminster, and others in the East India Company yard at Blackwall.

The Scots were not facing lifelong servitude – typically the fate of African slaves. Their terms were milder: roughly the same as those of indentured servants paying off the cost of their passage to New England. The prisoners could expect to regain their freedom after working for six or seven years without pay. In the meantime, however, they could be sold on the open market from one employer to another. Those transported to Virginia or Barbados might find themselves working in the fields, alongside African slaves, under a broiling sun. Theoretically they enjoyed legal rights and protections that the Africans never had, but some were unable to assert those rights with indifferent masters.

More fortunate were the 150 Scots put aboard the good ship *Unity*, entrusted to the care of its captain, Augustine Walker of Charlestown, Massachusetts. Many would end up working at the Saugus Iron Works in Lynn for a company founded by George Downing's cousin. Downing's father had been a major shareholder, and the current owners – Emmanuel Downing's longstanding business associates, Joshua Foote and John Becx – personally inspected the prisoners before they were shipped. Becx insisted he would only accept men who were well, sound and free from wounds. Five years after George and Emmanuel Downing had proposed slavery as the solution to the Bay Colony's chronic labour shortage – particularly for the ironworks – providence had supplied an eerily similar answer. To underscore the familial nature of the affair, the cavalry detachment guarding the Scottish prisoners in London was commanded by yet another of Downing's cousins, Major Stephen Winthrop. The ironworks' holding company also had a shareholder, or 'undertaker', well positioned to facilitate the trafficking of prisoners. This individual was likely the person who secured official approval for the scheme. He was Gualter Frost.

Indeed, the American friends and relations of George Downing were not the only beneficiaries of the Scottish prisoners' sufferings. Sir Arthur Hesilrige and George Fenwick sent dozens of Scots to work in the Wearside saltpans and collieries. Others were dispatched to west Norfolk, where a company set up by a middle-ranking official named John Thurloe was draining the Fens; while in a bid to stimulate the local economy of the North-East, Hesilrige set up a textiles enterprise using a dozen weavers to produce a linen-like fabric spun from nettle fibres, known as Scotch Cloth.

Meanwhile, several hundred prisoners were sent from Newcastle to France to fight in the French civil war known as the Fronde. This group was said to have been pressed into the service of the Vicomte de Turenne, one of the rebel generals. The Fronde was essentially a revolt of the nobility against the claims of absolute monarchy. Some of the convinced republicans in England's Council of State – including Sir Arthur Hesilrige, Henry Marten and Thomas Scot – were keen to topple all the crowned heads of Europe. But the Council was divided, with the majority cautious about getting on the wrong side of Cardinal Mazarin and the Queen Regent of France. Consequently the Commonwealth avoided making any clear commitment by way of military aid to the rebellion, instead sending an intelligencer, Edward Sexby, and several assistants to Bordeaux, a town with a large Huguenot population – therefore appealing to Puritan sympathies – and blessed with a fine port that England might one day find strategically useful. The team would send back intelligence reports to Thomas Scot twice per week. The Council's political calculations were further complicated by Turenne's decision in 1651 to swap sides. Somewhere amid the vacillation, the studied ambiguity and the treachery, the Scottish soldiers simply disappeared, seemingly never to surface again in any official record.

The sickest of the Dunbar prisoners would remain in custody for many years, detained in Tynemouth Castle until 1655. By then the war was long since over and Scotland and England had formed a more perfect union, becoming one republic under a Lord Protector. Nevertheless there was to be no returning home for the lost soldiers of the Covenant. These last remaining captives were sold to the merchant Martin Noell, John Thurloe's brother-in-law, who shipped them to Barbados.

# CHAPTER 6

# Capturing the Castle and Ending the War

## *Edinburgh, autumn 1650*

As the raggle-taggle column of defeated Scots tramped south from Doon Hill towards enslavement or death, the victors sped north to the capital, Lambert dashing ahead with his cavalry to secure key points along the way. The Lord General's party entered Edinburgh from Leith on Saturday 7 September, allowing George Downing, nursing the wounded arm that was his trophy from Dunbar field, the opportunity to retrace his steps to the Canongate; this time without fear of being set upon by footpads. On the High Street, Cromwell's message to the merchants of the city was to return to business as usual. The townsfolk were heartened by the exhortation, for a rumour had been going from house to house and shop to shop that the English general was coming to reduce Edinburgh to ashes and put all its inhabitants to the sword. The threat was credible enough, given that the first anniversary of the massacre at Drogheda was in just a few days.

In fact Oliver Cromwell had come to close down the horror show, not to re-enact it. At the Tolbooth he encountered the repulsive spectacle of the Marquis of Montrose's rotting, severed head and ordered it to be removed from its spike.[1] By nightfall, it had become clear that the English army had taken the city with a tally of zero dead and only one soldier wounded. The sole casualty had lost an arm to a cannonball fired from Edinburgh Castle. This stronghold remained in the possession of the Scots, a brooding hulk that might at any time erupt, spewing hot iron and terror across the city that it dominated.

Oliver Cromwell was under no illusions that the taking of Edinburgh Castle would be easy. The fastness had already been besieged no fewer than nineteen times in the past and the most encouraging lesson history could offer was that anyone aspiring to capture the castle should begin by preparing for a very long wait. The Lord General would have his prize by Christmas, but that was more than three months after it was first conceived and he would have to employ the most creative strategies. First, he sent for coal miners to be brought from Derbyshire; then he set his Scoutmaster General a challenge.

While penetrating Argyle's circle during the Breda treaty, George Downing appears to have flagged up to his handlers in London that Colonel Walter Dundas, recently appointed governor of Edinburgh Castle, was friendly to the Commonwealth and belonged to a family with republican leanings, something quite rare in Scotland at that time. Perhaps he developed a relationship with the colonel, maybe even effected a recruitment? Dundas certainly had affinities with others cultivated by Downing: men such as Strachan, Ker, Craighall, Stewart and Argyle.

The fact that only one solitary cannonball had found its mark as the English army approached the city was surely, upon a moment's reflection, downright fishy. The castle held sixty-seven artillery pieces, some of them the largest and most powerful in the country. What could account for the silence of the guns? Puzzlement turned to suspicion as this reluctance to engage continued. In October, a large English force returning from an expedition marched home through the vale below the castle's north wall. Once again the gunners unaccountably held their fire. Master Gunner Thomas Binning was always gung-ho to have a crack at the English soldiers, but Dundas constantly kept him in check, eventually forbidding him from discharging any gun without his personal sanction. Binning appears to have attributed his superior's refusal to shoot to timidity of character.

Binning was unaware that Walter Dundas's servant, John Home, was George Downing's secret agent. On one occasion Home had actually slipped out of the besieged castle for a surreptitious meeting with Downing at a house in the town. There, in the words of his subsequent indictment for Treason, Home 'made appointment with Mr Downing to cast his letters of intelligence over the wall to the mouth of the enemy's minds'.[2]

Thereafter, at 10 p.m. prompt on the appointed days, Home would take his night-time constitutional along the ramparts and, from a position where he could not be observed by other residents, let his letter drop down to Downing, who was lurking below in a yard off Castle Hill. By these means Cromwell received accurate details of the weapons and ammunition stocks contained in the castle, the number of soldiers quartered there and the exact location of every gunpowder store. Later he would receive actionable intelligence of a superior kind, which, owing to its political sophistication, is persuasive evidence that Home was only a go-between and Downing's real agent was the governor himself.

For the time being, Dundas continued to dampen his master gunner's enthusiasm, but Binning constantly found new outlets for expressing his patriotic hostility towards the Sassenach besiegers. When Cromwell's coal miners arrived from Derbyshire and began literally to undermine the castle, Dundas told Binning there was no point bringing up any cannon as it would not be possible to lower the gun barrels sufficiently to shoot down at the earthworks at the foot of the castle wall. Binning took this attempted deflection as a test of his resourcefulness. He had part of the wooden aprons at the front of six guns removed so that the cannons could fire almost vertically down from the battlements, blasting through the roof of the tunnel the miners had dug. Then, in place of medieval boiling oil, Binning deployed an early modern chemical weapon: a blazing cask filled with powders of esoteric formulation, exuding noxious smoke that swept through the mine, flushing the Derbyshire men, their lungs and eyes burning, out into the blessed relief of fresh air.

Yet when Cromwell responded by bringing up his big guns, siting them in a nearby churchyard and blasting away at the castle in retaliatory ire, Dundas still forbade any return fire. This time, an exasperated Binning demanded that Dundas repeat the order in front of his men, so that the baffled gunners would all know whom to blame for their enforced passivity. Dundas sheepishly complied.

From the perspective of those besieging the castle, the rationale for the governor's conduct was almost as opaque as it was to his own men. Cromwell knew that Dundas was handing over all his secrets to Downing and had taken care not to inflict many casualties on the Commonwealth army. These were surely the actions of a man who, at least in his own conscience, had crossed over to the Commonwealth side. Why he did not simply surrender the castle and walk away was a mystery. Cromwell wrote demanding a plain answer. Instead, like an evasive lawyer, Dundas denied that he had any authority to act. He asked if he could seek further instructions from his client, the Committee of Estates. Now it was Cromwell's turn to be exasperated. Scotland was a defeated nation; its army had been routed at Dunbar; its capital city was occupied. Oliver Cromwell, Captain General and commander-in-chief of the Army of the Commonwealth, was its master now. Dundas was refused permission to consult the Committee of Estates, whose authority was effectively nullified.

The situation at Edinburgh Castle reflected the national political dilemma. Why had God been so angry with the Scots that he had inflicted such a shameful defeat upon them at Dunbar? For the ultras in the Kirk party the answer was obvious. The King was not really a changed man at all. Breda, Heligoland and Garmouth were all a blasphemous performance. When Charles took the Covenant he was disingenuous, and God, they believed, could smell the insincerity in his soul. An omniscient God would also have comprehended that the commissioners at Breda, the political leaders in the Scottish Parliament and the Committee of Estates had all known in their hearts that the King was insincerely covenanted; accordingly, a wrathful God was extending his divine punishment to the whole nation. John Livingstone, the minister who administered the Covenant oaths, confessed his own culpability to his peers, saying that all the blood spilled at Dunbar lay upon his conscience.

This faction's army, the Western Association, based in the old Whiggamore heartlands of Ayr and Galloway, was, by and large, hostile to the English sectaries, but felt little or no allegiance to the king.

Charles's supporters, by contrast, blamed the debacle at Dunbar on the meddling zealots who had purged the army of its best and most experienced soldiers and recklessly thrown away the tactical advantage that Doon Hill had given them. God was punishing wilful stupidity, military incompetence and excessive religious enthusiasm. In between these two extreme positions lay the mainstream – accepting part, but not all, of each analysis and now genuinely wrestling with the question of whether to bring back the engagers and perhaps even sundry malignants into a new Scottish army.

The Lord General, for his part, made it an immediate priority to secure the west of Scotland. He marched towards Glasgow, sending Major General Lambert with more than 3,000 cavalry towards Ayrshire. Lambert's force encamped for the night at Hamilton. Colonel Gilbert Ker, hoping to win some credit with his fellow countrymen by inflicting a defeat upon the arrogant English sectaries, decided to enter the town at dead of night and fall upon Lambert's regiments as they slept.

The major general had posted vedettes some distance out, who heard the clatter of horses' hooves on the frosty ground (this being the end of November). They promptly notified Lambert. He stood down all the sentries to lure the enemy into an ambush in the town centre. While the commander of the Scottish troops, Gilbert Ker, stood off on open ground with his main party, a smaller force of Scots under Colonel Ralstoun rode into Hamilton, triggering the ambush. Hand-to-hand fighting went on for hours through the narrow streets, much of it in pitch darkness after the moonlight failed at 3 a.m.

According to one report from the scene, Lambert was knocked from his horse and taken prisoner. His captors, unaware of his identity or status, took him to Sarah Jean's Close, reportedly the best inn in town, where he remained a silent and cooperative prisoner, until he took an opportunity to dive out of the back door. Soon back in a saddle, Lambert used the English army's massive advantage in numbers to full effect. Next morning, in the fields outside the town, the English drew up behind a ditch that was not readily visible to the approaching Scots. Once Colonel Ker saw the obstacle before him, he tried to veer away, but the soldiers behind him misinterpreted his manoeuvre. Believing their commander to be in retreat, they all decided to cut and run. Soon Gilbert Ker was wounded and a prisoner, the English cavalry were pursuing the fleeing Scots for twenty-five miles to Kilmarnock and the Western Association army was destroyed. The next day, Archibald Strachan disbanded his force of two 200 cavalry at Kyle and rode in to Lambert to defect to the Commonwealth camp.[3]

## *Edinburgh Castle*

Lambert brought Strachan to Edinburgh, where he was at once recruited to the project of persuading Walter Dundas to quit the castle. By the second week of December, Cromwell's patience was stretched. A Captain Hammond, one of Colonel Goffe's officers, had been down to inspect progress at the mine – the Derbyshire men were fully recovered and back at the rockface. All of a sudden Hammond dropped down dead, shot by a sniper from the battlements.

This brutal reminder of unfinished business came as two members of the Council of State, Sir Arthur Hesilrige and Thomas Scot, came on a visit to Edinburgh. The latter's arrival provided Scoutmaster Downing with an opportunity to brief the spy chief in person about an operation that was, according to the most recent missive dropped down to him, heading towards a satisfactory conclusion. Ideally the visiting grandees would themselves be able to witness the long-delayed denouement of the siege.

On the Monday, Thomas Scot watched the snowfall leaving a thick covering all over the castle and reported back to London. On the Wednesday, he watched a *grenado* kill five of the enemy and wound half a dozen more. As it happened, these final noisy bombardments, though deadly and carried out with guns and mortars brought in from as far away as Holland, were mostly for show. They provided plausible military cover for decisions actually being taken for reasons of politics and religion. There remained an all-night negotiation to be held at Colonel Overton's lodgings between Colonels Monck and White for the English and two of Dundas's officers for the castle; but as Thomas Scot drily noted, these talks were 'chiefly on point of time' rather than about the substantive issue of capitulation. Strachan had done his work and the fix was in. Dundas was ready to hand over the castle.

It is not clear what argument had been the clincher. Perhaps it was the King's insincere covenanting, or the news that engagers and malignants were being allowed back, or Lord Craighall's resignation from the Committee of Estates over these same issues. What Dundas told his own soldiers was that he 'would not own the malignant interest'.[4]

So it was that on Christmas Eve 1650, the entire garrison of Edinburgh Castle marched out under their colours, dressed in their finest uniforms, heads held high and still bearing their arms. They faced no prosecution or sanction. All ranks were free to go home to their families. Their commanding officer, Colonel Walter Dundas, had an appointment that evening for dinner – at the Lord General's lodgings in the Canongate.

The generosity of these terms was all of a piece with Oliver Cromwell's recent charm sally aimed at overcoming the tendency among the Scots to conflate Independents with sectaries. He had invited Independent chaplains, including Robert Stapylton, to preach model sermons in Scottish pulpits in a bid to challenge the prevailing prejudice. For the Lord General still held out hope for a coalition-of-all-the-godly in Scotland. Mrs Wisdom had been saddened to lose her friends in the summer of 1650, but was prepared to be magnanimous if there was any hope of rekindling those *Great Expressions of Love.*

## *Royalist plots revealed*

During the early months of 1651 the English consolidated their position in the south of Scotland. George Fenwick's men cleaned out nests of moss-troopers in the Borders, George Monck stormed the Scottish fortresses of Tantallion and Blacknesse and the main body of the army kept David Leslie bottled up at Stirling. Colonel Okey's regiment was reconfigured after Dunbar as proper cavalry – a regiment of horse rather than dragoons. No more shooting from the hedgerows for John Okey; he would now be leading the charge.

Oliver Cromwell, meanwhile, having been out in the rain, hail and sleet, caught a cold, then a fever; and then another fever. Tucked up in the Canongate, he was able to read the numerous intelligence reports sent to him by Captain George Bishop. Finally, the answers to the long-standing questions about which Royalist plots were serious and what the Presbyterians were really up to were beginning to pour in. Lord Hopton, an Anglican who had refused to have anything to do with the Covenanters, was, post-Dunbar, back in Charles's service and masterminding plots and uprisings. He had summoned representatives of all the English regions to attend a conference in Utrecht to report on their states of readiness to mount an insurrection. Unfortunately for Hopton, the meeting was multiply compromised and the details of plots in many of the counties of England were now, courtesy of Thomas Scot's team, on Oliver Cromwell's desk.

Captain Bishop, whose unctuous manner sometimes detracted from the clarity of his communications, either feared that the Lord General was overly complacent about the current security threat or, finding the Council of State dilatory, was appealing to Cromwell to energize their response. He added some theatrics to entice him into becoming more closely engaged: a mysterious female courier carrying 'something of great concernment' to the King would pay a clandestine visit to Cromwell at his headquarters. Cromwell would know her by the word 'Prosperity'. Bishop knew full well who the woman was: he refers to her elsewhere as a Mrs Hamlin (aka Mrs Waters); but he did not give Cromwell either name in order to preserve her mystique, though he kept Thomas Scot fully briefed throughout.

Captain Bishop warned of an imminent uprising as he set out his most up-to-date elaboration of the threats facing the Commonwealth. Yet in many respects the latest intelligence looked very like the material Fauconer had brought back from Breda. The overarching plan was for a force of cavalry to ride out of Scotland, led by the King himself, to come into England near Carlisle and race down the western side of the country, picking up supporters all along the way. Meanwhile, key military strongpoints would be seized in every county. Foreign troops, supplied by friendly rulers, together with exiled cavaliers, would land from the sea. Once local objectives had been taken in the South-East, Royalist forces would converge on London and liberate the capital. In each district well-known Presbyterian figures would declare for the King alongside Anglican Cavaliers. Everything would depend on perfect timing and clever coordination.

Captain Bishop's fresh intelligence provided some, but perhaps not enough, of the fine detail: what sign would trigger an uprising, what plans had been laid for providing horses, weapons, ammunition, food and water? Many of the protagonists now had their orders in writing, signed by the King. Thanks to the penetration of the Hopton conference, the services of the ubiquitous Mrs Hamlin and successful surveillance of an enigmatic fellow styled 'Harloff Massyns, gentleman of horse', Captain Bishop had read the commissions. The most dramatic development related to imminent foreign intervention: 'We hear that there lie in Denmark thirty-four Swedish ships of thirty or forty brass guns apiece,' Bishop told Cromwell, 'that are to bring over Swedish and German forces into Scotland in March.'[5]

Cromwell had to recover from his ague and, in discussion with his senior officers, including Scoutmaster Downing, carefully assess the threats that Bishop had set out for their consideration. For those outside the charmed circle, it appeared that nothing very much was happening at all. Perhaps Cromwell was once again studying outward dispensations, the better to read the mind of providence.

If so, it worked. Based on some word-of-mouth intelligence garnered at the dockside at Ayr from sailors blown ashore by a freak tempest, Colonel Robert Lilburne and a troop of cavalry were dispatched by Cromwell to the port at Greenock, where they arrested a man carrying a heavy box. He was Isaac Birkenhead, brother of the well-known Royalist propagandist and newsbook pioneer John Birkenhead, sometimes known as 'Aulicus'. The heavy box contained letters and documents detailing the Royalists' planned insurrection, corroborating George Bishop's account and providing further particulars about how the rising would be brought off in Lancashire, Cheshire and North Wales. Isaac Birkenhead had been on his way to the Isle of Man for a secret conference with the Earl of Derby, who was to command the Royalist forces in the North-West and rendezvous with the King's party as they rode south. Birkenhead's box was found to contain a further prize: a sheaf of letters written by one Tom Coke (pronounced *Cook*), the son of one of Charles I's Secretaries of State, currently residing in London. The addressee was the Duke of Buckingham, one of the King's closest advisers. The letters gave off the unmistakable whiff of High Treason.

Major General Harrison arrested Coke in the Strand some days later. After an initial examination, Tom Coke was offered a clear choice: if he were unforthcoming, he would be hanged, drawn and quartered; if he talked, his life would be spared. Coke spilled the beans with an indecent thoroughness. He widened the scope of his own interrogation, disclosing secrets about matters that he was not even asked about. Coke had probably realized that he would face a terrible punishment for cooperating at all, if Charles Stuart were to prevail. By confessing, Coke was also shifting his own allegiance in the contest. It now made sense for him to tell the authorities anything that might help Parliament emerge the winner.

Thus the Council learned about the arms caches in the City of London and the names of the Presbyterian ministers who knew they were there. It discovered the names of the field commanders in each region and of the organizers in each county. Coke explained in what ways the revolt had been financed and who had put up the money. He also told them something they really did not want to hear: that Lord Fairfax, the founder of the New Model Army – Oliver Cromwell's patron and mentor, a revered national hero living in well-deserved retirement – was party to the plot.

The more the generals and the intelligencers learned about the Royalists' plans and the more they considered the generous gifts of intelligence that providence had lately bestowed upon their republic, the clearer it became that the smart move now would be to let it all play out.

## *Inverkeithing, 19–20 July 1651*

In Scotland, with Oliver Cromwell now recovered, the army itself had fresh energy. The English were trying to trap David Leslie and his Scottish soldiers in Stirling;

Cromwell was advancing on the city by the land route, along the southern shore of the Firth of Forth, and now launched an amphibious operation under John Lambert to cross the waters to the north side so that they could close on Stirling from two different directions. George Downing was sent to work alongside Lambert. We know that he had secret communications with contacts in the enemy camp, but quite what he was up to would never be entirely clear.

The Scoutmaster General had crossed the Firth to Fife in a small advance party well ahead of Lambert's main force, which would comprise Colonel Okey's cavalry together with 4,500 men who were being ferried over the waters right up to the day of battle. Downing had learned that the Scottish army, under Sir John Brown and Major General James Holborne, was only a few miles away and that the plan was to attack the English as they landed. He was so busy, Downing would later complain, that he had 'scarce been master of a moment's time to eat or sleep'.[6]

Warned that Scottish reinforcements would soon be on their way from Stirling, Lambert took the initiative. Leaving his own infantry dug in among the woods on the blind side of a hill, he rode boldly over the top, straight towards the enemy. After a rapid skirmish, Lambert pretended to flee, luring the Scots to follow him back over the hill right into the ambush. Captain Bramston's dragoons, Downing would later say, 'gave very good fire upon the enemy and to good purpose' and, where Okey's cavalry charged, 'the service was very hot at the sword's point'.

Downing's account of the Battle of Inverkeithing passes quickly over Holborne's actions – or failures to act. 'The horse being beaten, the foot presently threw away their arms' is almost all he has to say about it. Some other accounts suggest that Holborne pulled his punches and that there was evidence of collusion between him and Lambert, who made a show of firing only a few cursory shots at Holborne's men before the latter withdrew prematurely from the fight. Downing's dispatch notes that the battle had lasted only about fifteen minutes before the Scots fled.[7]

According to a local folk tradition, Holborne was seen conferring with the English commander through a speaking trumpet (surely an improbable thing to invent?), while it was widely rumoured that Holborne had played the traitor. The disgraced major general subsequently faced a court martial, but insufficient evidence could be found to secure a conviction. Those who would have been best placed to testify against Holborne were dead. Nevertheless, he was required to resign his command and go into retirement.

James Holborne was the first Scottish general that George Downing ever met. It was he who had ridden out to greet Cromwell's party at Seton in 1648 and who then conducted them all to the Canongate in a very fancy coach. Holborne had made an unusually lucky escape from the battlefield at Dunbar, before heading off for Stirling, where he was appointed governor of the castle. It came to the ear of the authorities in that city that some Englishmen were heard bragging that Cromwell had used the same keys to unlock Stirling as he used to unlock Edinburgh Castle: that is to say, Holborne, like Dundas, was in league with George Downing.

Downing offers a tiny clue in support of this conjecture in an official dispatch written after the battle, which begins with his signature rapture: 'Truly the Lord is now breaking out of the clouds in his brightness . . .' This happy state of affairs is in uplifting contrast with 'how we were tugging these past ten months, and still reaped nothing but disappointments'. This surely cannot have been intended to characterize English military fortunes since the rout at Dunbar in the autumn of 1650. Things had been going well enough during that time, with Edinburgh and its castle taken and a string of military successes in the west of Scotland. There had by no means been ten months of unremitting frustration. If, however, the time spent 'tugging' applied more narrowly to Downing's own project to get the Covenanters to fall away from the King and come into Cromwell's camp, then the Scoutmaster's metaphors make much more sense.[8]

There was a further mystery. A band of 400 Highlanders from Mull, led by Sir Hector McClean, received unusually savage treatment after the battle. They were taken prisoner and told they were going to be given quarter: that their lives would be spared. Yet only two hours later they were stripped naked, robbed of all their possessions and every man was appallingly mutilated with swords – while being told that they were receiving 'Cromwell's mark'. 'There were about 2,000 of them slain and seven or eight hundred taken [prisoner] . . .' ran Downing's almost nonchalant dispatch, reporting on the casualty ratios. 'Of their foot not 200 escaped and those that are prisoners, most of them are so desperately wounded that they will hardly live . . .' Yet the Battle of Inverkeithing raged for scarcely more than fifteen minutes before the Scots were beaten. It is impossible that so many men were killed or injured during that brief quarter of an hour. What Downing describes is altogether more consistent with a massacre of soldiers *after* the battle. That would explain why twice as many men were killed as captured, and why these prisoners were so badly wounded.

Downing records the numbers, avoiding any detail or honest explanation; nothing to see here. In his dispatch, however, Lambert makes a show of addressing the question candidly. 'The reason the slain exceeded the number of prisoners,' he volunteered, 'was because divers of them were Highlanders and got very ill quarter; and indeed I am persuaded very few of them escaped without a knock.'[9]

By ascribing the horrendous butchery at Inverkeithing to a reflex antipathy on the part of the typical English soldier towards Highlanders, one apparently so understandable it barely needs a gloss, Lambert exonerates himself and his officers from responsibility for the slaughter. His dispatch and Downing's own matter-of-fact report of what would now be a heinous war crime also remind us that the granting of quarter to those who surrendered was by no means universally established in custom and practice, let alone a law of war, in the mid-seventeenth century. Quarter was more readily offered by the English than by many other armies in Europe, but its application was understood to be discretionary.

'Our word was Providence, theirs Scotland,' Downing wrote of their battle cries. 'It seems they were sensible that Scotland lay . . . much at the stake.' Downing too, it seemed, intuited that this rapid battle had a significance beyond what was immediately apparent. *Mirabile dictu*: in his church at St Andrews, at the other end of Fife, the minister Robert Blair collapsed in a faint mid-sermon, reportedly at the very moment God gave victory to the English at the Battle of Inverkeithing.

The road to Perth was now open. If Cromwell took it, Charles and his generals would not be able to contain the urge to make a dash into England. Their plan had always been to tie up Cromwell's army in Scotland while they crossed the border near Carlisle and raced south, meeting up with local insurgents all along the way. This is exactly what Cromwell wanted, knowing that all these local plots had been rumbled by Fauconer and Captain Bishop.

## *Worcester, autumn 1651: the final battle*

The Commonwealth's stratagem had worked. Charles and the Scots had taken the road to England and made their dash all the way to Worcester. They were harassed along the way by Lambert's snarling at their rearguard and Lilburne disrupting the pitifully small parties of insurrectionists who came out to join them. The trumpeted Lancashire uprising was quickly extinguished by Lilburne in the lanes and hedgerows around Wigan. Captain George Bishop had upended the Royalists' designs in county after county. Those betrayed by Tom Coke or named in the Fauconer, Hopton, Massyns and Hamlin intelligence had been hauled in for questioning. There had been arrests and speedy trials, such as that of the Presbyterian minister Christopher Love, which resulted in a controversial death sentence, chilling the enthusiasm for revolt. Warships took up station to deter the landing of foreign troops; and government propaganda branded Charles's Scottish noblemen 'foreign invaders'. The uprising fell apart.

Meanwhile the King and his followers, exhausted by their long ride from Stirling, were blundering into the trap that had been set for them. Oliver Cromwell left Scotland at Kelso and marched briskly down the eastern side of England. He sent George Downing on ahead to Newcastle to deliver orders to Harrison, who was to march at once to link up with Lambert and join in the harassing of the Royalist column.

Forces from London and the West Country marched out to join Cromwell too and by the time he arrived at Worcester the Lord General had an army twice the size of Charles's Royalist forces converging on the town from all sides.

As final preparations were being made, important intelligence came to Cromwell's headquarters from inside Worcester concerning Royalist plans to mount a surprise attack on Commonwealth artillery positions. Thanks to the timely warning, an ambush was set and a stronger guard provided to the battery. When the attack came, it was immediately rebuffed. A local tailor, William Guise, a Puritan, had provided the vital information. This spy was caught and summarily hanged by the Royalists. Cromwell awarded Guise's widow a pension of £200 per annum.

The Royalists had destroyed bridges to the south of the town over both the Severn and the Tame, but the Commonwealth army had come well prepared. George Downing was there to witness Cromwell assisting the engineers in person. 'They had brought up the river with them twenty great boats, with planks. My Lord General fell presently to work and in half an hour one bridge was made over the Severn and another over [the] Tame, just where both rivers run into one.'[10]

The fighting in the fields west of Worcester raged all through a hot afternoon and, as at Dunbar, Downing appears, from his report, to have been in the thick of the action. Cromwell's plan to force the Royalists out of the town to fight in the surrounding country succeeded. Having beaten them in the fields, the Parliamentarians chased the Royalists back into the warren of narrow streets and turned their own artillery upon them. Before long even Charles himself was in a headlong rush to escape. Thomas Scot, in a dispatch, reveals that the intelligence operation had continued throughout the day, shifting its focus in the later stages of the battle to preventing certain individuals from escaping – especially the King. 'The greatest number,' he writes of the army attempting to escape Worcester, 'in the dusk of the evening, ran away at the north gate towards Bewdley, whither Providence led us to send one thousand horse and dragoons under the command of Barton and Mercer yesterday; and unto whom in the midst of the battle we endeavoured to give intelligence and trust it came to them.'[11]

'The Lord is still triumphing,' George Downing was elated to announce. Once again, 3 September had proved a charmed date in the calendar. 'This day last year was the great appearance at Dunbar, and this day again the Lord hath disposed for such a work.' Downing's colleague, Robert Stapylton, had also spotted Dunbar coincidences. 'The word was then the Lord of Hosts and so it was now . . . The same signal we had then as now, which was to have no white about us.' Stapylton had stuck close to the Lord General in the run-up to the battle, staying with him at Robert Berkeley's manor house at Spetchley in Worcestershire. For security's sake, letters for Cromwell from the Council of State in London were addressed to Stapylton, who sent out replies under his own name via Captain George Bishop, the secretary of the Council's close committee, still dealing with secret affairs.

The intelligencers were out in force that day: the

spymaster Thomas Scot himself was on the field of battle, describing himself as a spectator 'from beginning to end'. He noticed yet another curious echo of time past. That morning Lieutenant General Fleetwood's men had fought hedge-to-hedge, clearing enemy musketeers near Powick Bridge, eventually spilling into Wick Field, the place where in 1642 the parliamentary cause had sustained its very first fatality, when Colonel Sandys was cut down in a clash with Prince Rupert's Cavaliers. Hugh Peter, in a sermon to the troops a little later, would craft a mawkish line about Worcester being 'where England's sorrows began and where they are happily ended'.

By nightfall, Thomas Scot had already bestowed laurels on the hero of the day: 'Captain [Charles] Howard of Naworth, captain of the Life Guard, to his Excellency, [who] has received divers sore wounds . . . Captain Howard did interpose very happily at a place of much danger where he gave the enemy (though with his personal smarts) a very seasonable check, when our foot, for want of horse, were hard put to it.'[12]

## *Prisoners for profit*

Some ten days later the first column of Worcester prisoners arrived at Tothill Fields in Westminster. Bedraggled, many of them shoeless, they had been subjected to ribald mockery all along the 112-mile march. This time the captives had not been reduced to digging up cabbages to feed themselves, so most – though not all – survived the journey. Oliver Cromwell personally chaired the committee in charge of the disposal of prisoners of the rank of captain or below.

The committee once again proposed shipping the prisoners off to the Caribbean and Bermuda, earmarking more than 1,000 Scots for New England, all to face the same long years of indentured servitude as their wretched predecessors at Dunbar.

The very same traffickers reappeared to profit from these wretched lives, with Joshua Foote and John Becx this time sending their consignment of Scots to Thomas Kemble, who owned timber plantations in Charlestown and a chain of sawmills that extended from Maine to New Hampshire. Foote, Becx and Kemble had all been doing business with Downing's father, Emmanuel, trading in ships' masts. Foote later emigrated to Providence, Rhode Island, where Roger Williams suspected him of selling illicit liquor to Native American tribes.

Another consignment of Scottish prisoners from Worcester had a further battle to fight, for a group of Royalists had infiltrated the island of Barbados, and its assembly had now declared for the King. Parliament sent a squadron of ships under Sir George Ayscue to take it back. In November 1651, he found the Royalists on the island holding a party to celebrate a heartening piece of misinformation to the effect that Charles II had won a thumping victory over Cromwell at Worcester. Ayscue supplied them with newsbooks containing a disappointingly correct account of the battle. Later a ship full of Scots prisoners took shelter in the bay. Ayscue gave them arms and sent them ashore to attack a fort; astonishingly, they won.

## CHAPTER 7

# Rump to Barebone's

### *England, 1651–3*

THEY HAD SEX in public, frequently while drunk and often while swearing. Adultery, buggery: there were no limits, and they did not give a fig for decorum. Spitting in the face of pious Puritanism was precisely the point. To hell with Christian normativity; upside down was not enough – the Ranters wanted to turn the culture inside out. They preached that marriage was a shameful vice, and heaven a dreary destination, to be shunned. Emerging from various Anabaptist communities in the mid-1640s, the Ranters possessed a semi-coherent set of contrarian positions of their own within five years; and their readiness to transgress generally guaranteed them coverage in the newsbooks.

One of the best-known Ranters of his day was Abiezer Coppe, an alumnus of Merton and All Souls, Oxford. Coppe would stand bollock-naked, the better to draw a crowd, insisting that swear words were the language of angels. He published a book under the title *Some Sweet Sips of Some Spiritual Wine*, whose softly hissing sibilants hopefully soothed the circumstances that had occasioned it: four nights spent, as he described, 'utterly plagued, damned, rammed and sunk into nothing, into the bowels of the still Eternity'; which sounds like a dark night of the soul, but equally could have been a hell of a hangover. Certainly Coppe eventually recovered from his ranting. One day he just walked away, changed his name and spent the rest of his life as a respectable physician in Barnes.[1]

The Ranters themselves never presented a serious threat to the security of the Commonwealth, but the mere fact of their existence, and the messages it sent – that there was something deeply awry in the polity, that barbarians were within the gates – had a strong political salience. The war was over now and the old constitutional dispensation of King, Lords and Parliament gone. Only a part of the old Parliament remained after Pride's Purge. A new legislature would be needed and a new system of government to go with it.

In November 1651, the Rump Parliament gave itself a deadline, agreeing not to sit after 3 November 1654. A new Parliament would be elected, but the army and the politicians needed to agree about the most profound of fundamentals: who would be able to vote and how elections would be organized; how the executive functions of government would work in the future; and what were to be the true values and ethos of the new constitution.

But almost immediately Parliament began to slow-roll all consideration of its own replacement. The Levellers and the Fifth Monarchy movement brought forward plans that spooked the more conservative and Presbyterian members. Underlying their political unease was an awareness that Parliament did not yet have a proper system for financing either the government or the army. The soldiers, for their part, believed that many of the MPs were self-serving and corrupt. They demanded radical reform, extending all the way from the breaking-up of monopolies and cartels to an end to corrupt dealing among devious merchants in the City of London.

Weirdos such as the Ranters, and by extension other sects such as the Anabaptists and Quakers, were held up as the reason why a whole new Parliament should not be elected at this time – and why there should not be an unqualified franchise, either. The Ranters became the bogeymen in every discussion. Their presence on the lunatic fringe of public life was a reminder to those entrusted with designing the new constitution to gird it round with strong walls and gates. The Ranter scare strengthened the hand of the Fifth Monarchists, themselves an outlandish millenarian cult, but who were also arguing for a Parliament made up entirely of godly men of proven integrity.

In the spring of 1653, the army's patience with the Rump Parliament ran out. The Council of Officers met to discuss what to do with its replacement, which was termed the 'New Representative'. The Royalist writer James Heath, who was neither present in the room nor an impartial observer of the events, did nonetheless provide an account of the episode in the course of his biographical essay on Cromwell, 'Flagellum'. According to Heath, Cromwell and Lambert had already agreed a secret plan to dismiss the Rump and replace it with an appointed assembly. There were, though, some officers opposed to dissolution who were prepared to speak out against it. 'Of those that opposed . . . Colonel Venables, Scoutmaster-General Downing, and Major Streeter, were the most eminent,' Heath asserts, 'but Colonel Venables was soon wrought upon, and Mr Downing, offering to speak against it in the Council of Officers, and getting upon a table for better audience, was bid to come down by Cromwell, asking him what he did there: only Streeter persisted in his Resolution of giving reasons against it . . .'[2]

Downing's humiliation, it seems, was mild; Cromwell's tone one of avuncular correction. This misstep would have no discernible consequences for George Downing's future. But the same cannot be said for John Streeter, who was at that time Quartermaster General of the infantry in Ireland. Having spoken at the meeting, he crystallized his objections into 'Ten Queries' – the title of a pamphlet he proceeded to circulate among interested officers. For his trouble, Streeter was court-martialled, dismissed from the army and eventually committed to the Gatehouse jail in London. He managed to obtain a writ of habeas corpus and represented himself at the High Court, eventually even winning his freedom; whereupon he launched himself into a venture built upon his newly acquired talents, setting up as 'John Street: Printer and Publisher' of pamphlets and law reports.

The army sent a demand to Parliament to tweak the wording of a clause designed to keep out Royalists in such a way that only 'persons of known integrity, fearing God and not scandalous in their conversation' would be allowed to take their seats. The MPs agreed to the new wording. Cromwell intuited that Sir Arthur Hesilrige and Sir Henry Vane, who were both involved in the bill's consideration, must be up to something. He feared that they had already decided not to hold a new general election, but simply to recruit new members to fill existing vacancies; and perhaps even planned *never* to hold another election, but just to go on filling vacancies on the basis of their own assessments of who, under the new clause, was qualified to sit. This would give existing MPs secure positions for life and would turn

Parliament into a self-replicating body. Such a proposal would be sure to command a majority.[3]

On Wednesday 20 April 1653, Cromwell turned up at Parliament with a squad of soldiers, who were initially ordered to remain outside. He had been alerted by Major General Harrison that MPs were planning to pass the bill through its remaining stages that very day in a way that would leave no further possibility of amendment or challenge. According to one contemporary account, Cromwell wore plain black clothes, with grey worsted stockings, suggesting perhaps that when he dressed that morning he was not expecting it to be a particularly special day. For a while he listened, then he got up and 'told them of their injustice, delays of justice, self-interest and other faults . . .' At which Cromwell put on his hat and walked up and down, pointing at particular members and reproving them for their individual vices.

Time was when English schoolchildren were encouraged to learn Cromwell's words to the House that day by heart, as American schoolchildren learned the Gettysburg Address. The text was taken from a document that was specifically endorsed: 'Spoken by O.C. when he put an end to the Long Parliament'. It was first published in the *Annual Register* in 1767. Cromwell's resounding denunciations will be familiar to many readers:

> Ye are a factious crew, and enemies to all good government. Ye are a pack of mercenary wretches, and would – like Esau – sell your country for a mess of pottage, and – like Judas – betray your God for a few pieces of money. Is there a single virtue now remaining amongst you? Is there one vice ye do not

> possess? Ye have no more religion than my horse. Gold is your God. Which of you have not bartered away your consciences for bribes? Is there a man amongst you that hath the least care for the good of the commonwealth? Ye sordid prostitutes! Have ye not defiled this sacred place, and turned the Lord's temple into a den of thieves? You who were deputed here by the people to get their grievances redressed are yourselves become the greatest grievance.[4]

Alas, the document was a fake, its provenance a fiction. More than a century ago, the historian C. H. Firth averred that it was 'perfectly clear that this speech was not what it purports to be. It is not seventeenth-century English.'[5] Rather, Firth explained, it was a political squib written in the eighteenth century and employing eighteenth-century locutions to rebuke the Parliament that had expelled John Wilkes. Nevertheless, the speech does ring with what is sometimes called 'truthiness' – the quality of seeming to be true, even if not so, which perhaps explains its longevity as a myth.

In real life, what actually happened was that Cromwell ordered Harrison to bring in the soldiers. Lieutenant Colonel Charles Worsley appeared leading some thirty or so musketeers in red coats and grey breeches. As the House was cleared, Cromwell referred to the mace as a bauble, made some disobliging remarks to Sir Henry Vane, snatched the master copy of the elections bill from the clerks' table and stuffed it under his coat as he left.

The House was then locked up and Cromwell returned on foot to his apartments at the Cockpit in Whitehall, where his officers, almost certainly including his obedient

Scoutmaster General, were waiting. There he told them that he had not gone to Parliament fully resolved to dissolve the Rump, but while listening the spirit came upon him and he acted upon the spur of the moment. For many, this stretched credibility too far. Cromwell had, after all, taken thirty musketeers along with him. And yet there had been something extempore about his performance, and afterwards no sign of any guiding masterplan. The improvisation had to be kept up. For instance, it soon became apparent that the Council of State was planning to meet. Since that body derived its authority entirely from a Parliament that no longer existed, Cromwell dismissed it too. Until a new one was established, the Army Council ruled the land.

Almost at once, differences and rivalries developed among the protagonists. A number of turbulent preachers from Harrison's millenarian cult, the Fifth Monarchists, began bad-mouthing Cromwell and talking up their man as a more suitable leader to welcome Jesus Christ when He returned once more to Earth in glory; something they suggested could happen at any moment. All the fanatical talk wearied John Lambert, who was hard at work running the day-to-day affairs of government while devising by candlelight a new, written constitution. Meanwhile a more pressing priority for them all was to summon into being an impromptu assembly.

So it was that on 5 May 1653, George Downing's former Covenanter contact, James Hope of Hopetoun, was paying a visit to his gold mine in Lanarkshire and was nearly there when, in a clatter of hooves and a lather of horse sweat, his clerk, who had been chasing after him all the way from Edinburgh, thrust into his hands an urgent missive from Colonel Lilburne. Hope was bidden to return to Edinburgh at once for an urgent meeting; but when he arrived, Lilburne had already gone. Hope pursued him to the army headquarters in Dalkeith, where Lilburne explained that Hope's assistance was needed in London; but would not say precisely what this involved. Hope cried off, saying that he had too many projects in hand at that moment and it was not an opportune time for him to leave Scotland. Lilburne asked him to put his reasons in writing to Oliver Cromwell. Only a few days later a terse summons arrived from the Lord General himself, requiring Hope's attendance at Whitehall on 4 July. An attached paper made clear that he had been nominated to what in England would be known as Barebone's Parliament – named after one of its London members, the leather merchant and Fifth Monarchist, Praise-God Barebone. In Scotland some called it the Wee Daft Parliament.

As he got into his coach at Haddington for the long journey to London, Hope found that his travelling companion was John Swinton, who had also been nominated to the Parliament. Swinton, two years George Downing's senior, was another of the group that had opposed the Treaty of Breda and voted with Hope against the levy in 1650. Later he had followed Strachan, defecting to Cromwell's camp, and was soon given a series of positions under the occupation, working alongside Downing planning the settlement of Scotland. Another of his associates, Charles Howard, now recovered from his wounds, was appointed to sit for Westmorland.

That work continued during the summer of 1653, with the actual legislation being crafted for the creation of a complete union. Discreet talks had been held with the Marquis of Argyle at Dunbarton. The marquis had quietly withdrawn from public life when the Scottish army turned and made a dash for England. He had no part in the invasion and consequently was unsullied by the Worcester debacle. Soon the marquis was squared, the burgesses prepared and the legislation was ready to be enacted.

Downing remained in London for the rest of the year. From this vantage point he had seen how all the great soldiers such as Cromwell, Lambert and Harrison were now hanging up their swords and following a political *cursus honorum.* He too needed to march in a new direction. Downing had achieved a certain degree of eminence very fast, but from now on a peacetime army would offer only limited opportunities for advancement. His months as a political vedette or rapporteur – the eyes and ears of the government in Barebone's Parliament, while also acting as one of Scotland's main channels of liaison with Whitehall grandees – brought him an understanding of the pace and diversity of life at the political centre, as well as expertise in the minutiae of parliamentary procedure: ideal training for a future MP. Doubtless, observing all the carry-on in the Wee Daft Parliament, George Downing concluded that he could do it better himself. He saw Barebone's Parliament fail: the opportunity for significant social and political reform thrown away amid endless squabbling between the Fifth Monarchists and moderates over whether or not to abolish tithes. Even those among the public who had cheered the eviction of the Rump might now, as they perused their newsbooks, turn from a lampoon to a straight account of the Parliament's proceedings, then back again, finding it increasingly hard to tell one from the other.

During this period there was also a changing of the guard in the intelligence office. When Gualter Frost died of gangrene in the spring of 1652, John Thurloe became Secretary of State in his place. Thurloe was a lawyer by training; for years he had been the amanuensis to the judge and MP Oliver St John, a close friend of Oliver Cromwell, to whom he was related by marriage. St John had been on a recent diplomatic mission to Holland, and Thurloe had accompanied him there, winning plaudits for his subtlety of mind. After the dismissal of the Rump, Thurloe became secretary to the new council established under Barebone's Parliament. The late Gualter Frost's son, also called Gualter Frost, continued to mind the secret budget, providing the emerging service with continuity and institutional memory.

After the dissolution of the Rump Parliament, Thurloe added the intelligence brief to his portfolio when Thomas Scot, a visceral republican and champion of parliamentary government who had disapproved of Cromwell's coup, was removed from his oversight of espionage and security. There was a general clear-out of Scot's intelligence officers. Captain George Bishop returned to his native Bristol, where he became a Quaker. Colonel George Joyce, meanwhile, had become greedier and greedier in his speculation in delinquents' land and found himself in a dispute with one of Oliver Cromwell's sons over an estate in Hampshire. Joyce was stripped of his commission and briefly imprisoned.[6] George Downing, however, like William Rowe before him, had an independent claim to a place at high table as the Scoutmaster General. Nevertheless, he would certainly have to cultivate Thurloe, who by virtue of being both spymaster and Secretary of State, was Downing's new boss. Thurloe thoroughly professionalized the espionage department, massively expanding its capacity.

Meanwhile the appointed Parliament passed twenty-six mostly technocratic measures. One that would have considerable future significance transferred the power to conduct marriages from the clergy to civil registrars and justices of the peace. Another forbade bear-baiting; and Colonel Pride reportedly marched up to the huge bear at Southwark bankside and killed it with his sword. In the background the government was bringing an end to the First Dutch War of 1652–4, which was entirely fought at sea and towards which Cromwell maintained a degree of ambivalence. By instinct, he would not wish to fight the Dutch; he would have much preferred to bind them into a pan-European Protestant league. The war had started under the Rump, arising out of low commercial motives spiced with a pinch of piracy on each side. George Monck was sent to command the Commonwealth fleet and was, therefore, absent from Scotland for the duration of hostilities at sea. George Downing spent some time with him, visiting dockyards, ordering ammunition and consolidating a special relationship with the general.

One day in December, as a result of some cunning shenanigans directed from the wings by Lambert and confined to such a small number of officers that Cromwell could have no knowledge of it, a group of members of Barebone's Parliament stood up and walked out, taking the mace with them. They continued to the council room at Whitehall, where they ceremonially renounced and handed back to Cromwell all the powers and privileges he had entrusted to them when they first sat, declaring the Parliament to be no longer viable. Other members, including James Hope, were left behind in the room where Parliament met, trying to make sense of the walk-out. A few minutes later Colonel Goffe arrived and pointedly told them to leave on the double. When some of the Scottish members refused to budge unless their sitting could conclude with a prayer, Goffe marched in a dozen musketeers, whereupon James Hope and the rest meekly complied. It was not plain to see – perhaps least of all to Hope – to what extent this event was another coup.

Downing's own analysis of the failure of Barebone's Parliament was sent the next day to Robert Lilburne, the acting commander-in-chief in Scotland. The Parliament, Downing wrote, had consisted of men 'abounding with zeal but wanting a due balance of Christian prudence'. This had led to 'the majesty of authority being lost'. Downing went on to disclose that John Lambert's guiding principle in drafting his new constitution was the importance of political stability. 'Care is taken for a settled government,' he wrote, 'that we may not be every day at this work, which is both troublesome and hazardous.' He signed off with a rhetorical question that supplied the news in a nutshell: 'What think you of a chief Governor with a council, and a triennial parliament chosen by the people?'[7]

The following day, Major General Lambert presented his new, written constitution: the Instrument of Government. The title 'Governor' was changed to 'Lord Protector', a warmer, more caring designation that still spoke of authority, but sounded less bluntly authoritarian. Regents had previously used the title, so it carried a hint of the provisional, suggesting caretaker rather than usurper; but that notion was squashed flat by the explicit and unambiguous election of Oliver Cromwell for life. There was a council as well as a triennial Parliament; however, it would not be 'elected by the people' in the sense that the Levellers and other radicals wished – that is to say, universal manhood suffrage. Instead there was a property qualification for the shire seats, while the boroughs continued to restrict the franchise to aldermen and burgesses. The constitution provided for religious liberty, 'provided this liberty be not extended to Popery or Prelacy, nor to such as, under the profession of Christ, hold forth and practise licentiousness', which excluded the Ranters as well as Catholics.

Three days later, with only a very few adjustments to Lambert's draft, Oliver Cromwell walked to the Palace of Westminster to be installed as Lord Protector of the Commonwealth of England, Scotland and Ireland. He went in tastefully restrained pomp, protected by his lifeguard, which was commanded by Charles Howard. It had all, Cromwell maintained, come as a complete surprise.

# CHAPTER 8

# A Marriage and a Settlement

## *Naworth Castle, Cumberland, 1649–50*

BACK IN THE autumn of 1649, the year they killed the King, twenty-seven-year-old Colonel Joseph Bampfield encouraged his lover, Anne Murray, to get out of London with some friends to avoid trouble. Bampfield and Murray had aided and abetted Charles I's second son, James, Duke of York, in his dramatic escape from Parliamentarian guards across the North Sea to The Hague, dressed as a woman, and the authorities might now be on their tail. Sure enough, Bampfield would be caught in a security dragnet and committed to the Gatehouse. Anne Murray, for her part, set off from London on 10 September and travelled safely beyond York in the company of her childhood friend Anne Howard, daughter of Lord Howard of Escrick, and her husband, Sir Charles Howard of Naworth. The party came at last to Henderskelfe, now known as Castle Howard, where Charles's two sisters were staying.[1]

After staying put in Yorkshire for several weeks to shake off an infection, the whole party, including the sisters, carried on north beyond Carlisle to Naworth in the West March of England, where Anne Murray would remain for approximately six months. At the castle was a resident chaplain, Roland Nicholl, who said prayers twice a day and preached sermons on Sundays, but whose main role was to apply a plausible veneer of Protestantism to the two sisters, who had of course, like Howard himself, been raised as Catholics.

Nicholl was endowed with all the theological and liturgical flexibility, or dexterity, required for the job. He could pitch high or low. An alumnus of Queen's College, Oxford, Nicholl became chaplain of Magdalen College and was said to have preached before the King himself when Charles I and his court removed themselves to the city in the early 1640s. By the time of the republic, however, Nicholl was seen by much of the county of Cumberland as an Independent; though after the Restoration he would swiftly conform, becoming chancellor of the diocese of Carlisle. Anne Murray's first impression of the chaplain was favourable: 'He was a man of good life, good conversation,' she remembered, 'and held in such veneration by all as if he had been their tutelar angel.'

One day a 'discreet woman', who acted as governess and chaperone to the two sisters, approached Murray wishing to confide a brooding anxiety. Each evening, she said, the young ladies used to attend Mr Nicholl in his chamber to receive instruction in the creedal heritage of Calvinism. But the elder sister, Mistress Frances, had recently taken to staying late, sometimes not emerging until after midnight. Clearly the canny chaperone doubted that all this time was spent on a painstaking exposition of predestination, but she had no solid evidence upon which to hang a charge.

Murray too was reluctant to raise the matter with Sir Charles and Lady Howard and was still mulling over what to do when her old friend slipped into the room, lay down on her bed and asked for help in heading off something that threatened 'great disorder' to the household. She explained that for some time she had observed that Frances was 'looked upon more kindly' by Mr Nicholl than was 'usual with his gravity'. On the previous evening she became aware, on departing from the dining room at the end of dinner, that she was leaving the two of them alone together. On an impulse of curiosity, she looked back through the 'cranny of the door' and saw the chaplain pulling Frances to him and 'with much kindness lay her head in his bosom'.

Roland Nicholl was thirty-six years old at this time. Frances Howard's date of birth was not properly recorded, as only too common for girls at that time. Equally, Catholic children were frequently not entered in Church of England baptismal registers. Taking account of the ages of her siblings, it seems likely that Frances was between fifteen and seventeen. An exchange between Anne Murray and Lady Howard suggests that she may have looked even younger. To Murray's suggestion that the girl is 'too much a child' for the chaplain to be seriously considering marrying her, Anne Howard responds that Frances's petite frame makes her appear more of a child than she actually is.

It so happened that Nicholl was up to other mschief at the same time, involving Iago-like manipulation designed to turn Anne Murray against Anne Howard, and vice versa. Yet even when the drama was brought to its denouement in the middle of an actual earthquake, which saw Howard and his chaplain clinging to the walls of the house to keep their balance, Sir Charles remained oddly reluctant to part with the doctrinally complaisant Nicholl, who had perhaps acquired too many family secrets. In the end Sir Arthur

Hesilrige found a solution, ejecting a nearby clergyman from his living on the grounds of culpable ignorance and installing Roland Nicholl as rector. That put the predatory chaplain safely beyond the castle walls, while leaving him dependent on Howard's continuing good favour.

## *The cousinhood*

Four years after these events the wedding took place between Frances Howard, daughter of the late Sir William Howard and the late Mary Eure of Naworth Castle, Cumberland, and Mr George Downing, late of Salem, Massachusetts. The marriage brought Downing, in his early thirties, into what was probably the most extensive and powerful aristocratic clan in Britain at that time, encompassing the dukedoms of Norfolk and Suffolk; the earldoms of Arundel and Berkshire; and connecting him to Lords Howard de Walden and Howard of Effingham – and to the Howards of Escrick for good measure. There was probably not a noble family in England, Wales, Scotland or Ireland that had not at some time married a Howard. The family's relational web stretched up the drive and through the gates of every substantial house in the Protectorate.

George Downing was now part of this cousinhood. It meant that people who had no reason to notice him before now had no option but to pay him attention and respect. One contemporary remarked that Downing had grown enormously in self-confidence as his career successes followed so rapidly one upon the other and enabled him to marry a beautiful woman of very noble birth. This glancing reference to Frances's beauty – and another tribute in a more hyperbolic vein – represent all we know of the bride's looks, for there is no surviving portrait of Frances Downing, if indeed one was ever painted. Despite many years as the wife of an ambassador to the Netherlands during the Dutch Golden Age, when anything and everything was praised in paint – the inner courtyard of a terraced house, a dish of glowing strawberries, a dead herring on a pewter plate – Frances, Lady Downing, remained undepicted.

Her wedding, on the other hand, was wholeheartedly celebrated. An epithalamium in Latin was commissioned for the occasion from Payne Fisher (sometimes Fitzpayne Fisher), who was fast becoming known as the Protectorate's poet laureate.

Fisher's poem is extravagant in its appreciation of Frances's beauty, which it claims surpassed anything seen in all previous ages. The fact that the bridegroom's recent past had been spent carrying out secret business could have posed an insurmountable problem for the composer of a panegyric. But not on this occasion, for Fisher was clearly briefed. He praises Downing for his watchfulness; for his bravery on behalf of his country in Scotland; for placing his own life in true peril on behalf of others. He singles out certain qualities in Downing: intellectual ability and ingenuity among them.[2]

Fisher came from a family that was ardently Royalist and staunchly Anglican. His father was a captain in Charles I's Life Guard. After studying at Hart Hall, Oxford (later Hertford College) and Magdalene College, Cambridge, Payne Fisher enlisted as a junior infantry officer in the King's army for the Bishops' Wars of 1639–40, where he became a friend of the Cavalier poet Richard Lovelace. He went on to serve in Ireland in the war against the Catholic rebels, serving under Sir John Clotworthy, the would-be trafficker of children to New England.

In July 1644, Fisher fought under Prince Rupert and the Duke of Newcastle, on the Royalist side, at the Battle of Marston Moor. After the defeat he was sent as a prisoner of war to London. There he made contact with Clotworthy, who was in a position to help, being an MP and prominent Presbyterian. Fisher made his plea in verse, recalling their time as comrades-in-arms in the Irish bogs, up to their waists in mire and mud, suffering privations that he claimed were as nothing in comparison to his present griefs in Newgate jail.

Once freed, Fisher became a literary turncoat, using his poem 'Marston Moor' to signal a shift of allegiance. Given that he already employed both John Milton and Andrew Marvell in an office just down the hall, Cromwell hardly needed a poet laureate. Fisher, though, had found a champion in General Monck's secretary William Clarke. Having spent ten months in Scotland in 1652–3 gathering material for a planned epic on Cromwell's victory at Dunbar, Fisher clearly made a strong impression upon Clarke, who composed a series of enthusiastic testimonials on the poet's behalf. These he sent to people who might help: Cromwell's assistant William Malyn; the senior administrator John Rushworth; the impulsive red-headed propagandist Henry Walker – a close friend of Hugh Peter; the newsletter writer Gilbert Mabbott, Clarke's own brother-in-law; and Richard Hatter, the secretary to the Army Council. This group was very much George Downing's coterie and he was in constant touch with Clarke, so it was almost certainly via this route that he was alerted to Payne Fisher's talents and new-found celebrity.

Downing's life had changed. His former patron, Sir Arthur Hesilrige, could not bring himself to approve Cromwell's personal concentration of executive power. Hesilrige was a 'Commonwealthsman' to the core, a true believer in parliamentary government and the spirit of the early rebellion carried in the idea of the 'Good Old Cause'. Hesilrige's idea of a model republic was in fact Venice. He wanted England to become a great trading nation with a sensible and moderate Parliament, where the real power was exercised by plutocrats such as himself. Neither Hesilrige, Thomas Scot or Sir Henry Vane was in a state of outright or visible rebellion, but they had all sunk into what would become a prolonged political sulk, during which they could be of no practical use in furthering Downing's career.

George himself could play the patron now, of course, given his successes. As his first act of patronage, Downing installed his brother Joshua in the customs office at Glasgow. There would be further opportunities to exploit. He had been spending a good deal of time with George Monck since the beginning of the Dutch War, visiting shipyards and passing time with the fleet. The Council, likely at Monck's behest, entrusted Downing with a massive budget and gave him the authority to procure cannonballs and shot for the navy, as well as the powers to requisition wagons for their transportation. The Scoutmaster General still had work to do in Scotland, but his day-to-day correspondence was increasingly concerned with foreign affairs and matters of national security – the comings and goings of ambassadors, the Dutch peace negotiations, Royalist plots – all within the bailiwick of Mr Secretary Thurloe, now the primary focus of Downing's desire to please.

'My brother Howard is ordered for the borders,' Downing chirpily informed his colleagues in a memo, just in case anyone had forgotten whom he had married. But there were still some personal matters he kept out of the public eye. Where had all his money come from? Not even his own mother knew. Since arriving in England without a shilling, he had somehow acquired a fortune. In 1651, Lucy Downing heard from her brother-in-law, Richard Kirby, that young George was 'the only thriving man' of his generation and that he had purchased an impressive acreage of land. How? Emmanuel Downing had learned something similar, thanks to an in-law taking a surreptitious glance at some private papers casually left out on a desk in a lawyer's office in London. These revealed that George Downing now had property yielding an income of £300 per annum – equivalent to a colonel's pay – and that was on top of his own salary. In October 1652, Hugh Peter was writing back to New England adjusting the figure to a full £500.[3]

These gains were modest compared with the wealth accumulated by some senior army officers. Major General Lambert became the owner of Queen Henrietta Maria's former palace in Wimbledon, which had recently been remodelled by Inigo Jones. Colonel Pride acquired the palace built by Henry VIII at Nonsuch in Surrey. Colonel Okey bought up countless acres in Bedfordshire.

In the North-East, Sir Arthur Hesilrige assembled an enormous portfolio of land in the counties of Durham and Northumberland, much of it from the sale of church estates after the abolition, in 1646, of all bishops and archbishops in the Church of England. In the late spring of 1648, a few weeks after he had first arrived in Newcastle to take up the post of governor, with his chaplain-cum-secretary

George Downing at his side, Hesilrige wrote to the Speaker of the House of Commons pointing out that the overwhelming majority of those living in the county who had fought for the Royalists in the First Civil War had mysteriously managed to avoid having their estates sequestered, and these same men were now joining the Royalist forces for the Second Civil War. Hesilrige wanted a new team, approved by himself, to sequester all Royalist property at once. Sequestration required a local committee appointed by Parliament to take charge of the property of a Royalist soldier – as a kind of trustee – and then let the property out to tenants for a fair rent. A proportion of the income was reserved for the upkeep of the owner's dependants; the rest went straight to the state, which used it to help meet the costs of government and war. But the Royalist could choose to go for a 'compound' – that is, pay a set fee, calculated on the value of the estate – and thereby release the asset from sequestration.

The system offered plenty of scope for corrupt individuals to enrich themselves without having to put up any initial outlay. An agent of the committee might, for instance, accept a bribe to understate the value of an asset, or look aside while it was transferred to a relation. He might establish two rents for a farm: a nominal one that was declared to the committee and was used as the basis for distributing the proportion reserved for the owner's family; and a true one – the one actually paid by the tenant, which would include something extra for the middleman. Rents or compounding were not the only ways to generate an income: for example, shooting a proportion of the deer on an estate and then selling the venison meat could produce returns that were easily hidden from the government; the same applied to felling timber. It was rumoured that some of the most sophisticated City merchants made vast profits from delinquent land without their names ever appearing on any register, either as buyer or seller. This was because they traded in mysterious abstractions, similar to the futures and derivatives markets today.

George Downing was living and working cheek by jowl with two of the most egregious expropriators of them all – Sir Arthur Hesilrige and Colonel George Fenwick, who were carrying on their enterprises on what was quite literally an industrial scale. The wealth went to Sir Arthur's head and he took to dressing his servants in velvet livery and having himself driven around the country in a magnificent coach. The joint enterprise of Hesilrige and Fenwick included coal mines, salt mines and textile mills. In April 1649, Fenwick acquired the colliery at Harraton on Wearside. Indeed, he bought the whole town too, as part of a package of assets formerly belonging to the episcopal manor of Houghton-le-Spring and Morton. After 1651, measures were passed by Parliament freely allowing the sale of Royalist estates; yet this came too late to explain Downing's earliest land acquisitions. Oddly, some of the most assiduous of purchasers turned out to be the Royalist owners themselves. There was no great shift of property from one social class to another during the so-called English Revolution; nothing like what occurred following the Dissolution of the Monasteries. Indeed, some of the noble Royalist families ended up with as much as 90 per cent of what they had owned when the Civil Wars began.

The players in the shadowy world of security and espionage, however, were particularly well placed to spot opportunities for acquisitions. For example, Colonel Joyce and George Bishop conspired to frame Lord Craven for Treason and subsequently confiscate all his estates in Berkshire. Craven had never fought on the Royalist side, nor was he part of the King's exiled court; rather, he lived at The Hague as a member of the household of Queen Elizabeth of Bohemia, in whose late husband's army he had once served. It made not the slightest difference.

Joyce and Bishop suborned perjured testimony from Fauconer, implying that Craven took part in seditious talk. This gave them the grounds to snatch his property. Lord Craven, however, was politically shrewd and highly litigious. He hired John Rushworth to assist his legal team and at one point even had the support of Oliver Cromwell in a Commons vote relating to the case. Craven kept his challenge going in the courts for many years and his land was at last returned to him at the Restoration. On it he built a palace for the woman he regarded as his own Winter Queen, for whom he had long felt a chaste *tendresse*; but she died before they could move in.

William Rowe had even higher aspirations than Joyce for upward social mobility. After his promotion to a senior civil-service position, he began to sigh for a coat of arms. A quaint survival of the adoption of the new form of republican government had been the position of Garter Principal King of Arms, held by Edward Bysshe. To obtain gentry status, Rowe, who came from a modest home in Pontefract, had to persuade the nation's social gatekeeper that he somehow passed muster. Bysshe declared himself satisfied, largely on the basis of Rowe's service as a 'General Officer of the Army, namely Scoutmaster General, under the command of their Excellencies Lord Fairfax and my Lord General, Oliver Cromwell'. When it came to land, not for William Rowe some mouldering Royalist estate perched up on the Ridgeway; he wanted sun-kissed islands: it was Bimini or bust. So it was that Rowe formed the Eleutherea Company with, among others, John Rushworth, Gualter Frost and the Independent MP Cornelius Holland, to take ownership of the Bahamas. According to a legal document citing the original bill, 'the said persons, their heirs and successors should enjoy and possess the islands forever'.[4]

George Downing was exposed, by the example of his colleagues, to a variety of enticing schemes for self-enrichment, and the moral climate of his times and profession was apparently indulgent towards a little gentle peculation here and there. It was seen as a way of recalibrating a man's financial equilibrium amid the vicissitudes of war. William Rowe once remarked to Cromwell that his work as Scoutmaster had in recent years drained his personal resources, but hurried to assure the Lord General that he wasn't complaining, acknowledging that in good times he had filled his boots, and implying that he expected to do so again when things looked up. Sir Arthur Hesilrige had personally met the running costs of his entire cavalry regiment – horses, fodder, uniforms and ammunition – through much of the First Civil War, before making himself whole from the bishops' lands. Parliament, the Council of State and Cromwell himself all recognized that a flexible approach to recoupment and reward was preferable to observing legal formalities. At least it was among godly men. As Hesilrige's secretary, Downing would have had broad discretion to agree or vary the terms of tenancies and an opportunity to piggyback on his patron's deals. As an intelligence officer, he would have been privy to knowledge that could be exploited for personal gain.

Downing was fortunate to have a very useful contact at the hub of the sequestration operation. A family friend, Edward Winslow, was one of the commissioners for Compounding with Delinquents at Goldsmiths' Hall, and was later a member of the committee that managed sequestered estates. Winslow was, moreover, one of the trustees for the sale of Crown goods. It was at his office in fact that the private papers detailing George Downing's property portfolio had been left open to view by inquisitive relations. Winslow was a fellow New Englander: he had been among the original Pilgrim Fathers, sailing to America aboard the *Mayflower* in 1620 and later serving for five years as governor of Plymouth colony. After his return to England in 1646, he remained in close and cordial contact with the Winthrops and with Emmanuel Downing, whom he had got to know well.

Their shared New England experience was by no means the only social thread connecting George Downing to the Compounding Committee. The tiny village of Clapham, three miles from Westminster, was at this time the home of a cluster of Independent Puritans who figured in Downing's story.

Winslow lived there; and so did Gualter Frost (secretary to the Council of State), Joshua Foote (one of the shareholders in the Saugus ironworks) and Richard Salway, a member of the Council and spymaster Thomas Scot's fellow intelligencer on the battlefield at Worcester. As it happened, two other members of the Compounding Committee – Samuel Moyer and William Molins – were Clapham residents as well. In all respects, Winslow was an ideally placed mentor for George Downing to consult.

In July 1650, Emmanuel Downing complained that he

had not had any letters from his son George for a year. Lucy Downing recorded that she had not been able to have any sustained contact with George for a long time, either. The protracted silence corresponded with the period of the Breda Mission and the initial phase of the invasion of Scotland before the Battle of Dunbar. Emmanuel was particularly keen to get hold of George because he had a money-making scheme in play that he hoped might have been brought to fruition. 'When I was last in London I left a business with Sir Arthur Hesilrige and George, who both promised to get it dispatched for me,' he told the younger Winthrop. 'When Sr Arthur read it, he said it was very honest and of great use to the Commonwealth. It's of more value than I will speak of.' What the project was – and how much, if anything, came of it – appears not to have been mentioned again.

In December 1654, Oliver Cromwell sent Winslow to the Caribbean as one of the commissioners of his Western Design – an ill-starred expedition to seize some Spanish colonies in the Americas. During an attempt to take Santo Domingo, providence seemed to turn against the project – and, by extension, the Protectorate. General Venables caught dysentery, got lost in the woods and became a laughing stock among his men. His officers displayed shameful incompetence, and his soldiers ran not just from the Spanish, but at Fort San Geronimo from Colonel John Murphy's cow-killers. Murphy was believed to be an Irish Catholic, expropriated by Cromwell and now out for blood. His little army consisted of 200 hunters, whose day job was to catch and kill cattle that, having heard the call of the wild, had made off to the forest. By the end of the engagement Venables's men had turned so faint-hearted that they panicked at the approach of two of their own African bearers; whereupon it was decided to move on and try conquering somewhere else instead.[5] Rotten luck pursued them. Out of the blue, Edward Winslow was bitten by a mosquito, took sick and died, probably of yellow fever. At the end of the first week of May 1655, the commissioner was buried at sea somewhere between Hispaniola and Jamaica, taking the secret of George Downing's wealth to Davy Jones's locker.

## *The Trossachs, August 1654*

At the very time when General Venables was receiving his orders from the Lord Protector for the Western Design, George Downing was spotted in a remote part of the Trossachs. Cornet John Baynes, a commissary officer with General Monck's forces, recorded Downing's arrival in mid-August at a camp near Duchray Castle in Aberfoyle.[6] Monck and his men had been destroying farms and settlements nearby, hoping to bring an end to an uprising that had been launched by the Earl of Glencairn more than twelve months before. The English general's plan was to ensure that there would be no food to sustain the insurrectionists through the coming autumn and winter.

It was at Duchray, in August of the previous year, that Glencairn had held his first rendezvous and set up his headquarters. The castle belonged to his stalwart, John Graham – known as the Highland Hector and the Tetrarch of Aberfoyle, who carried everywhere a silver pistol that had been a gift from Montrose. The rebels turned out many-hued and motley. Covenanters rode beside Catholic

Cavaliers; Lowlanders marched cheek by jowl with Highlanders . . . and even Islanders; some of the most exalted noblemen in the land made common cause with simple cotters; all pledged to serve their king. This may have had the appearance of a hastily improvised revolt, but the core group of Royalists in touch with the exiled Charles had been carefully laying their plans since early 1652. The rebels' horses were bought, begged and borrowed from every point of the compass; some were even stolen from right under the noses of the English as they watered at the Town Loch in Edinburgh.

Edward Wogan, an astonishingly daring Irishman fresh from France, joined the insurrection some weeks later. Wogan was a turncoat, who had begun his military career in the New Model Army, serving as a captain in Colonel Okey's dragoons at the time when George Downing was chaplain. In 1648, hearing that his company was to be disbanded, Wogan swapped sides, joining the Engagement and fighting with Hamilton's army against Cromwell at the Battle of Preston. Despite his Roundhead past, Wogan came to epitomize the Cavalier spirit. He had been kicking his heels at court since helping the King escape from the battlefield at Worcester. Hearing gossip about an upcoming rising in Scotland, he pleaded with Charles to let him take a few bored and frustrated young blades like himself and join in the action. Having landed secretly from the continent, the plucky band gathered a score of extra horsemen in London and headed north to join Glencairn, wearing purloined Roundhead uniforms. Wogan rode boldly through Berwick, even taking a number of prisoners there, before going on to recruit dozens of moss-troopers to his buccaneering squadron during its progress through the Merse.

Meanwhile the Tetrarch had led a charge of twenty Highlanders armed with broadswords, which got the better of a much more numerous column of Roundheads who had ridden out from Stirling to police the pass at Aberfoyle. In the following months Colonel Lilburne succeeded in containing the uprising, but really only scorched the snake. Just when one district seemed pacified, another would break out in rebellion as the contagion of revolt spread through the heather from glen to glen. Wogan, though, was soon killed. In a clash with Colonel Rich's regiment, he received a wound that turned septic. Despite the best efforts of a surgeon, his flame guttered and he died at Wemyss Castle on 4 February 1654.

The Marquis of Argyle was most devious and serpentine throughout the uprising. For a while at least he was actively providing intelligence to the English, even about the movements of his own son, Lord Lorne. On the other hand, Monck became more and more convinced that Argyle had such an animus against England that he could never be believed, and some of the junior officers began referring to him as the Marquis of Arch Guile. Given their previous connection at the time of the Treaty of Breda, it is likely that Scoutmaster General Downing would have been involved either in running Argyle as an agent or in helping Lilburne analyse and interpret the intelligence he provided.

The shadow of Joseph Bampfield fell across the rebels' plans. Bampfield visited Fyvie, where they gathered before Glencairn received his commission. The colonel became an active supporter and confidant of Lord Balcarres, who believed that he, rather than Glencairn, should be leading the uprising. The two were genuinely committed to the Presbyterian interest, an affiliation that, in their own consciences at least, excused betraying the more decadent varieties of Royalist.

Bampfield appears to have asked Balcarres to make representations on his behalf to the King, seeking a return to royal favour. The King's reply was an emphatic negative. Three weeks earlier Charles had signed a warrant for Bampfield's arrest, describing him as 'a person trusted and employed by our enemies',[7] and ordering his interrogation. The earl and his confidential agent quit Scotland for Paris. From there, Bampfield sent reports on Royalist activity to his new master, Secretary Thurloe.

When General Monck returned from fighting the Dutch in the spring of 1654, he and his deputy, Major General Morgan, inflicted serious defeats upon the rebels. The insurrectionists had already fallen out among themselves, with Glencairn actually fighting a duel with George Munro after a dinner-table spat – reportedly over the relative merits of the Lowland and Highland soldier. Charles II replaced Glencairn as commander-in-chief with the Earl of Middleton, who had fought well at Worcester but proved no match for Monck, who came storming back with renewed vigour after his adventures at sea.

Morgan routed Middleton's column at Dalnaspidal near Loch Garry, pursuing their commander first into Badenoch and later into Caithness. There he got the jump on Middleton once again, driving the Royalist cavalry into a bog, where they were compelled to dismount, hamstring their own horses and tramp off onto the hill like infantrymen.

General Middleton would eventually surface at the King's court in Cologne. He had, however, left behind on the battlefield a portmanteau containing the detailed orders that Charles had provided to him, along with further prize intelligence, which Oliver Cromwell, who was paying very close attention to the detail of the campaign, asked to be brought to him in London.

*General Monck*

George Downing arrived at Duchray with secret orders from the Protector. He also had a hand in concluding the surrender of some of the rebel leaders. Downing's signature appears on the Articles of Submission of the Earl of Atholl, who was surrendering to Monck, as 'consenting' to the terms of the capitulation – probably on behalf of the Protector. While Downing was with him, Monck wrote to Cromwell asking to modify the scheme whereby prisoners taken in the Highlands were being sold via a London merchant to sugar plantations in Barbados. The prospect of seven years of slavery, he explained, was deterring Scottish soldiers from surrendering. Monck proposed setting up a penal regiment, which could be leased to 'some foreign prince or state', thereby matching the Barbados option in terms of earning revenue, while offering an attractive inducement to men who had known no other profession but soldiering. 'I humbly conceive it would rid the nation of most of them,' the general concluded, 'who will otherwise trouble the country by robbing in small parties.'[8]

Once the country was largely pacified, the Lord Protector could develop new plans for the governance of Scotland. While these were cooking, the First Protectorate Parliament sat at Westminster. George Downing was elected as Member of Parliament for Edinburgh. Doubtless the Scots saw it rather differently, but it was nevertheless apt that this formal ratification of Downing's change of status should be associated with the city where he undertook his first clandestine operation.

The following year, a council for the government of Scotland was announced. It was headed by a Lord President: Roger Boyle, Lord Broghill, a son of the Earl of Cork. Broghill had become a favourite of Cromwell's in Ireland, where he had fought hard and effectively for the Protestant interest. He was a man of Downing's generation – thirty-four years old, to Downing's now thirty-two. Educated at Trinity College, Dublin, Broghill was a cultured man who had, in his youth, anticipated the Grand Tour, seeing the great art of France and Italy, then pausing for some weeks in Geneva to sit at the feet of a Calvinist divine. Later in life, he would write a novel and several plays. As well as being his intellectual equal, Broghill had one more thing in common with George Downing. He too had married a Howard.

Downing's brother-in-law, Charles Howard, was also appointed to the Scottish Council. As was Samuel Desborough, a recently returned New Englander from New Haven. General Monck was a member and remained the commander-in-chief of the army in Scotland. The identity of the Clerk to the Council must have come as something of a surprise to almost everyone. It was Emmanuel Downing, George's father, now back from Salem, who became the most senior civil servant in Scotland. It may have seemed that there were more New Englanders involved in the government of Scotland than Scots. The governor of Edinburgh Castle was George Fenwick of Saybrook. The governor of Stirling was Thomas Reade, a stepson of Hugh Peter and a former neighbour of the Downings in Salem. Reade's sister was married to one of Downing's Connecticut cousins. Joshua Downing was managing the customs in Glasgow; Richard Saltonstall, from Watertown, Massachusetts, whose son Henry had been in George Downing's class at Harvard, was in charge of sequestrations.[9]

George Downing had found his place and his people. His new political network, made up of Broghill, Monck, Howard and Thurloe, would be his allies in the years ahead. But his work in Scotland was now done and in the autumn of 1655 the Protector gave him a taste of something very different.

CHAPTER 9

# A Diplomat Abroad

Avenge, O Lord, thy slaughtered saints, whose bones
Lie scattered on the Alpine mountains cold,
Even them who kept thy truth so pure of old,
When all our fathers worshiped stocks and stones;
Forget not: in thy book record their groans
Who were thy sheep and in their ancient fold
Slain by the bloody Piedmontese that rolled
Mother with infant down the rocks. Their moans
The vales redoubled to the hills, and they
To Heaven. Their martyred blood and ashes sow
O'er all th' Italian fields where still doth sway
The triple tyrant; that from these may grow
A hundredfold, who having learnt thy way
Early may fly the Babylonian woe.

## *The Savoyard atrocities*

JOHN MILTON'S SONNET 'On the Late Massacre in Piedmont' expresses his moral revulsion at the genocide perpetrated against a community of Calvinists in Piedmont known as the Vaudois or Waldensians, who had long lived in the valleys at the foot of the Alps, but were now being forcibly expelled if they refused to become Catholics. Oliver Cromwell shared the poet's indignation and his own prose, in a letter to the Dutch parliament, powerfully condemned the atrocities. The Vaudois were, he wrote, 'a needy and harmless people, many being slain by the soldiers, the rest plundered and driven from their houses together with their wives and children to combat cold and hunger among deserted mountains and perpetual snow'. The Protector went on to declare his emotional and political solidarity with the Protestant refugees: 'These things with what commotion of mind you heard related, what a fellow-feeling of the calamities of brethren pierced your breasts, we readily conjecture from the depth of our own sorrow.'[1]

The crimes were allegedly committed by both French and Savoyard troops. According to a least one account, several companies of Irishmen, expelled from their homeland by Cromwell, also took part in the massacre – although that assertion may well have been made by a propagandist or news writer and there appears to be no supporting evidence. There was eyewitness corroboration of the infamy itself. 'Some were flayed alive, some were disembowelled; or tied to trees in their own orchards and their hearts cut out . . . others were buried alive.'[2]

This report was sent to Samuel Morland, an ambitious young former fellow of Magdalene College, Cambridge and Samuel Pepys's tutor. Morland had accompanied Robert Stapylton on Bulstrode Whitelocke's embassy to Sweden in 1653–4 and was well on his way to becoming one of the most senior intelligence officers on Thurloe's staff. In 1655, Cromwell ordered Morland to Turin to negotiate with the Duke of Savoy and deliver a formal remonstration in Latin, which Milton had a hand in drafting. He was to liaise with the mathematician John Pell, late of the Orange College at Breda, now Thurloe's Resident at Zurich, who would go on to act as the Protectorate's political agent in Geneva. Cromwell had a notion to create a Protestant union in Europe, bringing together parts of the Netherlands, Germany, Scandinavia and the Protestant cantons of Switzerland under British leadership. Pell was charged with exploring the possibilities. Cromwell chose Piedmont as the cause around which Protestant Europe might rally.

In August, George Downing was sent to meet Morland and Pell in Geneva. On the way there he was to call in on the French court, present a letter for Louis XIV from Cromwell and, if possible, speak to Cardinal Mazarin, Louis's chief minister of state. In the years since his first visit to Edinburgh in 1648, Downing was so involved in back-room politics it would hardly be surprising if he had not developed a carapace of cynicism. Yet his report to Thurloe is inspired with the same ingenuous enthusiasm, even with regard to the hospitality, as *Great Expressions of Love.*

The French court was then gathered at the town of La Fère in northern France, which the queen had used as a place of safety during the Fronde. Downing stopped en route to attend a church service at the enormous Huguenot temple at Charenton; and made sure to report the fact to Thurloe. After all, the impetus behind the expedition was Protestant solidarity, and Downing wished to be seen to be aligned with the policy. He was not attending church out of piety.

Foreigners' access to La Fère was tightly controlled. Downing was met on the road by a messenger – a '*Courier du Cabinet du Roy*', perhaps liveried to the nines, Sir Arthur

Hesilrige style. Downing was impressed. The messenger conveyed the English visitor to an inn, he wrote to Thurloe, 'where the Queen's train were'. A Monsieur Bosc, 'one of the King's secretaries', duly arrived with 'the Comte de Brienne's coach' (Brienne was the Foreign Secretary) to take Downing to the cardinal. The French officials withdrew, leaving the two principals alone.

*Cardinal Mazarin*

Harvard's rule requiring undergraduates to converse at all times in Latin prepared Downing well for this encounter, which lasted two hours and was conducted entirely in that tongue.

'He told me, that of all things in the world he desired a right understanding with his Highness; that he would do anything in his power to evidence it.' Downing stressed that Mazarin was keen to conclude a full strategic alliance with England that went far beyond a mere trading agreement. He declared that Charles Stuart's blood relationship with the King of France was no obstacle to a deal with the Protectorate. After all, France was at war with Spain even though the queen was Spanish. The cardinal promised to treat the Huguenots in a kindly fashion and disclosed that the King had sponsored a peace deal in Piedmont. He promised French support, should Cromwell wish to appropriate any Spanish-held towns in Flanders – probably hinting that Dunkirk was an option.

Mazarin also made a down-payment on an intelligence-sharing agreement, revealing the presence of a mole in Cromwell's navy. 'He told me, that as a pledge of his goodwill to his Highness, he would tell me a secret, which he said could no other ways come to his Highness,' Downing reported. 'To wit, that a person, who should have commanded in the fleet that is gone with Penn [to Hispaniola], went about two months ago to Brussels, and from thence embarked for Spain, to reveal what he knew concerning the [Western] Design.' Mazarin stressed that this information was highly classified. 'This, he desired, I might let his Highness know as a great secret . . . and if it were in any way known what is here written, his intelligencer would be destroyed.'[3] Mazarin had one last piece of information to impart: 'He said moreover, he knew the Spaniard had now some notable design in hand against his Highness; that as any particulars thereof should come to his hands, if he saw me again, he would impart them to me.'

That evening Downing was moved out of the inn – this time in the queen's coach – and put up in greater splendour at the governor's house. Demonstrating true diplomatic courtesy, it being too late for anyone to cook, the cardinal sent Downing his very own supper. 'He also sent his own plate and servants to wait and the captain of the guard and Monsieur du Bosc to keep me company.'

With his business completed, Downing made ready to go post-haste to Geneva. 'The Cardinal offered me a guard, but I refused it, but have accepted a Courier du Cabinet du Roy to go along with me,' he boasted to Thurloe in a postscript, along with a parting plea. 'I pray send me an order or letter of credit for more money. I am, I am sure, as good an husband for his Highness as I can be, but I shall spend per mensem 500 l. sterling; and the letter of credit I had was but for 12000 livres.' Mindful of the sensitivity of the contents, Downing entrusted the packet not to the fancy French messenger, but to his own man – a Mr Warcub – with orders to put it in the hands of Secretary Thurloe only.

On his arrival in Geneva, Downing and Morland went to meet the Dutch agent. It quickly became clear that the French-sponsored peace treaty had killed off any chance of uniting the Protestant interest. The Dutch were keen to ensure the atrocities had ceased and, though willing to help the survivors financially, were not interested in any kind of punitive crusade against the killers of the slaughtered saints. The Swiss, for their part, were privately relieved that the French were prepared to take charge of keeping the peace. They claimed to have no money, in any case, and had already embraced the French proposals with shameless alacrity. They now felt they could hardly revoke their consent, so there was very little Downing and Morland could do to amend the treaty. The Duke and Duchess of Savoy were not minded to be humiliated. The French plan offered them a face-saving solution, whereby they were not required to express contrition for the massacres.

Morland was furious. He wrote to Pell to brief him on the latest developments:

> Sir, – On Tuesday last, Mr Downing and I received each of us a letter from Mr Secretary Thurloe, the substance whereof was, that they have received all our packets and informations concerning the [*treaty*]; that my Lord Protector was extremely troubled at it, and now begins to see that his neighbours are not so hearty and affectionate for the deliverance and establishment of those poor people as himself; and that 'they are so little sensible' (I put Mr Secretary's own words) of the blood that has been shed, and the great calamities which the protestants undergo, that they forthwith set themselves rather to compose by any means the difference, than to hazard anything, either to avenge the bloodshed or to undertake the rights of those who do survive . . . In sum, and upon the whole, my Lord Protector is extremely troubled, and will take no resolution before he has spoken with Mr Downing, and received an account from him of all things, and therefore has ordered Mr Downing with all possible speed to return back to London. As for yourself and me, we are to stay at Geneva for further directions, as well for the distribution of the money as for what else may occur hereafter.
>
> Samuel Morland.
> Geneva 13 September 1655.[4]

The money referred to in the final sentence was a considerable sum of humanitarian aid for the survivors of the massacre, provided by the British people. Money, an end to hostilities and a guarantee that they could from now on worship in their chosen way were all the Vaudois would ever get. Oliver Cromwell, while deprecating the timidity of continental Protestants, switched his own attention to the opportunities extended by Cardinal Mazarin. In November 1655, the British Republic signed the Treaty of Westminster with France, a limited defensive alliance that enabled Britain to pursue hostilities against Spain with greater confidence.[5] German and Swiss Protestants, John Pell assured Thurloe, 'will be glad to hear of England's peace with France, and war with Spain; for it is in these countries a general observation with hardly any exception, the Papists are for Spain, the Protestants are for France'.

*Samuel Morland* (left) *and John Pell* (right)

Meanwhile, Thurloe's staff had intercepted a letter of intelligence from George Ratcliffe, an adviser to Prince James, Duke of York, to a 'Mr Harrison' – probably a pseudonym:

> Much talk we have of an ambassador come to Paris well attended, who, they say, hath taken a lodging [in the] Rue de Seine, with two Swiss at his door, where no English, Scots, or Irish may enter, but only French. He is said to be a gentleman of great credit, scoutmaster general, and called Downing. His first pretence was for Savoy: now men guess (and but guess) that he means to reside at Paris. Hence most conclude, that the next news will bring the desired peace between England and France, and then have at Flanders the next year . . .[6]

Ratcliffe was a shrewd fellow. The Britain–France reset had its apotheosis in 1657 with the Treaty of Paris, providing for Anglo-French military cooperation by land and sea, leading a year later to the Battle of the Dunes and the British acquisition, with French help, of two Flemish prizes: Dunkirk and Fort Mardyke.

## *Coda: the mole*

Before setting out to see Mazarin at La Fère, Downing believed he would be travelling onwards to Turin to link up with Samuel Morland at the ducal palace of Savoy at Rivoli. For some reason the Scoutmaster General was more apprehensive about visiting that city than Paris or Geneva. It was understandable that he should take precautions. Two Commonwealth envoys, Isaac Dorislaus at The Hague and Anthony Ascham in Madrid, had been killed by Royalist assassins. Sir George Ratcliffe had noticed how tight Downing's personal security was in Paris: Swiss guards at the door and a complete ban on any English, Irish or Scots. Yet Downing, wishing to be extra-vigilant, made use of some ultra-secret intelligence. At that time Thurloe had an agent in place at Charles II's court at Cologne. He had produced a stream of information about Royalist movements, aliases, meeting places and communications that had proved to be reliable. If anybody knew whether a Royalist assassin had been dispatched to kill the Scoutmaster General, it would be Henry Manning.

When Manning had first turned up at Charles II's court in early 1655, someone should have spotted that he was too good to be true. First, there was the perfect pedigree. Manning was a Catholic. His father had been a colonel in Charles I's army and had been killed in action at the Battle of Cheriton during the First Civil War, quite likely by Arthur Hesilrige's Lobsters. Manning himself had been wounded in the same engagement. He appeared not only to know everyone in the Royalist family back in England, but, as Henry Hyde recalled, 'spoke as if he were much trusted by them and held correspondence with them'. And while the court had become increasingly ragged and down at heel, Manning 'had a store of good clothes and plenty of money'.

Manning had served as a captain in the Royalist army and consequently found it easy to establish a rapport with the frustrated young swordsmen in exile, who were desperate to assassinate the Lord Protector or, at the very least, mount an insurrection. Manning always had the latest newsbooks from London and fed items of gossip to his new friends. Not only did he appear to share their impatience for action, but he claimed to know a new generation of Royalists back in England – men who had come of age during the Civil War and were unknown to the Protectorate's spies – now armed and ready, just waiting for the signal. In this way, he became first interesting, then influential. Manning's time in Cologne coincided with a real plot, known as Penruddock's Uprising, which collapsed into farce as one after another regional rebellion fell apart. The result was that the authorities were on the highest alert and many Royalists were arrested, sometimes because of smart intelligence work by the state; but mostly through their own incompetence.

Eventually the King learned that mail was regularly being left for Manning's collection at the premises of a merchant named David Wicket in Antwerp. The young courtier also used the same address as an outgoing mailbox for letters he dispatched to England. Agents went to scoop up whatever was on the premises. They returned with a packet of letters that left no doubt of Manning's duplicity. That night the King's most trusted grooms raided his apartment, catching the spy *in flagrante delicto* with a cipher.

On the King's orders, Sir Edward Nicholas, the Secretary of State, and Lords Ormond and Colepepper conducted an interrogation. Manning tried his best to pretend that he was, essentially, a fabricator of intelligence who had fed the Protectorate's spymasters wild stories of his own invention, most relating to non-existent plots or risings. His motive, he admitted, was money. He had lost his patrimony and found himself in serious debt before coming to the exiled court. He claimed that his intention was to work for Thurloe only long enough to restore his financial equilibrium. He denied passing any substantive information of value: any truthful report he had passed on was already in the public domain, common gossip from the Exchange.

Yet one of the most striking things about Manning's intelligence, when considered in the round – including material later found in Thurloe's papers that was not available to the interrogators – was the evident enthusiasm he felt for his work. It was with a partisan glee that he set about frustrating Royalist schemes, and the indignation he expressed to the Protectorate authorities if he found them slacking appeared entirely genuine. Yet Manning had every reason to be a loyal Royalist and to disdain the Republic. The parliamentary army had, after all, killed his father and left Manning himself sorely wounded. It was the Commonwealth and Protectorate, with their sequestrations and compounding, that accounted for his lamentable financial circumstances. Only in his own unreliable narrative, squeezed from him under the psychological pressure of a formal interrogation, did he ever appear as a reluctant turncoat. Off-guard, among friends, as it were, he was gung-ho. Consider, for instance, his chiding of the security apparatus for its failures at the port of Dover: 'Your Governor at Dover must be either knave or fool, for he hath lately let pass Wilmot and Philipps, Armorer, Halsey and Daniel O'Neill . . .' Later, as if he had taken it upon himself to look into the matter, Manning disclosed that it was not the governor who was choosing to look the other way when Royalist agents came and went. Manning named the guilty man, identifying one of the port searchers, Andrew Day. In his interrogation he was questioned about his betrayal of two further port officials who had been allowing Royalists either to pass or even escape custody: Foster, at Dover; and Singleton, at Rye. Not only had he revealed these two names, he badgered his handlers to take action against them.[7]

Asked for details of the intelligencers who ever wrote to him, Manning named only two. The interrogators clearly sensed there might be a third and pressed him, and for a while the identity of an 'old handler' hung in the interrogation room like a spirit at a seance where Manning was the medium; but *poof!* . . . It was dispelled. The two names he did vouchsafe were Hawley, his regular handler, and George Downing, whose request for details of agents travelling to Turin he disclosed in full.[8]

The interrogators were careful to keep Manning's arrest a state secret. Nevertheless, on 7 December 1655, an urgent message from another agent at Cologne was sent to Thurloe alerting him to the fact that Manning had been taken during the night of the fifth. The agent added that the spy was said to have confessed to having secret correspondence with the Lord Protector. Fearing lest the authorities in London should respond by arresting an important Royalist, perhaps with a view to a prisoner exchange, Henry Manning was taken out into the forest somewhere near Cologne and shot by Major William Armorer and Sir James Hamilton.[9]

# CHAPTER 10

# Politician and Envoy

## *Westminster, 1656–7*

THE SECOND PROTECTORATE Parliament met in September 1656. It sat for only two convulsive and divided sessions before Cromwell, under the Lord Protector's prerogative, dissolved it in February 1658. But during this time George Downing, the elected member for Carlisle, took part in two of the most notorious debates: whether Oliver Cromwell should now be made king, and what should be the appropriate punishment for blasphemy in the case of James Naylor. Formerly a quartermaster in John Lambert's regiment of horse, Naylor fought at Dunbar, but had now become a roving Quaker evangelist with messianic pretensions.

England at this time was effectively a military dictatorship, divided into ten regions, each ruled by a major general answerable to the Lord Protector. (George Downing's brother-in-law, Charles Howard, governed the northern counties of Cumberland, Westmorland and Northumberland.) The Rule of the Major Generals was a response to an ineffectual Royalist uprising; former Royalists now had to register their movements and forfeit a decimation tax of

10 per cent of income from their property to pay for a standing army and, now, a maritime war against Spain. Some of the more godly major generals (though not Howard) also waged their own particular war on vice, especially gambling and fornication, but also bear-baiting, cock-fighting, horse-racing and card games, plays and even football. This did nothing to make the government more popular with the people, who had lived through war and revolution already and were also now enduring bands of roving religious cranks: Ranters, Fifth Monarchists, Anabaptists and the new wave of Quakers, who appeared to have taken over from the Ranters the habits of importuning strangers in the street and going about naked, for shock effect.

Since leaving the army, James Naylor had taken to performing a literal *imitatio Christi*: styling his centre-parted hair and beard to resemble Jesus and deliberately offending the Puritans. He repudiated all forms of social deference, in particular refusing to take his hat off. He spoke out against the slave trade, chided the rich and those who lived in large houses. Naylor had a cult following among Quaker women. The civil authorities considered him an outright menace.

It came to a head in Bristol in October 1656 when Naylor, looking his most Christ-like, cheered along by women singing hosannas, rode into the city on a horse in a symbolic re-enactment of Jesus's entry into Jerusalem. Was it a performance, a parody or an actual blasphemy? Some argued that it did not matter which, for his was the 'freedom of conscience' that Cromwell and the army had championed. The provincial authorities recognized the public outrage, but had no clear idea with what offence to charge James Naylor.

A parliamentary committee convened in the Painted Chamber in the Palace of Westminster to establish the facts. Naylor was brought from Bristol for several days of questioning. At some point during the proceedings, George Downing was heard to declare, 'We have gotten enough out of him.'[1] On 7 December, after some reflection, Naylor asked to address the committee about this remark, which he said clearly demonstrated prejudice.

Downing was fast becoming a family man; his wife Frances was newly pregnant. He looked upon Naylor as a flagrant satyr, who believed that sex was as holy as going to church and led women to abandon all decorum. Fast ascending the Lord Protector's ranks, Downing may also have believed that he was one with Cromwell in condemning Naylor's flouting of discipline and deference.

The House spent a full nine days considering Naylor's case. A fellow MP, Colonel Sydenham, said that the Quaker belief that Christ could be found in every believer was 'akin to a glorious truth' and that although Naylor's theology was not entirely orthodox, it would hardly be wise to punish someone for a doctrinal difference, lest everyone do it. But the House eventually decided that Naylor was guilty of 'horrid blasphemy' and proceeded to debate the punishment.

Naylor escaped the death penalty by a margin of fourteen votes. He was sentenced to be put in the pillory, his back whipped through the streets to a bloody pulp, to have a hole bored through his tongue and to be branded with a letter B for 'blasphemer'.[2] The boring of the hole with a red-hot poker was the suggestion of George Downing.

The Lord Protector wrote to the House asking for a rationale for the sentence and why Parliament had gone ahead without his fiat. This challenge split open the great question: what was the extent of Parliament's authority, and what were the prerogatives of the Protector? Downing favoured subtlety, sophistication and restraint:

> The Instrument of Government is but new, and our jurisdiction is but new too. It is dangerous either for him to question our power, or for us to question his, in matters that are for the public safety: we must both wink. If we should enter upon such a moot point, I dread the consequence. What bred all the former differences, but points of jurisdiction? I would have us to return a short answer to the letter, for I understand not that my Lord Protector does at all question, or desire an account of our jurisdiction. As I said before, we must *wink* at one another.[3]

*James Naylor*

All through 1656, MPs worried about would happen to the country – and what would happen to them – if the Protector suddenly died. There had been so many plots and assassination attempts that this was a real and urgent concern. It forced consideration of a drastic issue: the succession. Senior army officers were in favour of elective succession; but this was not just a matter of principle for a man like Charles Fleetwood, cocksure that he would win an election, but disadvantaged in any hereditary system since he was only Cromwell's son-in-law. Naturally there was an equal and opposite reaction against election, in a country that still remembered the rule of the major generals, prompting the counterintuitive idea of a return to monarchy and hereditary succession. As it happened, Cromwell had two sons who made plausible successors but, inconveniently, the better candidate by far was the younger son. Nevertheless, a group led by Lord Broghill and George Downing, in whose own house the pro-kingship faction met, pressed ahead with a draft constitution under which Cromwell would take the title of king and his elder son would be king-in-waiting. The popularity of this proposal was easily explained by universal anxiety about the eruption of a new civil war if the question of succession was not definitively settled.

Oliver Cromwell himself, however, with his usual feline ambivalence, indicated that he would need to be persuaded to accept such an arrangement. He encouraged Parliament to consider various refinements. One was to accept the succession proposal, but keep the title Lord Protector; another was to find a third way, which would avoid the disadvantages of both election and hereditary succession. This was a nominative system under which the king or Protector would declare his successor in his will. A document, which ultimately became the new constitution of the Protectorate – entitled 'The Humble Petition and Advice' – which both Downing and Broghill were involved in drafting, finally became law, but only after the monarchy clause was excised. So the Protector got his way: keeping his old title while acquiring the right to nominate his successor.

## *The Hague, 1658*

George Downing took a barge down the Thames from London on Saturday 2 January 1658 to Gravesend in Kent. In the middle of the river, riding in the Hope, an anchorage off Tilbury, he boarded the frigate *Newcastle*, a large vessel of 700 tons, carrying forty-four guns. Captain Curtis greeted Downing and pointed out the frigate's companion vessel, a Dutch *bouyer* called the *Dort*, which carried all the goods and chattels, horses and servants that the Protectorate's new envoy to The Hague would need in his next post.

Downing was to be ambassador to the Netherlands in all but name. He could not have the title because that was how the Dutch got around the conundrum of the British having both a king and a republic at the same time. Easier for them both to have envoys or residents. No one would care, except the French ambassador, who was a stickler for precedence.

No wind came for four days, so the new envoy had to pace the decks and twiddle his thumbs. Then it blew up just enough to reach Queenborough on the Isle of Sheppey. There on the 9 January, fully one week into his journey, Downing decided to go ashore for the weekend. It did the trick. On the Monday morning the wind had come around and off they set for the continent. At around noon on the Tuesday, Downing transferred to the flat-bottomed *bouyer*, and the frigate with its forty-four guns stood off until the *Dort* signalled that it was crossing the bar and lay beyond reach of pirates.

The plan had been to sail down the River Maas to Rotterdam; but there was too much ice and the *Dort* had to put in at Maassluys. The arrival of the *bouyer* was enough to bring out the burgomeister, and Downing received a proper civic welcome to soothe his humiliated dignity. He sent a letter explaining his circumstances to Lord Nieuport, who had until recently been the Dutch ambassador in London. In a trice, Downing had the *Dort* emptied of its cargo, which was carried off to The Hague on thirteen wagons, while he made for an inn at Delft, where a formal letter of welcome from the States General was waiting. The letter referred to him as the Resident.[4]

Nieuport soon afterwards came to convey Downing to his new lodgings, just across the tree-lined street from the Mauritshuis and close to the gates of the Binnenhof, the palace that housed the States General – the Dutch parliament and the offices of all the senior ministers of the government. He was at the epicentre of The Hague.

Once all the flummery of welcomes and introductions was over, Downing quickly got down to work. One of his first challenges was already being solved. The British Resident had orders to pursue Cromwell's overarching project of uniting the Protestant powers. Until now the Dutch had taken the side of the Danes against the Swedes. In a remarkable coup, in February, the Swedish army marched over a sea that was frozen solid by the Little Ice Age to take the Danish island of Funen, capturing Danish ships and the King of Denmark's own brother. This put the Swedish army within alarming reach of Copenhagen; the Danes were quickly brought to the negotiating table.

*Binnenhof, The Hague*

It appears that Downing managed to get this news back to London before anyone else. Samuel Hartlib, who worked closely with Thurloe, told a colleague that:

> Last Thursday night, there arrived an express from our resident Downing at the Hague, that the King of Sweden hath beaten also the army in Fueren, taking prisoner the general, and is now master of that whole island, and of eight Danish men-of-war which he found there frozen in. He writes also, that the Swedish general in Livonia, De la Gardie, hath beaten

> the Polonian army near Riga. The King of Sweden hath written with his own hand, that the peace is made between him and Muscovia. We long extremely for the confirmation of Mr Downing's news, but the post of last week is not yet arrived. At Whitehall, the news is firmly believed, for he would not send . . . the express, till the news were confirmed.[5]

Another issue that Downing had been ordered to address with dispatch was the shady dealing between the Netherlands and Spain. The Protectorate was at war with Spain, but the Dutch – in flagrant violation of their existing treaty obligations to the British – were secretly supplying the Spaniards with weapons. Downing formally alerted the Dutch authorities about an arms dealer called Tysen who was operating out of Amsterdam. But instead of arresting him, the Dutch let him go with a warning.

Downing was keeping Thurloe closely informed about another illicit arms-trafficking operation being run out of Rotterdam. Five ships carrying munitions to the Spanish Netherlands were intercepted at sea by the Protectorate's navy. Thurloe saw the value in building up The Hague as a regional intelligence hub and provided Downing with an enormous budget to run agents against the Spanish as well.

Shortly after his arrival, the new Resident wrote to John Pell in Geneva suggesting that they keep in touch via occasional letters. Pell's reply is instructive for its extraordinary condescension. He presumes to give Downing instruction in elementary spycraft and the principles of operational security as if he were a neophyte. This suggests that Pell cannot have known about Downing's extensive undercover past, though one might think that the title Scoutmaster

General – which Downing still had when he went out to work with Pell and Morland to assist the Waldensians – would have been hint enough that the newly appointed Resident in The Hague had some familiarity with the fundamentals of espionage.[6]

Had Pell only known what work Downing was presently engaged in (though perhaps his apparent ignorance was to some extent reassuring). For Downing had re-entered the clandestine world with evident relish and was burgling, bribing and blackmailing his way across the Low Countries.

## *Aggressive surveillance*

One of his first targets was the bookshop in The Hague owned by Samuel Browne, frequented by Royalists and which doubled as the editorial office of an anti-Cromwell newspaper. Downing first had the premises watched and then, having identified some likely prospects, recruited agents to report on who came and went, and what was said. The Resident then targeted the church serving the English expatriate community and the Stuart family members, some of whom lived in The Hague. He had the house of the Princess Royal put under surveillance and was able to report on a secret visit by her brothers, James, Duke of York and Henry, Duke of Gloucester.

As Downing's network of agents grew, he began to score some real intelligence successes. He was able, for instance, to provide early warning of a plot to stage a Royalist uprising in the North of England. Downing had an agent at the heart of the conspiracy in the exiled court; when he finally induced him to defect, Downing smuggled Sir John

Marlowe out of Holland so that Thurloe could question him in London and arrest those involved. Another agent, a Mr Palmer, was sent to investigate a merchant in Brussels who was in fact an arms dealer supplying the Royalist forces in exile. Downing discovered the whereabouts of the arms cache and was able to prevent the sale.[7]

Downing arrived at The Hague nine years after the execution of Charles I, and seven years since Charles II had been forced back into exile on the continent. The city was home to significant members of the royal house of Stuart. The *grande dame* was Elizabeth, Queen of Bohemia. She was a daughter of James I of England and therefore the late King Charles I's sister, and was mother of Prince Rupert, the Cavalier general. Elizabeth had lived in exile in The Hague after being expelled from Prague in 1621.

Then there was Charles II's sister, Mary, the Princess Royal, also known as the Dowager Princess of Orange, whose husband had died of smallpox in 1650, just nine days before the birth of their son, who would later become William III of England. In The Hague, Mary lived less than three minutes' walk from George Downing's house. The queen mother, Henrietta Maria, who normally lived in Paris, and Charles II's brother, James, Duke of York, made occasional, discreet visits. Surrounding these grandees in The Hague was a vast number of extended family, courtiers and hangers-on. Among them were some very dangerous individuals, members of secretive organizations who were planning assassinations and uprisings.

Downing had been ordered to penetrate the circle of exiled Royalists and obtain early warning of their plots. To do this he focused on the household of the Princess Royal. Among the frequent visitors were Daniel O'Neill and Nicholas Armorer, whose names had been linked to plots by Henry Manning. Keeping track of the princess was difficult because she was frequently out of town. She had her own country estate at Honselaarsdijk and a palace at Breda, but also liked to escape to the home of her old friend and former governess, Lady Stanhope, who lived at Teilingen, near Leiden. It was a place for the princess to get away from her interfering and controlling mother-in-law, Amalia of Solms. Katherine Stanhope was married to a Dutchman, Lord Heenvliet, who was Master of the Princess's Household. His illegitimate daughter, Walburg van den Kerckhove, was the governess of the now eight-year-old Prince of Orange. As it happens, Walburg was, like Downing, married to a Howard. Her husband was Tom Howard, Master of Horse to the Princess Royal. He was a younger brother of the Earl of Suffolk, and his sister, Margaret, was married to Downing's friend, Lord Broghill.

*Mary, Dowager Princess of Orange* (left) *and Elizabeth, Queen of Bohemia* (right)

These social connections were not George Downing's only way to approach Tom Howard. The courtier had once made a very serious mistake. He had become entangled with The Hague's most notorious and volatile *femme fatale*. Lucy Walter, also known as Lucy Barlow, had been the mistress of Charles Stuart when he was a young prince of seventeen. She had his love-child, who became the Duke of Monmouth. Mrs Barlow was the mistress with babe-in-arms paraded up and down to shock the 'bigot clergy' at Breda.

*Lady Stanhope* (left) *and Lucy Walter* (right)

It is not clear whether Tom Howard's relationship with Mrs Barlow was genuine – in the sense that he really was smitten by her charms – or whether he thought he was performing a service for the King by keeping her away from court, but at the same time under observation. Either way, in May 1656, just after taking her young son to visit his father the King, Lucy Barlow travelled from Flushing to England, along with Tom Howard, her brother Justus and her two children. Barlow's maid, Anne Hill, had already gone on ahead. The group stayed at lodgings above a barber's shop by Somerset House in the Strand.

Thurloe's agents arrested them. Barlow and Howard were questioned by John Barkstead, the Lieutenant of the Tower and the chief interrogator for the close committee of the Council of State. Barlow and Howard had clearly agreed their stories. They both claimed to have met for the first time, and entirely by chance, on the boat from Flushing. Barlow admitted that she once had a child by Charles Stuart, but said he died. Howard admitted knowing Charles Stuart and working for the Princess Royal, but said he had not seen the King for a year or more.

The maid was questioned twice, having been recalled after the others had been interrogated. She told an altogether different story: that the child was Charles Stuart's and that they had seen him recently; that Mrs Barlow had plenty of money and a coach to take her about in The Hague. She also disclosed that Barlow and Howard knew one another well and went about frequently together.

Thurloe had all the information he needed. The only good reason to release the miscreants would be a successful recruitment. And they were released. So we can draw our own conclusions.[8]

## *The Hague, summer 1658*

In June, Downing was at last able to savour the fruits of his meeting with Mazarin at La Fère and congratulate himself on a job truly well done. The Battle of the Dunes had one of the oddest line-ups imaginable. On the one side was the Spanish army under Don Juan of Austria; a group of French rebels from the Fronde led by the Condé; and the English Royalist army in exile, backed by a fleet of Spanish pirates. On the other side was Louis XIV's French army; some units of the New Model Army commanded by William Lockhart, Downing's friend from Scotland and Barebone's Parliament; and the English navy under Edward Montagu. It ended with a rout of the Spanish coalition and the Protectorate taking Dunkirk.

The Princess Royal was so upset by the outcome that she could not get out of bed for several days. Eventually she felt well enough to go to Zevenbergen to meet her brother. But Charles was bounced out of Zevenbergen when Downing made a formal complaint arguing that Charles Stuart's presence on Dutch soil was expressly forbidden under an agreement between the States General and Oliver Cromwell. He demanded that Johan de Witt, the Dutch prime minister, should prevent any further treaty violations of this kind.

The Resident kept as many of the Royalists under surveillance as he could afford to and resolved to complain every time another surfaced. He railed at de Witt about Charles Stuart, accompanied by the Earl of Ormond, going on a tour of the United Provinces; Sir Edward Hyde residing at Breda and sundry Royalists moving to The Hague. Downing requested that they should all be deported.

The princess was so outraged by this that she threatened to leave The Hague herself, forever; though she never did. Downing devised yet another ploy to further annoy his enemies. He obtained an order in council from London preventing any English ministers abroad saying prayers for their king. They were to pray instead for England's welfare.

Such pointed provocations almost invited a violent

response. Downing found a premature news report that felt uncomfortably portentous. 'I perceive, there hath been a report at London, that I was stabbed,' he told Thurloe, 'and I find it very often true, that when the Cavaliers give out any news as done, that they have at that time some design for doing it.'[9]

One night a Dutch gentleman, of similar height and girth to Downing, left the ambassador's house after dinner and was set upon by three men speaking English. One pulled a knife and was about to stab him, but realized in the nick of time that he had made an almost fatal error. Alerted by the dinner guest to the attempted assassination, Downing requested round-the-clock bodyguards for himself and his family, which Thurloe duly approved.

## *September 1658*

Charles II was playing tennis with Don Juan of Austria when word came that Oliver Cromwell was dead at fifty-nine. The news apparently came as a surprise to the King, but George Downing was expecting it to happen. Some weeks earlier he had urged Thurloe – and Cromwell, if there was still time – to consider the children: by which he meant England, Scotland and Ireland.

Cromwell had died of what the author John Johnston – the leading medical authority of the day – called a 'tertian bastard ague'. This was held to result from 'excrementitious cholor putrefying in the mesaraick veins'.[10] Today we would most likely be looking for signs of a urinary-tract infection combined with an infection of the liver. According to Thomas Burton's contemporary account:

> His body, presently after his expiration, was washed and laid out; and being opened, was embalmed, and wrapped in a sere cloth six double, and put into an inner sheet of lead, enclosed in an elegant coffin of the choicest wood. Owing to the disease he died of, which, by the by, appeared to be that of poison, his body, although thus bound up and laid in the coffin, swelled and bursted, from whence came such filth, that raised such a deadly and noisome stink, that it was found prudent to bury him immediately, which was done in as private a manner as possible.[11]

The funeral that George Downing attended, with its wax and wooden effigies, was essentially a charade. Nevertheless, its imagery was powerful and its scale impressive. There was order, respect. Ambition was held in check. Things would soon fall apart; but for now society was holding itself together. The new Protector was Oliver Cromwell's eldest son, Richard. Downing could look around and find that he had affiliations with several emerging factions: the Republicans – Sir Arthur Hesilrige and Thomas Scot, his old patrons, making a comeback; the Soldiers – John Lambert and Charles Fleetwood (Downing had served with both at Dunbar and Worcester); and the new Protector's Praetorian Guard – Lord Broghill and Charles Howard. Which way would General Monck jump? Or Edward Montagu, general at sea? What was Secretary Thurloe thinking?

Some had already made dramatic and surprising choices and these were beginning to be revealed. Sir Richard Willys was known as a cavalry officer of the old school. Knighted way back in 1642 at Shrewsbury, he was made a colonel of horse. But his main contribution to the Royalist cause had been top secret: his membership in the Sealed Knot – in theory a wise and level-headed group responsible for promoting workable plots while restraining wild men who threatened to do more harm than good to the king's cause. The point of the Sealed Knot – the name rather gives it away – was that it put security first. The supreme irony was that Willys turned out to have been working for the Protectorate, handing information about plots, uprisings and assassinations to Thurloe's office since August 1656. But equally shocking to supporters of the Protector was the discovery that the man who exposed Willys's treachery to a disbelieving King and a sceptical Hyde was none other than Samuel Morland. Not only had he handed over details of Willys's treachery, but he had given Hyde George Downing's cipher. The beating heart of Thurloe's intelligence office was himself a double agent. Morland later told friends that the fear of exposure had been difficult to live with and that he rarely slept without fearing he would be taken out and 'have the flesh pulled from [his] bones with hot pincers'.[12]

Richard Cromwell did not last long as Lord Protector, but was forced out by a military coup. His last loyal supporters were Broghill and Downing's brother-in-law, Charles Howard. The army was divided – partly by personal ambition and partly by ideology. Both Lambert and Fleetwood thought of themselves as plausible national leaders. In both cases, however, what they could offer was essentially military dictatorship, a reversion to the rule of the major generals.

Meanwhile the republicans or 'Commonwealthsmen', such as Hesilrige and Thomas Scot, revived old parliaments in search of constitutional legitimacy: first, the Rump was recalled. Then the Long Parliament, taking things right back to square one. Politics spiralled out of control as the army and Parliament clashed. The most surprising people became important once more. Even Lord Wariston found himself back in the sun – with a seat on the Council of State and the Committee of Safety. Downing took pains to keep up with all the latest intrigues, treating Sir Arthur Hesilrige to dinner at the French Ordinary, a Huguenot restaurant at Charing Cross.[13]

The people of England wanted an end to civil war and religious enthusiasm and were prepared to consider a restoration of the monarchy. Meanwhile they were forced to put their faith in General Monck and the promise of a new, freely elected Parliament. Monck, along with Broghill and Charles Howard, was quietly beginning to explore through secret channels what sort of deal might be done with the King.

These people were George Downing's intimates. What he did not know was that his friend William Lockhart had carelessly left a copy of the cipher he used to correspond with Downing at his lodgings in Dunkirk. He had to ask someone to find and return the document to him. The letter making this request came into the hands of one de Marcès, a spy working for Edward Hyde (later Lord Clarendon). The cipher was intercepted and copied. It is clear from de Marcès's reports to Hyde that Lockhart's letters to Thurloe were frequently read by Hyde as well. As two of London's ambassadors abroad were nervously asking friends for news and reassurance, it was as if Edward Hyde were eavesdropping.

One might think the mood in England was already febrile enough without further moral panic, but the country seemed to need an identifiable bogeyman to justify cleaving to General Monck and the King. The Quakers stepped unwittingly onto the stage. It was in response to the coup against the Second Protectorate that the Quaker Dorothy White proclaimed that '[God] has come to turn the world upside down'.[14] Such utterances alarmed even tolerant Baptists. Hostility to Quakers was mounting. Erstwhile radicals would rather bring back the king than allow Quakers their liberty. Conservative Presbyterians in Parliament and the City of London traditionally formed the party of order; now that coalition was gathering Englishmen of all classes who were fed up with both political radicalism and religious extremism.

## *The Hague, 1659–60*

Here are three stories about George Downing. Each of them shows him on the turn, shifting allegiance, betraying one master and embracing another. None of these stories can be wholly and literally true. Considering all three together, however, shows us what a plausible account of Downing's dramatic defection would look like.

### I

King Charles II is travelling in disguise through Holland, attended only by Lord Falkland [or, in another version, by Lord Fleming], to meet his mother and sister at Honselaarsdijk. He puts up at an inn. Some time after his arrival the landlord comes to his room and announces that there is a beggar or tramp at the door, very shabbily dressed [or 'an old reverend-looking man, with a long grey beard and ordinary grey clothes'], who is very importunate to be admitted. The King is curious and bids the landlord bring the man in.

As soon as the beggar enters the room, he pulls off his false beard and announces himself as Sir George Downing, the Resident at The Hague. He warns the King that assassins are waiting to ambush him near the gates at Honselaarsdijk. Downing asks for no specific favour or reward, but says he may have occasion to offer further assistance at some future date. With which, he puts his beard back on and leaves.[15]

## II

Back in The Hague after their troubling experience in London, Tom Howard and Lucy Walter's relationship has deteriorated. The volatile Lucy hires someone to stab Howard with a knife. The attack actually happens, though it results only in a flesh wound. But Tom has entrusted a box of sensitive papers to his mistress and needs them back or he could face ruin.

A certain unnamed person, let us call them X, some time later tells Downing about the compromising papers, claiming to be in possession of them. Downing asks to see them and is allowed to do so; but then refuses to give them back to X. Instead Downing uses the papers to blackmail Tom Howard into spying for him.[16]

Tom Howard does not know that Downing has also copied the documents to John Thurloe, along with a commentary written half in cipher. Downing asks Thurloe to keep the matter very secret: 'If it should be known that I have given you this account . . . he [Howard] would endeavour to have me killed.'[17]

Later, in the spring of 1660, Downing summons Tom and tells him he must make representations to the King on his behalf. We can assume that he is told exactly what to say:

> Your Majesty,
>
> Yesterday, Downing the Parliament Resident sent twice to speak with me so earnestly . . . he told me . . . that he wished the promoting of your Majestie's service, which he confessed he had endeavoured to obstruct, though he never had any malice to your Majesty's person or family . . .

Not a word about Downing actually fighting against the King at the battles of Dunbar, Inverkeithing and Worcester, let alone his years of spying. Howard then gives the slyest of excuses – he blames America:

> [*Where he was*] engaged in a contrary party by his father, who was banished into New-England, where he was brought up, and had sucked in principles that since [*then*] his reason had made him see were erroneous, and that he never was in arms but since the [*old*] King's death, nor had ever taken oath or engagement of any kind. In short, he told me his desires were to serve your Majesty if you would be so graciously pleased as to pardon his past faults and error . . .

Howard then sets out what Downing is offering the King: to use his influence among the senior officers to get Parliament's army onside. This will be critical if the Restoration is to be achieved:

> . . . to assure me he was real in his proposition to serve your Majesty, he showed me a letter he received that morning (all in cypher which he had deciphered from Thurloe); which gave him an account of the intention of the army . . . and that the generality of England was for your Majesty: but that those who most endeavoured your coming in, desired it upon such terms as that you would have no more power than a Duke of Venice, and that no person now about your Majesty abroad should be suffered to come into England in many years . . .

This piece of intelligence could not have been better calculated to ensure that the King's courtiers, sitting up in alarm at this news of a threat to their own positions, would advise His Majesty to agree to Downing's engagement. And here he is, moreover, ever so humbly proposing himself as the loyal solution:

> This he bid me give your Majesty an account of, telling me he wished your restoration upon better terms, and that he wished to see you a King that might oblige and punish, and that he would make no conditions for himself; but desired to be looked upon according to the merit of his services, and he would for the future hazard his life and fortune for your Majesty . . .
>
> Your Majesty's etc.
> T Howard
> The Hague, April 5, 1660

The reply came as follows, from the Marquis of Ormond to Mr Howard:

> Sir
>
> The King was pleased to shew me your letter to him of the 5th of this month, containing the discourse Mr Downing had with you; to which he commands me to return his answer, which is that having nothing more in his thoughts and wishes, than to become according to his duty the principal author of the peace and happiness of his people next after God, he is prepared to receive and encourage all persons that in their respective capacities and conditions shall be able and willing to contribute towards so happy a work; and therefore without looking back on past deviations, or examining the causes of them, he desires you would assure Mr Downing (to whose person he has no particular prejudice, and of whose carriage he knows not that he has any particular reason to complain) that he willingly receives the overture he makes of returning to his duty, and is not only well pleased to receive services from him, but resolved to reward them . . .

Ormond concludes by saying that the King leaves it to Downing to decide what should be done, and how and when to do it.

## III

The Marquis of Ormond's son, Viscount Thurles, became engaged to Emilia van Nassau-Beverweerd, a natural granddaughter of the late Stadtholder, Maurice, Prince of Orange. Ormond paid a discreet visit to The Hague to discuss arrangements for the marriage with the family of the bride-to-be. While he was in town he was approached by Downing, offering to supply secret intelligence to the King, on condition of the strictest secrecy. As a taster, Downing provided details of a source in the King's entourage who was generally considered to be above suspicion, but who had long been passing his royal master's secrets on to the Resident. Downing wanted no money or other reward beyond an assurance that if the Restoration were brought about, he would keep his sinecure as a Teller of the Exchequer and continue in his diplomatic post at The Hague.

Story I, the first of these accounts of Downing's turncoat moment, comes in various versions, printed in a variety of popular publications over the centuries, and reportedly derives from a manuscript note setting down some of Charles II's table talk. The author of the original note was not born until after Charles II's death, so certainly could not have recorded the anecdote himself. It cannot be denied that Downing comes out of the story remarkably well. Such chutzpah cries out for applause. In saving the King's life from the fabled assassins, the Resident performs an undeniably humanitarian act; and he asks for no reward. Such altruism wins him further credit, but is by now surely stretching credibility to its limit. The story was given credence for a time, especially in New England, but is nowadays generally held to be apocryphal. What is self-evidently true is that whatever means Downing employed to draw the King's attention to his pitch, it will have required the kind of audacity and resourcefulness demonstrated here.

Story II appears, on the face of it, much more believable. Bullying, blackmail, purloining documents – these were all known to be in George Downing's repertoire. There is quite a lot of corroborative evidence for parts of the story – Downing's letters to Thurloe; the fraught relationship between Howard and Lucy Walter, which was aired in the Dutch courts in the course of a long-running legal process; and the two letters: one from Howard to the King, and the reply from Ormond to Howard, which have well-attested provenance.[18] The nagging problem with this account is the tightness of the schedule. Howard's letter is not sent until 5 April 1660 (New Style). The Council of Officers gave their assent to the Restoration on 2 May (Old Style), so there was little time – just over five weeks – for Downing to earn the very generous rewards he did end up receiving. Moreover, there is a subtle but discernible performative quality to the exchange, as if the aim of the exercise were to regularize an already existing relationship – perhaps between Downing and Ormond himself – providing cover for actions taken extempore and in secret. However, the part about erroneous principles being put into Downing's head in New England has the ring of authenticity about it, and we can be confident that it was genuinely part of Downing's plea in mitigation, wherever and whenever that speech was delivered.

The third version, which is provided by Lord Clarendon some years later, resolves the timing issue nicely.[19] Ormond's son's wedding took place on 14 November 1659, so any pre-nuptial discussions would have been before that date, giving Downing plenty of headroom to work his magic with Monck – and likely with Broghill and Charles Howard too. It may well have been that both parties to the bargain felt that the cause of the Restoration would be best served by keeping Downing's defection from a notoriously leaky court, even if that meant forging ahead with the arrangement without the King's explicit permission. All this operational security might have been for nothing: Clarendon (or, as he still was then, Edward Hyde) was, after all, reading the Resident's post.

*Edward Hyde, Earl of Clarendon*

Charles II left Holland on 23 May 1660 for his triumphant return to London. In his last two or three days in Holland he conferred with the men who would lead his government, attended a banquet at the Mauritshuis and danced with both his sister, the Princess Royal, and his aunt, the Queen of Bohemia. Somehow he found time to bestow knighthoods upon two turncoat spies, Samuel Morland and George Downing. Once back in England, he would make General Monck the Duke of Albemarle; Lord Broghill the Earl of Orrery; and Charles Howard the Earl of Carlisle.

The King appears to have made no special effort to disguise the fact that Morland owed his knighthood to duplicity; by some accounts, making it plain to all. A greater discretion was shown in Downing's case, but it did him little good. Most of the court was as astonished as the wider public that Downing was received with such good favour. Indeed, many expected he would be dismissed in disgrace. Ormond's original promise of strict confidentiality had been well kept by all privy to the secret. The Dutch were dismayed, but were bound by protocol to swallow their consternation in public. Yet as Clarendon later recalled, '[The States] . . . could not forbear to lament in private that his majesty would depute a person to have his authority who had never used any other dialect to persuade them to do anything he proposed but threats if they should not do it; and who had several times disobliged most of their persons by his insolence.'[20]

# CHAPTER 11

# Rendition

## *London, September 1660*

AT THE BEGINNING of September, intelligence reached the Secretary of State, Sir Edward Nicholas, that the fugitive Hugh Peter had been sighted in Southwark. The wanted man was hiding out in a nest of Quakers somewhere in St Thomas's parish. Nicholas dispatched John Wickham, one of the King's Messengers, to investigate. It was not the business of Messengers of the Chamber in Ordinary to deliver the royal mail; rather, these servants of the Crown, working from an office in Whitehall, were 'instruments of intelligence and discovery', searchers and seizers, wielders of the coercive powers of the state.

Wickham was new to the work and doubtless keen to make a success of it. In the years ahead, on secondment to the magnificently titled Surveyor of the Imprimery, Wickham would specialize in regulation of the press – hunting down the publishers of seditious books and pamphlets. That line of work would bring him back to Southwark seven or eight years later to arrest the owner and operator of a secret unlicensed press. When Wickham and his team broke in, they found two women cranking the machine. One was Elizabeth Calvert, widow of Giles Calvert, the radical printer of George Downing's *Great Expressions of Love*, back in 1648. The Widow Calvert's accomplice was Elizabeth Poole, a mysterious prophetess who had twice addressed the Council of Officers between 1648 and 1649 at the invitation of Oliver Cromwell, during debates about whether Charles I should be tried and put to death. Claiming to be directly in touch with God, she advised in favour of a trial but against execution.[1] If there is a single thread connecting all the figures in this circle – Downing, the Calverts, Oliver Cromwell, Wickham and now Poole – it begins and ends with Hugh Peter.

During the summer of 1660 the King's Messengers were focused on the hunt for the regicides – the men who had signed the late king's death warrant or played a significant supporting role in his trial and execution. Two opposing sentiments divided the nation: the first, irenic, inspired the Act of Free and General Pardon, Indemnity and Oblivion – magnanimity written into law, encouraging the whole nation to put the pain of the Civil War behind it. The second sentiment was a overwhelming fear that the regicide put the times out of joint; the veil of the Temple had been rent and it could not be made whole without expiation. 'The Presbyterians were now the white-boys, and according to their nature fell a-thirsting, then hunting after blood . . .' wrote Lucy Hutchinson, the wife of a Roundhead colonel. 'God's blessing could not be upon the land, until justice had cleansed it from the late king's blood.'[2]

Hugh Peter's name was not on the death warrant. Nor had the King listed him among those especially exempted from the general pardon. But Parliament added his name to the death list, after foolish rumours in the press that Peter was the masked and hooded executioner at the Banqueting House who had personally killed the King. Hardly anyone believed it, but many knew the real truth: that apart from Cromwell himself, no one had striven so hard as Peter to secure the conviction and execution of Charles I.

So it was that on the first Saturday of September 1660, John Wickham, who had teamed up with Stephen Harris, the local constable, was down in Southwark tapping Harris's confidential informants for the latest scuttlebutt. After dark, acting on information received, the searchers descended upon the home of a Mr Broad, allegedly a Quaker, whose daughter, Mrs Peach, had two days previously given birth to a child and was now lying-in. According to a scurrilous report in a newsbook, Hugh Peter crept into the young woman's bed, which the King's Messenger was too chivalrous to have stripped and searched. Wickham and Harris found a secret passage leading to the home of another Quaker next door. While they were busy checking out the neighbouring property, Hugh Peter, so it is said, slipped out of Mrs Peach's bed and made off into the night, leaving behind his cloak, sword-stick and Bible.[3]

It is possible – indeed probable – that none of those identified in the press reports were Quakers at all. The area was known more for its leanings towards the Particular Baptist sect. But although the threat of a Quaker insurrection had subsided after the Restoration, the Quaker-as-bogeyman was still a useful smear against a defendant ahead of his trial.

Hugh Peter had escaped out into the Maze. This was not as it sounds: a bewildering network of streets and alleys filled with tall, crowded tenements. In 1660, the manor of the Maze, stretching from Tooley Street in the north to the bottom of Weston Street in the south, was still semi-rural.

Cattle drovers, who had brought their animals on a long, exhausting journey to market, would rest and fatten their beasts on the grazing land at the Maze for several days before taking them onwards to Smithfield. Urbanization of the area would not advance until after Thomas Guy had built his Hospital for Incurables in 1721.

*Hugh Peter*

The vista before Wickham was a series of fields, each having one or two buildings of various sizes. The low density gave the residents a high degree of privacy. There was an ever-shifting, itinerant population of drovers, a number of refugee families from France and the Netherlands, and many Baptists and sundry Nonconformists. It was not a community disposed to cooperate with the authorities and consequently made an excellent place to hide. Indeed, as it turned out, the Hugh Peter investigation ruined Stephen Harris's career. He found himself unable any longer to discharge his duties as constable because 'the factious people of Southwark' denounced him as 'a Saul and a persecutor' after Peter's arrest and he had to petition the King for a new job.[4] Yet somehow, on Sunday evening at around 6 p.m., John Wickham was given an address to go to. The King's Messenger tried to open the front door of a house belonging to a certain Nathaniel Mun, a ribbon-maker; but found Mun's wife was barring the door against him. After a good deal of shoving, he managed to force his way inside and climb the stairs, only to find Hugh Peter himself pushing back at the bedroom door. Eventually the outlaw was taken and escorted to the Tower of London, protesting all the way that he was not Hugh Peter at all, but 'Mr Thomson'. His friend, Maurice Thomson, perhaps?

Peter had only a perfunctory trial in which it was necessary for the prosecution merely to show that he had 'compassed' or 'imagined' the king's death for him to be convicted of High Treason. Not only were there witnesses to his preaching against the King, but Peter had made no secret in the wider world of his opinions. When Bulstrode Whitelocke, accompanied by Samuel Morland and Robert Stapylton, went on their diplomatic jaunt to Sweden in 1654, Hugh Peter had sent along some gifts for the Swedish queen: a mastiff; an enormous cheese; and a letter explaining why it had been necessary to execute Charles I. In any case, Hugh Peter had made a realistic appraisal of his circumstances and concluded that 'Apologias rarely reach their ends because their game is an aftergame.' Prejudice, he explained, is strong and 'apologias can hardly be put into hands that have [already] . . . received the first tincture'.[5]

On 16 October, Hugh Peter was taken with John Cook, who had been the chief prosecutor at Charles I's trial, to the gallows at Charing Cross, which afforded a line of sight down Whitehall to where Charles had been executed. Cook was the first to be subjected to the appalling punishment they both faced. First, he was hanged, but was taken down when not quite dead; then the executioner cut off his penis and testicles and disembowelled him; his intestines were thrown on a fire and burned in front of his eyes; his head was then cut off and his body divided into four parts. It is likely he remained alive until decapitation. Hugh Peter was required to watch all this amid the jeering and whooping of the crowd and taunts from the executioner as he rubbed his bloody hands together. Then it was his turn.

He said a prayer, made a brief speech and may even have surprised himself with his impromptu collectedness, in the teeth of the barracking and laughter and the unthinkable ordeal ahead. He had been sustained in his last weeks in the Tower by daily visits from his daughter and he wrote a pamphlet for her entitled 'A Dying Father's Last Legacy to an Only Child', which he entrusted to Giles Calvert, who published it after the execution. The pamphlet contained much sage advice. He exhorted Elizabeth to 'keep the best company', 'read the best books', seek out a special friend and move to New England.[6]

There is no reason to believe that George Downing was present to bid his former mentor a safe journey into the afterlife. Or to say farewell when Thomas Scot was dragged to the gallows the following day. Downing must have been acutely aware of how fortunate he was to have avoided reprisal. Hugh Peter, Colonel Okey, Sir Arthur Hesilrige, Sir Henry Vane, Thomas Scot – all those who had helped him when he first arrived from New England were exempted from pardon.

Downing used his time in London wisely, in the autumn of 1660 and the early months of 1661, to refashion his political image. He got himself appointed to the Council of Trade as a commissioner, where he sat alongside men such as Nicholas Crispe, a pioneer of the African slave trade; William Thomson, Maurice's younger brother; and the merchant and slaver Martin Noell. One day in January 1661, at the Mercers' Hall, he ran into his former clerk Samuel Pepys, who was there with the Comptroller of the Navy. 'To Mercers' Chapel and so up to the great hall,' Pepys recorded in his diary:

> where we met with the King's Council for Trade upon some proposals of theirs for settling convoys for the whole English trade, and that by having 33 ships . . . settled by the King for that purpose, which indeed was argued very finely by many persons of honour and merchants that were there.
>
> It pleased me much now to come in this condition to this place, where I was once a petitioner for my exhibition in St Paul's School and also where Sir G. Downing (my late master) was chairman, and so but equally concerned with me.[7]

At this time Downing also acquired his first proper country house and estate, purchasing the manor of East Hatley in Cambridgeshire from Robert Castell, a down-on-his-luck former Parliamentary colonel, and his brother Edmund, a

Semitic philologist, later to become professor of Arabic at Cambridge University. Downing had his land planted with apple and walnut trees – Harvard-style – and installed his mother in the manor house to mind the farm when he and Frances were away.

*The heads of Cromwell, Ireton and Bradshaw are on the poles marked 1, 2 and 3 respectively*

A few weeks later at Westminster, on the twelfth anniversary of the late king's execution, the corpses of the dead regicides Oliver Cromwell, Henry Ireton and John Bradshaw were disinterred from their resting places in the abbey, dragged through the streets to Tyburn and hanged. Cromwell's head was set on a spike above the House of Commons. Later in the year would come a further round of disinterments, with the bodies of Cromwell's wife Elizabeth, his sister Jane, Sir Arthur Hesilrige's brother Thomas, and the regicide Isaac Dorislaus (who was assassinated in 1649 while on a diplomatic mission to The Hague) all hauled out of their tombs in the abbey and flung into a pit in St Margaret's churchyard next door.

## *Envoy Extraordinary*

After the coronation of King Charles II in April 1661, Downing was sent back to The Hague as Envoy Extraordinary, arriving in early June. He found the country greatly changed, full of republican riff-raff, recalcitrant loyalists to the 'good old cause'. 'It is not to be credited what numbers of disaffected persons come daily out of England into this country,' he reported to Lord Clarendon, who as Lord Chancellor led the government and was broadly the equivalent of a prime minister today. The Nonconformist chapels, Downing explained, were where the troublemakers lurked. 'They have settled at Rotterdam an Independent, Anabaptist and Quaker church and do hire the best houses and have great bills of exchange come over from England to them.'[8]

Over and above Downing's pay and generous expenses, the King agreed to provide him with an allowance designated for 'intelligence and other private services'. Part of this would be used to monitor the 'disaffected' British expats. This was a complete about-turn from Downing's first embassy at The Hague, when he used to spy on Royalist plotters and their bookshops, disrupt Anglican prayers for the King and needle the Queen of Bohemia.

One month after he returned to The Hague, Downing received orders in cipher from London requiring him to make every effort to 'lay hands upon the rogues'[9] – these being the wanted regicides and other excepted persons who had escaped to the continent. One of the first to be spotted, in June, was George Joyce, then apparently living in Rotterdam. 'One who saw Cornet Joyce within these two days,' Downing reported to London, 'tells me that he talks very high.'[10] The envoy added that he was currently recruiting an agent in Rotterdam to keep under surveillance.

Joyce was by no means a high-value target. He had not been exempted from the Act of Indemnity and Oblivion for snatching the late king from Holdenby, nor for running messages between Cromwell and Ireton as they made plans for the King's trial; or even for his recent return to intelligence work for Thomas Scot under the Commonwealth revival of 1659. What had, in fact, put Joyce on the wanted list was the testimony provided to a gullible parliamentary committee by the charlatan astrologer William Lilly, who claimed that the second masked executioner on the platform at the Banqueting House had not been Hugh Peter, as otherwise rumoured, but George Joyce. Lilly told MPs that his source for this information was Robert Spavin, the secretary whom Cromwell dismissed in 1649 for forging his master's signature on a pass.

George Downing had seen Joyce rise over the years to the rank of lieutenant colonel, so it is peculiar that he should still be describing him as 'Cornet Joyce'. Maybe he encountered him at Holdenby when he was a chaplain with Okey's dragoons, or afterwards in the vicinity of Childerley, and Joyce became for ever imprinted on his mind as a young cornet.

Downing needed to reconcile a number of sensitive diplomatic considerations all at the same time. A treaty with the Netherlands was now in prospect. And a treaty between the Netherlands and Portugal, in which the King was taking a particular interest, ahead of marrying a Portuguese princess, was almost ready for signing. But Downing found some technical problems with it. The King was especially concerned with the well-being of his nephew, the Prince of Orange – in particular with the tutors chosen to teach him, his prospects and titles of honour. Some in Holland resented English patronage of the Orange faction within Dutch politics, seeing it as meddling in their internal affairs. Downing identified the Dutch prime minister Johan de Witt's priorities and adroitly made progress in one strand, dependent upon concessions in another.

Although the sympathies of the Dutch Republic leaned towards the regicides more than to a Stuart king, Downing was nevertheless able to have an extradition clause inserted into the draft of the forthcoming agreement, along with an assurance that even before such a deal was concluded, the Dutch would be cooperative in bringing the regicides to justice. He tested de Witt by asking first for a 'dormant order' – essentially a blank arrest warrant that Downing could fill in as the opportunity arose. De Witt was not keen, raising legal and constitutional impediments. Rather than retreat, Downing advanced, asking what then his reaction would be if some fugitives were simply kidnapped off the street and bundled aboard a ship to England. The statesman replied that was the surest way and although it might provoke some outrage, it would all be over fast and could not be reversed. Encouraged by this reply, Downing looked to Clarendon for political cover for such a move. He had already asked to be supplied with a snatch squad of three or four committed English officers and a ship, with a view to acting outside the law. But Clarendon prevaricated.

Soon afterwards Downing received confirmation that his watchers in Rotterdam had found one of the organizers of the late king's trial. This was Edward Dendy, formerly the Serjeant-at-Arms of the Rump Parliament. Downing had been auditioning for some military muscle among the English mercenaries in Dutch service, but was turned down by one leathery veteran after another, each afraid that the mob would tear him limb from limb. With not even a wink of reassurance from Clarendon, let alone the letter of instructions signed in the King's own hand that he had requested, there was nothing for it but to apply to de Witt for an order. Given their previous frank exchanges, Downing naturally reminded him of his promise of cooperation. But de Witt feigned total incomprehension, refusing to acknowledge that any such conversation had ever taken place.

Downing refused to back down. He found an alternative method to have his application put before the States General and set about browbeating anyone who opposed it. Remarkably, the order was granted on condition that Dendy's name be written on the face of the warrant. Downing was told that the paperwork would be ready for collection at noon on the following day. Unfortunately for the persistent envoy, there was a leak at the Binnenhof. That night Edward Dendy was alerted by a magistrate in Rotterdam that an order for his arrest was expected to arrive the next day. He quit the city at once and headed north to Amsterdam.[11]

George Downing had his own man in Amsterdam: Sir William Davidson, a wily Scottish merchant. The two met at Downing's house in The Hague and came up with a promising scheme. Rather than attract attention by applying for a politically contentious order, they would have

Dendy arrested for debt. Such arrests happened every day in the course of ordinary commerce and might well pass without notice. Downing accordingly prepared a writ for an entirely fictitious debt of 200,000 guilders. But by the time Davidson got back to Amsterdam to serve it, Dendy had fled. After one further brief appearance in the city, the regicide left for Switzerland and safety.

A short time afterwards Sir William Davidson reported that sixty people attended the funeral in Amsterdam of the regicide John Hewson, following his death from natural causes. Alluding to the disinterments of Cromwell and Ireton et al., Davidson only half-jokingly suggested that perhaps the best thing he and Downing could do would be to dig up Hewson's body and send it to London. For the first time it seemed that Downing had run out of puff. He wrote to Clarendon rehearsing the difficulties of arresting or kidnapping the regicides and asked the question that oft was thought, but never expressed out loud. 'What if,' he enquired innocently, 'the King should authorize some trusty persons to kill them? Let me have the King's serious thoughts about this . . .' Clarendon replied that the King could never countenance such a thing. Whether this was diplomatic caution or naivety is not clear. For assassination would eventually become the King's policy.

## *Dragnet*

As someone who had lived the secret life himself, George Downing knew that to find someone in hiding you should follow the post. This realization brought him Abraham Kicke, an Englishman living in Delft. Many of the fugitives had left their wives and families in England. Accordingly, letters and money had to move both ways. A merchant's premises made an ideal *poste restante.* And, for a fee, the merchant might provide other services: banking, asset management and so on. Downing's spies reported that a number of different targets had been observed visiting premises associated with Kicke. One of them was Miles Corbet, who was thought to be living in Zwolle or Campen. Rather than maintain surveillance for months, Downing jumped straight in. He arranged a meeting with Kicke and told him that he knew what the merchant was up to. He gave him a choice: either accept a bounty of £200 per regicide he entrapped or face total financial ruin and possible imprisonment.

Kicke would be up against the power of the English Crown. By comparison with his own limited resources, those of the state were almost unlimited. Downing could bring any number of legal actions against him and his business; he could fund others to sue at arm's length; he could bribe officials in the Netherlands, make complaints, call in favours, buy up Kicke's debts, pay his customers to go elsewhere. At the very least the merchant would be bankrupt within a few months; at worst he would be deported to England, where he would face prison, or worse, for aiding and abetting traitors. Kicke had only one anxiety: what if the townspeople of Delft found out and came after him? Downing had a ready answer, it seems, perhaps based on his own experience. His brother Joshua had been a merchant in Barbados, and Downing subsequently got him a job as a customs officer in Glasgow. The one turned out to be a good preparation for the other. If things did not work out in Delft, Kicke would have not only his money, but a guaranteed position in the Customs House. Downing's appeal to greed, combined with an overwhelming threat and accompanied by a safe route out, clinched it.

Before long, Kicke and Downing had located six fugitives and made a plan to lure at least two of them to Delft the following March. Downing had been badgering Clarendon to send him a certain Colonel Griffith, a man of renowned resourcefulness and martial talent, a kind of one-man special-forces unit. Griffith duly arrived at The Hague and Downing was impressed. The soldier and the envoy talked through the plans: Colonel John Okey, a former cavalry colonel and unambiguously a regicide, and John Barkstead, also a regicide, a former Lieutenant of the Tower of London and accomplished interrogator, would be invited to Delft by Kicke to discuss a possible investment scheme. There was a good chance that another regicide, the former MP Miles Corbet, might also be taken. When the targets were safely installed, the trap would be sprung, the outlaws arrested and shipped to England.

Colonel Griffith quite suddenly made his excuses and left. He needed, he explained, to speak to Lord Clarendon in person. He did not return. Clarendon never revealed quite what it was that put him off. Was it that Griffith did not think it honourable to take part in so serious a deception? Or that he did not like or trust Downing and Kicke? Or perhaps he thought the plan itself was fundamentally misconceived and sure to unravel? His replacement as the project's military consultant, Colonel Killigrew, was adamant about one thing: Downing must put away any thoughts of kidnapping and go through the proper process of obtaining a warrant. If the townsfolk of Delft were to think this was an unlawful abduction, they would swarm out onto the streets and overwhelm the snatch team. With some reluctance, Downing agreed to take Killigrew's advice.

## *Delft, March 1662*

The time of 9 p.m. prompt on Thursday 7 March (Old Style) was set for the arrests. At 2.30 p.m. that afternoon, Downing visited de Witt at his house and invited him to do the King of England a kindness by providing a warrant for the arrest of three regicides. The treaty between England and the Netherlands was at that time being finalized and de Witt had a very powerful incentive to ensure it was concluded. Downing declined to disclose the names of the regicides or the name of the town where they were living. He said only that he must have the order by 7 p.m. De Witt presented it to the States of Holland at 6 p.m. and it was approved subject to the names being written in by de Witt. Downing sent his secretary round with the names and the warrant was back with him by the appointed hour.

Downing decided to lead the arrest team himself. He took the boat to Delft with a Major Miles, Lieutenant Willoughby, Lieutenant Ogle and a number of servants from the embassy. He left them in the area of the Nieuwe Kerk for a few minutes while he presented his warrant to the town bailiff. Then the party went to Abraham Kicke's house, arriving at about 9 p.m. They knocked on the door and when it was opened, 'the crowd rushed in tumultuously and found the three men sitting by a fireside with a pipe of tobacco,' Downing wrote in his report to Clarendon.[12] 'Immediately they started up to have got out at a back door, but it was too late. In a moment the room was full.'

Downing discovered that he had indeed netted three of the regicides, arriving just in the nick of time to catch Miles Corbet, who was preparing to leave, with the candle for his lantern already lit. Corbet was so shocked and terrified by the arrest that he lost control of his sphincters, soiling himself front and back. The prisoners were placed in leg-irons and shackles and taken to the town jail where, according to their own account, they were 'cast into a nasty, moist and dark dungeon having nothing but the damp earth to repose upon'.[13]

The arrest, it turned out, was the easy part. There then began almost a week of bureaucratic and political argy-bargy, requiring further interventions on Downing's side by de Witt, two further orders from the States General and a vigorous campaign of bribery. Downing bribed the bailiffs, the police, the officers of the watch, the jail staff . . . almost anyone who would take his money. On the other side, Messrs Dawson and Welch, two rich English merchants from Rotterdam, were paying off magistrates and local aldermen in an attempt to have the prisoners released. The regicides became a *cause célèbre*, with politicians travelling down from The Hague to meet them.

Downing had members of the embassy staff literally camping out in an office at the jail in order to provide warning in case a release appeared likely. He learned from Kicke that an advocate named Oynions, at The Hague, had been approached to represent the three accused. Oynions was one of a number of lawyers retained by the British Crown through the embassy. Instead of telling him to recuse himself, Downing told him to take the case, but act only on instructions from him. The prisoners believed that thanks to their rich friends in Rotterdam they now had the best attorney in The Hague on their side, while all along he was secretly working for the King's Envoy Extraordinary.

Eventually the envoy obtained a further order from the States of Holland narrowly addressed to the bailiff of Delft, whom Downing had inevitably bribed, requiring him to hand over the prisoners. He brought his fresh order to the jail between three and four o'clock in the morning and demanded that the prisoners be surrendered at once. If the officials on the nightshift appeared reluctant to comply, Downing doubtless threatened and cajoled and, by sheer force of personality, shepherded the shackled prisoners down the back stairs of the jail just before dawn and onto a small boat waiting at the adjacent canal. At a rendezvous just outside the harbour of Delft, Downing transferred the prisoners to Nicholas Armorer, whom he instructed to ensure the captives did not set foot on land at any point, but were taken all the way through a maze of inland waterways to the Dutch naval base at Helvetsluis. There the English frigate *Blackamoor* was waiting to conduct them to Harwich and thence by riverboat to the Tower of London. This was likely the first recorded case of extraordinary rendition.

The King wrote Downing a congratulatory letter, to which his loyal servant made this fulsome reply:

> What I have done is no more than my duty, and therefore had no reason to expect any acknowledgement thereof, but to have it and that immediately from yourself under your own hand and in such terms is a favour and honour altogether surprising and confounding, such as I could not in my whole life have hoped to have attained, nor can sufficiently admire and esteem. I do from the day of the receipt thereof

> account myself perfectly and completely happy, as having lived to see my King upon his throne, and myself not only pardoned but received into his grace, employed and trusted by him and my poor endeavours thus accepted . . . [And so on in the same vein.][14]

It did the trick. Charles gave Downing a baronetcy, £1,000 in cash and eventually, in 1664, a fresh lease on some undistinguished land in Westminster that Downing seemed to want, for some obscure reason.

Unlike the King's response, Lord Clarendon's message to Downing after the rendition was sharply double-edged: 'You never did anything more advantageous to yourself and your reputation than your conduct in this business.'[15]

A couple of years later the government was persuaded to try what it had previously considered one of Downing's more outrageous ideas, reportedly at the urging of Queen Henrietta Maria. The regicide Sir John Lisle, who had sat alongside Downing in Parliament during the Protectorate, was walking to church in Lausanne, thinking himself entirely safe, when a death squad shot him at close range. Their leader was James Cotter, who had fought on the Royalist side at the Battle of Worcester. He was later appointed governor of the Caribbean island of Montserrat.

Three regicides escaped to America. Two of them, William Goffe and Edward Whalley, who was Oliver Cromwell's cousin, fled to Massachusetts straight after the Restoration. Both had been senior military officers and had served alongside George Downing at Dunbar and Worcester. The colonists in Massachusetts and New Haven were sympathetic to the fugitives. They would not have received the same kind of welcome in Virginia, however.

There the colonists were copying the most extreme gestures of the Cavaliers back home: they dug up the body of the Puritan whom Cromwell had briefly installed as governor and hanged his skeleton.

In Massachusetts, Goffe and Whalley were given refuge in basements and outbuildings from the agents Charles II sent to extradite them to England. To avoid capture, Whalley and Goffe had to spend a year in a cave, way out in what was then wilderness (and is now West Rock Ridge State Park) north-west of New Haven in Connecticut. They later moved to the cellar of a house in the town of Hadley, Massachusetts, where they were careful to ensure that none of the locals, other than their host, ever set eyes upon them. Many years later, according to popular legend, when the town was attacked at night by Wampanoag Indians, the elderly white-haired General Goffe emerged from his hiding place in a nightshirt brandishing a sword, rallied the defenders and saved the town. No one knew who the strange figure was, thereafter known as the 'Angel of Hadley'. Whalley and Goffe evaded capture for their rest of their lives. There was a third regicide who escaped to America. John Dixwell had been the Roundhead governor of Dover Castle. He took few precautions to avoid capture beyond adopting the pseudonym John Davids. Under this name he lived a conventional life as a citizen of New Haven and was never troubled by agents of the king. In fact Dixwell's name did not appear on any arrest warrant. By a stroke of good fortune, he had been listed as already dead as a result of a clerical error back in London.[16]

# CHAPTER 12

# Rise and Fall

## *Westminster, 1661–8*

AT THE NORTH end of Westminster Hall rose a pair of staircases, one in the north-west corner; the other in the north-east. If you took the former, it led up to where the actual exchequer lay: being the giant chessboard tablecloth that gave the institution its name. The table it covered was enormous and around it sat men doing sums and resolving tax and loan disputes. If you took the other staircase, it led you to the Exchequer of Receipt, where George Downing was one of four tellers who inhabited the grey zone between picturesque medieval tradition and early modern corruption. It was a bizarre world of parchment teller's bills and wooden tally sticks carved with notches of esoteric significance. Your stick might be cut in half, one part becoming the foil, the other the tally. If the two were later found to click together, you were entitled to a *quietus est* from the Pipe Office.[1] All of that just to pay money to the government.

George Downing very much enjoyed being a Teller of the Exchequer – it was one of two positions he made a special point of asking to retain when he made his deal with Charles II. The job brought a retainer of £400 per annum and who-knows-how-many times that sum in fees. Downing particularly liked one of the perks: each teller was given his own small town house in St Stephen's Cloister, adjacent to the chamber of the House of Commons. For someone who was both a teller and a Member of Parliament, nothing could be more convenient. But Downing was not only interested in the money, the perks and the status. He genuinely wanted to change the system for the better. He had ideas for reforms across the piece: in the Treasury, in the way public finances were run, and in international trade.

When the King set up his new trade council in the autumn of 1660, he signalled that he wanted 'knowing, active men' and 'understanding, able persons'.[2] Downing had been on the Protector's council since 1655 and had many personal and family connections among the new wave of London merchants who had made their fortunes trading with the colonies. In 1657, his father's friend Maurice Thomson was made governor of the East India Company – an enterprise that Downing believed had enormous potential, but which needed to be supported and nurtured by the government. He became its foremost parliamentary champion. As Resident in The Hague, he had watched resentfully as the Dutch turned themselves into the richest and most dominant trading nation in the world. Now he wanted to apply Dutch techniques to England's economic management.

Downing recognized how crippling a shortage of money was for a ruler. So many of the problems of the Civil War – arguably the Civil War itself – stemmed from the King not being able to afford what he wanted to do. The Commonwealth had been perennially short of cash too; and missteps such as the Western Design, though the product of many interwoven factors, might well have been avoided if Cromwell had access to more money at that time. Downing's ambition was to ensure that Charles II could easily raise all the money he needed, either by taxes or through loans. To this end, Downing helped devise reforms that would make people less frightened to lend money to the King. One innovation was a system of 'appropriations' whereby money would be voted for a specific use – the Dutch War, say – and it would be unlawful to fritter it away on anything else. A second scheme guaranteed that people lending money to the government were repaid strictly in the order in which the loans had been made. A register would be kept and every lender would know their place in the order of precedence. Previously the sequence of repayment had been at the discretion of the Lord Treasurer. His cronies knew they would get their money back promptly, while everyone else feared they might be left to whistle for it.

Lord Clarendon was by nature averse to innovations, or schemes of improvement, believing they inevitably threw up unforeseen problems. The Lord Chancellor also felt instinctive disdain for George Downing, calling him 'a man of an obscure birth and even more obscure education'.[3] He thought Downing rated his own intellect and ability too highly. Downing was, he said, 'a very voluminous speaker, who would be thought wiser in trade than any of the merchants, and to understand the mystery of all professions much better than the professors of them'. Clarendon tried to put a spoke in the wheels of Downing's treasury reforms at a special debate attended by a group of senior ministers and the King in 1665.

The Lord Chancellor was suffering from gout at the time, so Charles commanded that the meeting be held in Clarendon's bedroom. The Lord Treasurer also had gout, but was persuaded to shuffle along to join the meeting at which Downing was made to defend his policies, as if before the Board of Overseers at a Harvard *viva*.

Clarendon's opening shot was on the dangers of novelty. This got him nowhere with the King, who was noticeably leaning towards Downing. 'The King had in his nature so little reverence or esteem for antiquity,' Clarendon ruefully recorded afterwards, 'and did in truth so much contemn old orders, forms, and institutions, that the objections of novelty rather advanced than obstructed any proposition. He was a great lover of new inventions, and thought them the effects of wit and spirit, and fit to control the superstitious observation of the dictates of our ancestors: so that objection made little impression.'[4]

Clarendon paraphrased Downing's pitch thus:

> Downing . . . told them . . . by making the payment with interest so certain and fixed, that . . . it should be out of any man's power to cause any money that should be lent tomorrow to be paid before that which was lent yesterday . . . he would make [the] Exchequer . . . the best and the greatest bank in Europe . . . and all nations would sooner send their money into [it] . . . than into Amsterdam or Genoa or Venice. And it cannot be enough wondered at, that this intoxication prevailed so far that no argument would be heard against it . . .[5]

The King decided that any objections should be written up as constructive amendments to the bill before Parliament. Clarendon could feel victory slipping through his gouty fingers. He would later blame 'the extremity of the pain which at that time he endured in his bed' for a sudden and terrible outburst against George Downing.

'It was impossible for the King to be well served,' Clarendon declared with more than his usual grandiosity, 'whilst fellows of [Downing's] condition were admitted to speak as much as they had a mind to; and that in the best times, such presumptions had been punished with imprisonment.'[6] The King was furious and upbraided his Lord Chancellor, indicating that his own position was now 'on slippery ground'.

Downing's reforms went through and in 1667 he was made Secretary to the Treasury. Before his promotion, he ran into Samuel Pepys in Westminster Hall:

> Sir W. Pen and I towards the Exchequer and in our way met Sir G. Downing . . . and he would go with us back to the Exchequer and showed us in his office his chests full and ground and shelves full of money, and says that there is 50,000*l.* at this day in his office of people's money, who may demand it this day, and might have had it away several weeks ago upon the late Act, but do rather choose to have it continue there than to put it into the Banker's hands, and I must confess it is more than I should have believed had I not seen it, and more than ever I could have expected would have arisen for this new Act in so short a time.[7]

## *The Manhattan and Long Island land grab*

Downing Street runs between Varick Street and Bleecker Street in New York's Greenwich Village. It is fitting that there is a street named after George Downing in Manhattan, for he played a significant part in transferring control of the island from Dutch settlers, led by Peter Stuyvesant, to the English Crown. Under the Dutch it was known as New Amsterdam and, together with Long Island, formed the New Netherlands. The English renamed it New York, after James, Duke of York.

In 1661, when George Downing had returned to The Hague to serve the newly restored King Charles II, he received a discreet visit from his cousin John Winthrop, the governor of the Connecticut colony.[8] This was a somewhat more modest affair than the state that bears that name today. Winthrop's Connecticut did not include New Haven, which had been established as a separate colony. The governor, by nature an expansionist, was looking to make some radical changes to the map. As well as a merger with New Haven, he had his eye on acquiring Long Island and Manhattan. He had come to The Hague to ask George Downing to help him wrest control of these territories from the Dutch. Downing was able to oblige. Indeed, he saw in Winthrop's plan for a new charter a chance to advance England's international trading ambitions at the expense of the Dutch. With Downing's support and introductions, Winthrop went on to London and secured from the King and the Duke of York a new charter giving Connecticut vast new territories covering all of what is now New York state, plus parts of New Jersey and Delaware. New Haven was tidied into greater Connecticut too. This gave Winthrop the legal rights to New York, but not the possession. George Downing understood that it would probably take a war to get what they both wanted.

In the summer of 1664, a squadron of English frigates sailed into New Amsterdam's harbour and called upon the settlers to surrender. Remarkably, they did so without putting up a fight. Some weeks previously agents had landed on Long Island with pre-printed handbills offering generous terms to the Dutch settlers if they would accept British rule. The agents were quickly followed by troops, who secured the key points of the island and advanced to Brooklyn to await the arrival of the frigates. The operation had been carefully planned by a special commission set up back in London. The Dutch settlers of Manhattan, under their leader Peter Stuyvesant, surrendered to a group of commissioners that included John Winthrop.

Although he did not yet know it, in Charles II Downing had met his match in terms of guile. The King had his own agenda for New England. He planned to bring all the colonies more tightly under his control and that of his brother, the Duke of York, who was a Catholic. To this end, he picked for the commission former Royalist officers, Catholic sympathizers and a Massachusetts colonist called Samuel Maverick, who had complained that he had been persecuted during the Civil War on account of being a Royalist and a mainstream Anglican. The commission had two sets of orders: one, openly avowed, involved taking Long Island and Manhattan from the Dutch; but it appears there was also a submerged agenda to restore royal authority and control throughout New England. Once again, Downing had to demonstrate that his loyalties lay with the new dispensation and no longer with his Massachusetts past. He needed no persuading. By now, mercantilism had become Sir George Downing's new religion. He took the initiative in revamping the Navigation Act to ensure that colonial goods were carried only by colonial or British vessels, preventing Dutch or French ships from taking a share.

A similar jingoistic spirit animated both Lord Arlington, one of the King's closest advisers, and Charles's brother, the Duke of York, who commanded the navy. They aimed to seize Dutch colonies and trading posts in the Caribbean, Africa and the Indies. Downing's role was to advance their schemes by exploiting political divisions among the Dutch and once again providing London with timely intelligence from the Netherlands. He also used his position as an MP for Morpeth, George Fenwick's old seat, which was now in the gift of his Howard in-laws. 'And when he sat afterwards as a member of the House, returning still in the interval of parliament to his employment at the Hague,' Clarendon observed, 'he took all opportunities to inveigh against their usurpations in trade and either did or pretended to know many of their mysteries of iniquity.'[9]

Downing was indeed able to catalogue Dutch failures to compensate for unlawful seizures of ships and cargo going back to the 1640s. Many of the cases still extant featured in his numerous testy memorials to the States General, under both the King and Oliver Cromwell. Downing had developed a loathing of the Dutch and became driven by his ideological mercantilism, whereby he not only tried to keep the Dutch out of home and colonial trade with navigation laws and tariffs, but out of any economic activity that he could.

Anti-Dutch feeling was particularly rife among the merchants, especially those such as Maurice Thomson with interests that spanned the globe. Thomson resented Dutch dominance in West Africa, as the East India Company wanted to use bases in the Gambia and on the Gold Coast for provisioning its ships bound for India. England's close relationship with Portugal, arising from the King's marriage to Catherine of Braganza, created new opportunities for the company. The King received Bombay as part of the queen's dowry.

Thomson and his merchant friends were indignant at Dutch breaches of the Navigation Acts in the Caribbean, and began to intrude upon the Dutch monopoly in the Spice Islands. Thomson, acting on his own account rather than that of the East India Company, was involved in 'interloping' in Guinea, muscling in on the Dutch-controlled trade in African slaves.

The perils of commercial buccaneering were made startlingly evident by the curious fate of the late Martin Noell's disappearing wealth. The man who had made a fortune selling Scottish prisoners into slavery, and whose family owned vast sugar estates in Barbados, suddenly seemed to leave nothing behind. 'It seems nobody can make anything of his estate, whether he be dead worth anything or no,' Samuel Pepys recorded in October 1665, 'he having dealt in so many things, public and private, as nobody can understand whereabouts his estate is, which is the fate of these great dealers at everything.'[10]

In the spring of the previous year, an expeditionary force under the command of a Royal Navy officer, Robert Holmes, seized a string of trading posts and slave castles along the west coast of Africa, including the main Dutch fort. In The Hague, de Witt tried to engage the English in a mediation process. As a token of his peaceful intentions, he instructed his fleet to stay in port. But this was just a sham. He had sent secret orders to Admiral de Ruyter to break away from fighting Barbary pirates in the Mediterranean and head for Guinea, Gambia and the Gold Coast to seize back all the forts from the English.

These raids, combined with England's invasion of the New Netherlands, with a soundtrack of George Downing's blowhard rhetoric, tipped the two sea powers into formal conflict. The Second Anglo-Dutch War was declared in 1665, while Downing was still at his post. Under the Crown – just as under the Protectorate – George Downing brought to the practice of everyday diplomacy the special skills of the professional spy.

During the course of March and April 1665, he was able to send back to London intelligence of the very highest quality and importance regarding the disposition of the enemy fleet and the intentions of the Dutch commanders. He discovered that the Dutch would initially divide their force into two, with ninety ships at the Texel and thirty at Weylingen. He obtained this information from a highly placed agent who appears to have ready access to the most sensitive information. Downing refers to his agent only as 'my friend'. In early April his friend brings important news that the two flotillas are to link up. Downing has other intelligence about Dutch ships heading to Africa and New York. He describes holding a meeting with his agent at The Hague, just before the source went on to join the Dutch fleet at Texel.

In addition to reporting on naval matters, Downing was also keeping London informed about Dutch propaganda and psychological warfare. A letter had been read out in the States General detailing alleged British atrocities in Guinea involving 'frying Dutchmen by the fire and cutting off the ears and noses of others'. Downing believed this letter was a fake and had been forged at The Hague. He also informed Arlington that 'They have some at work penning books in English, which they intend to scatter through England, Ireland and Scotland . . .', ending with the mordant punchline, 'and with these paper bullets they intend to kill ye all'.[11]

During this period, Downing later revealed, he employed a servant in de Witt's household to take the prime minister's keys out of his pocket while he slept, open the closet and remove his secret papers to Downing, for an hour, before returning them and slipping the keys back.

*Battle of Lowestoft*

In mid-June, as the Battle of Lowestoft raged out in the North Sea, Sir George Downing barricaded himself in the British Embassy. 'Between 10 and 11 at night sitting in my dining room (though my house be in the middle of the Hague) there was such a blow that it made all my windows rattle and blew open my casements, and about one at night it shook the whole house, and the very beds as if it had been a great earthquake.'[12] The sound he heard was the magazine exploding on a Dutch man-o'-war out at sea.

*Lange Voorhout, The Hague*

Downing took elaborate steps to protect himself. He reported to London thus:

> I provided myself well with all sorts of arms, and powder, and things like Granadoes, and from the time that I did perceive that the fleets might be engaged, I neither stirred out of my own house myself, nor suffered any of my people to stir out, but sent some others that I could trust of all messages so that there might be no pretence of picking any quarrel with them . . . I had carried up such quantities of great

> stones, and placed them at the top of the stairs and other convenient places, as also great barrels of earth made up in strong casks at the top of the stairs, to be ready to tumble down upon any that should adventure up . . . but I thank God I have not yet met with the least occasion to make use thereof, nor so much as an ill word spoken before my door, nor a stone cast at any of my windows.[13]

It was truly an extraordinary thing that an envoy should be able to remain in place at the height of a shooting war; but Downing continued to send back military intelligence of the highest quality. He had agents in each of the maritime provinces, whose sole task was to count ships: ships at sea and ships in port. On any given day he probably knew at least as well as any Dutch admiral the precise disposition of the enemy's fleet in home waters.

Ghosts from Downing's past made fleeting visits around this time. Joseph Bampfield was back on the scene and, as always, it was hard to be sure whom he was working for; it transpired that much of the time he was in the pay of de Witt. The loyalties of William Scot, son of Downing's old spymaster Thomas Scot, were equally opaque. He and his friend Aphra Behn were both spying for England in the Netherlands and may well have been instructed to liaise with Downing.

The conflict between England and the Netherlands was as much one between the English East India Company and the Dutch East India Company. Downing was always striving to find new ways for the English to get an edge on the Dutch, copying whatever the Netherlands did well. English freight ships were more expensive than the

Dutch equivalent because the English spent so much on naval gunnery. For relatively safe neighbourhoods, such as the Baltic, Downing encouraged the commissioning of ships built merely for bulk, without guns or roundhouse. 'If England were once brought to a navigation as cheap as this country,' he wrote from The Hague, '[then] good night, Amsterdam.'[14]

Downing's political masters had their war, and for a while it looked as if they were going to win. But early successes turned to dust. The Dutch mounted a spectacular raid on the English fleet in the Medway in June 1667, where they destroyed more than a dozen vessels and captured the English flagship, towing her back to the Netherlands as a trophy.

When the warring parties met to negotiate peace and sign the Treaty of Breda in July, the Dutch chose not to press their claim for the restoration of New York. Instead they preferred to have the British accept Dutch ownership of all of Suriname. Johan de Witt was hailed for winning both the war and the peace settlement.

Soon Sir George Downing would be back in The Hague, with orders to foment yet another war. This one was not so much propelled by economic forces or commercial ambition as by Charles II's determination to receive the respect that he considered his due. Downing received instructions from London to pick a quarrel, and even how he should do so. As so often, Downing thought he knew better. Dilatory in following orders from Lord Arlington, he could be downright recalcitrant. A succession of nudges, delivered through the chain of command, had failed to persuade Downing to do what was required of him. The King himself sent a severe letter. 'I find you are sometimes divided in your opinion between what seems good to you and what my instructions direct,' Charles wrote. 'I have thought fit to send you my mind on the last hinge of negotiations in my own hand, so that you may know it is your part punctually to obey my orders instead of putting yourself to the trouble of finding reasons why you do not do so.' The King signed off as 'Your loving friend, Charles R'.[15]

Nevertheless, when instructed to stay put in The Hague at all costs and continue sending intelligence in the run-up to the outbreak of the Third Anglo-Dutch War in 1672, Downing once again disobeyed his loving friend's orders and, fearing for his life, made a run for it back to London. The King was furious and had the disobedient envoy locked up in the Tower of London for six weeks to teach him a lesson.

During the course of the war a Dutch expeditionary force recaptured both New York and Long Island. However, under the Treaty of Westminster, which brought an end to the conflict, the Dutch chose to swap New York for the island of Run in Indonesia, which produced vast quantities of nutmeg and mace. The Dutch were convinced they had got the better part of the bargain.

There would be no more diplomatic missions for George Downing. He was allowed to keep his seat in Parliament, and a couple of lucrative sinecures, but had lost the King's trust on abandoning his post. But Downing left in the nick of time to save his own skin. For the Dutch mob that had so loudly cheered Johan de Witt at the triumphant outcome of the Second Anglo-Dutch War now turned against him. Inflamed by the very political divisions Downing had sought to exacerbate, a crowd of The Hague's civil militia seized de Witt in the street, shot him and then left him to

*Jan de Baen's masterpiece depicting the mutilated corpses of Johan and Cornelis de Witt, hanged on the stake on the Groene Zoodje in The Hague*

the mob, who tore him limb from limb. His stripped and mutilated body was strung up on a gibbet, alongside that of his brother Cornelis: a scene that would become one of the most frightening paintings in seventeenth-century Dutch art. According to some accounts, de Witt's liver was gouged right out of his body, cooked and eaten by the Orangist mob.

Downing may have fallen from royal favour in England by now, but he remained an active – even hyperactive – Member of Parliament. He sat on scores of parliamentary committees and was personally involved in passing more than a hundred bills during his Westminster years. His parliamentary work was extraordinarily broad in scope, ranging from the predictable – measures to encourage the export of cider, or to protect the wool industry by making it a legal requirement for all bodies to be buried inside woollen sacks – all the way to the unexpected. Downing took the side of pedlars and hawkers against the corporations and was even involved in a horrifying and bizarre plan to assess the efficacy of a Swedish measure for castrating Jesuits.[16]

He also seems to have had time to accumulate yet more wealth, even though he was already one of the richest men in the kingdom. Just as his mentor Sir Arthur Hesilrige had once bought great tracts of Northumberland and County Durham, so Downing now invested in vast swathes of Cambridgeshire, including the whole area around East Hatley, where he lived, Gamlingay and Croydon, where he was buried in the parish church beside his wife. He was the largest landowner in the county.

Yet for all his enormous wealth, Downing was stingy. His elderly mother was forced to rely upon the kindness of far poorer friends and relatives when her son refused to provide her with an adequate allowance in old age. Downing was miserly with his alma mater, which he had once so generously endowed with an apple orchard. In a year when he had earned more than £20,000 – a colossal sum for the times – he responded to a fundraising appeal to Harvard alumni with a donation of a paltry fiver. He appears to have been far freer with the money, however, when it came to his own physical pleasures. A fellow MP claimed that George Downing's concupiscence kept no fewer than six prostitutes in business, but that was Westminster gossip, not proven fact. And yet, even the King was a little jealous. Sighing regretfully when a young actress rebuffed his advances, he ruefully remarked that he would have to be as rich as Sir George Downing to have any chance of obtaining her favour.

Downing kept his family life private, sealed up in silence. The world rarely catches a glimpse of his wife, Frances. She is occasionally mentioned in Lucy Downing's letters, recovering from childbirth or suffering some undisclosed ailment: 'I found my Lady Downing very weak and wears much and daily takes the air in her coach and wants no means that art and nature can afford for her comfort.'[17] Unlike her husband, Frances was generous to her mother-in-law, encouraging Lucy to 'have what I like . . . upon her cost'.[18] Frances Downing gave birth to three sons and five daughters. George, the eldest boy, became a Teller of the Exchequer just like his father. He married Lady Catherine Cecil, daughter of the Earl of Salisbury, joining the Downings to another of England's great aristocratic families. Charles, the next son, emigrated – as his grandfather once had – to Massachusetts, becoming comptroller of the customs at Salem. William, who was born in The Hague and had the great advantage of having King William III (formerly the Prince of Orange) as his godfather, appears to have left no mark in the public documents and died childless. George Downing's three younger daughters married well, in Ireland, Suffolk and Devon, but his two elder daughters predeceased him. Francis had married Sir John Cotton, Bt and was widowed; she died in 1681. Philadelphia married Sir Henry Pickering and had three daughters before her death in 1676. There are no documents to give us any sense of Downing's capacity for grief.

# CHAPTER 13

# *Si monumentum requiris . . . circumspice*

## *Downing Street*

IN 1682, TWO years before he died, Downing built the street of houses that represents his monument. They were then, as they are now, at the heart of politics and power in London.

Sir Christopher Wren had a supervisory role in surveying the project. From the surviving documents, it appears that Wren was acting more in the role of a planning officer, cautioning Downing not to exceed his bounds and intrude onto the green lawns of St James's Park, where so many British prime ministers now take ostentatious daily exercise. Downing built four great red-brick houses, of which numbers ten and eleven survive. Today's 10 Downing Street is formed of two houses, the garden wing being originally a separate house that was not part of Downing's development.

Downing's name first appears in connection with the land that would become his eponymous street on 24 November 1654, when he purchased the equivalent of a freehold of a property known as Hampden House. This shrewd acquisition was made in the same year as his marriage, while

Downing was living in next-door Axe Yard. The vendor was Robert Thorpe, who had bought out the Crown's interest in the house in the sell-off of Crown land in 1651.[1] A Mrs Elizabeth Hampden was still in residence when Downing made his initial investment. Indeed, she had a lease that would not expire until 1682. Mrs Hampden was the mother of the MP John Hampden, one of those who had been allocated a reserved plot at Saybrook. As it happens, she was also Oliver Cromwell's aunt. And another of her nephews was the regicide Edward Whalley, who had fought alongside Downing at Dunbar and later fled to New England. It is possible that Downing knew Elizabeth Hampden and had made a cold-blooded assessment of her potential longevity, always playing the long game. As the transaction had been made under the 'usurping powers' – that is to say, the Commonwealth – it was almost certainly void after the Restoration; hence the need to ask the King to issue a new lease. Yet even when that was supplied, Downing had to wait another eighteen years before he could demolish the old house and start building.

Were he comfortable with his past, Downing might have seen the development of the street as gathering together the disparate strands of his life. On one side of the plot had stood Oliver Cromwell's original lodgings in the Cockpit, where Downing had once waited for his patron to come back from the House of Commons with eyes agleam and blood up after dismissing the Rump in 1653. Those same rooms later housed Downing's old army pal George Monck, as he tried on his finery in front of the mirror before going out into the world as the Duke of Albemarle. On the other side of the development was Downing's own former house and first marital home in Axe Yard, where his sometime clerks of the Exchequer, Mr Hawley and Mr Pepys, had also lodged. From the corner of his Downing Street plot, he could look straight across to the palace of Whitehall, towards the offices that once housed the intelligencers and the Council of State. More disturbingly, he only had to turn his head to see the Banqueting House, outside which they had erected a platform on a winter's day to sever the old king's head from his body. There was no day when Downing the developer was not put on the spot by his own project: brought face to face with the sites of bloodshed and terror. Had he looked to the left, up what is now Whitehall, he would have seen the very place where his own spymaster Thomas Scot was hanged, drawn and quartered at Charing Cross.

If the memories sent a cold frisson down his spine, there is no evidence that Sir George allowed the associations a second's thought. He never lived in Downing Street himself. It was built entirely as a cold-blooded business venture, not a legacy project. His builders worked quickly – the houses were up in just over a year. A later occupant, Sir Winston Churchill, would tartly observe that the buildings were 'shaky and lightly built by the profiteering contractor whose name they bear'. Downing stinted on the mortar and faked up the effect of stonework by drawing artificial lines, prefiguring the cynical political deceits of later occupants.

Who names a street after himself? Westminster addresses take the name of English aristocrats: Buckingham, Jermyn, Villiers, Northumberland. But Downing, born without a title, elevates himself by association. Whether he intended it or not, the street has become his legacy by default. Most of his best work was carried out in secret, and it is an almost universal rule that those who practise the profession of espionage must forgo renown. Much of his worst work was morally heinous, hypocritical or cynical. An uneasy conscience does not much care to reflect upon the past.

Downing's contemporaries were clear-eyed in their judgements of his character. Samuel Pepys, who tried hard to like Downing, nevertheless marked him down as 'a perfidious rogue' in his diaries. To the Earl of Shaftesbury, Downing was 'real vile'. Americans have been no kinder. In New England for some years after his betrayal of the regicides, committing an act of gross treachery was described as 'doing a George Downing'. Another notable critic was John Adams, second President of the United States and a Massachusetts man himself, who wrote of him in 1818:

> This 'dog' Downing must have had a head and brains. Or, in other words, genius and address. But, if we may believe history, he was a scoundrel. To ingratiate himself with Charles II . . . he betrayed to the block some of his old republican and revolutionary friends. George Downing! Far from boasting of thee as my countryman, I should wish that thou hadst been hanged, drawn and quartered instead of Hugh Peter and Sir Henry Vane. But no! This is too cruel for my nature. I rather wish that you should have been obliged to fly and repent among the rocks and caves of the mountains of New England.[2]

Yet the world should resist holding George Downing to a different standard than his contemporaries. He was a turncoat when turncoats were ten a penny. He is understandably excoriated for capturing regicides and delivering them up for execution. Yet should not the largest measure of blame for what was done to Okey, Barkstead and Corbet be laid at the door of the King and his ministers? Why do we not hear anyone condemning Charles II, or Lord Clarendon for the acts of unspeakable savagery carried out at Tyburn and Charing Cross? And as for being a turncoat, only a few months after Downing shifted his allegiance from republic to Crown, so did the whole country, repudiating a failed revolution and restoring the nation to an older and surer footing as it hailed its returning monarch.

Nevertheless, it would be wrong to portray Downing as some kind of sly-yet-endearing rogue with a brazen front and a taste for black humour, a plump metropolitan Autolycus. His hands were forever stained with blood. In the end, acuity was George Downing's only engaging virtue; and that is never enough. The best hope for his reputation is that time will pardon him for spying well.

# Notes

## *A note on online sources*

In order to avoid congestion in the endnotes I have not generally provided full web addresses or access dates to platforms with stable URLs. Such sources are identified either by name or by abbreviations. Details of the main relevant online resources are listed below. Some are open-access, but others may have full or partial paywalls or require personal or institutional subscription.

British History Online (BHO): www.british-history.ac.uk/
Diary of Samuel Pepys: www.pepysdiary.com/
Early English Books Online via ProQuest Platform (EEBO): about.proquest.com/en/products-services/eebo/
Early English Books Online via the University of Michigan Digital Collections (UMICH): quod.lib.umich.edu/
Early Modern Letters Online, Bodleian Library (EMLO): emlo.bodleian.ox.ac.uk/
History of Parliament Online: www.historyofparliamentonline.org
Oxford Dictionary of National Biography Online (ODNB): www.oxforddnb.com/
Wikisource: Dictionary of National Biography 1885–1900 (DNB): en.wikisource.org/wiki/Dictionary_of_National_Biography,_1885-1900

## Introduction

1. These reproofs have been attributed to Anthony à Wood, John Lane and Andrew Marvell respectively. See *Collections of the*

*Massachusetts Historical Society: Vol. I, 5th series*, Boston, MHS, 1871, Preface, p.xxxiv. J. Beresford, *The Godfather of Downing Street: Sir George Downing 1623–1684: An Essay in Biography*, London, Richard Cobden-Sanderson, 1925, p.93.

2. E. Peacock, 'Notes on the Life of Thomas Rainborrowe, Officer in the Army and Navy in the service of the Parliament of England', *Archaeologia*, Society of Antiquaries of London, Vol. XLVI, 1880, p.9 (paper read 14 December 1876; emphasis added).

## 1: An Unsentimental Education

1. B. Pierce, *A History of Harvard University*, Cambridge, MA, Brown Shattuck and Co., 1833, pp.1–4. S. E. Morison, *The Founding of Harvard College*, Cambridge, MA, Harvard University Press, 1935, pp.181–228.
2. M. Parker, *John Winthrop: Founding the City upon a Hill*, New York, Routledge Taylor and Francis Group, 2014, pp.58–9.
3. Letter from Lucy Downing to John Winthrop, March 1637. *Collections of the Massachusetts Historical Society: Vol. 1, 5th series*, Boston, MHS, 1871, p.18.
4. J. Winthrop (J. K. Hosmer, ed.), *Winthrop's Journal: History of New England, 1630–1649*, New York, Scribner's, 1908, Vol. 2, p.84, see note 2.
5. Ibid., Vol. 1, p.203.
6. Ibid., Vol. 1, p.270.
7. Morison, *Founding*, pp.271–4.
8. J. L. Sibley, *Biographical Sketches of Graduates of Harvard University*, Vol. I, Cambridge, MA, Charles William Sever, 1873, pp.1–14.
9. Morison, *Founding*, pp.228–40.
10. *Winthrop's Journal*, 1908, Vol. 1, pp.311–14.
11. James Savage (ed.) and John Winthrop, *The History of New England 1630–1649*, Vol. I, Boston, 1825, p.254.
12. J. Latimer, *Buccaneers of the Caribbean, Cambridge*, MA, Harvard University Press, 2009, pp.86–8. See also P. G. E. Clemens, 'The World of Maurice Thomson', review of R. Brenner, *Merchants and Revolution: Commercial Change, Political Conflict, and London's Overseas Traders, 1550–1653*, in *Reviews in American History*, Vol. 21, No. 4, Dec 1993, pp.575–83.

13. F. Bremer, *John Winthrop – America's Forgotten Founding Father*, New York, Oxford University Press, 2003, pp.127–9.
14. *Winthrop Papers*, Massachusetts Historical Society, 1943, Vol. 3, pp.133–4.
15. Ibid., Vol. 3, p.165.
16. M. Kishlansky, 'Martyrs' Tales', *Journal of British Studies*, Vol. 53, No. 2, April 2014, pp.334–55.
17. R. C. Winthrop (ed.), *Life and Letters of John Winthrop*, Vol. I, Boston, Ticknor & Fields, 1864, p.304.
18. *Collections of the Massachusetts Historical Society*, 3rd series, Vol. 7 (1838), pp.33–48.
19. R. Stearns, *The Strenuous Puritan, Hugh Peter 1598–1660*, Illinois, The University of Illinois, 1954, p.98.
20. Charles Upham, *Salem Witchcraft, Volumes I & II, with an Account of Salem Village and a History of Opinions on Witchcraft and Kindred Subjects*, Project Gutenberg EBook #17845, 2006.
21. J. Felt, *Annals of Salem From Its First Settlement*, Salem, Ives, 1827, pp.233–4.
22. Charles Pope, *Pioneers of Massachusetts*, Boston, privately published, 1900, p.4.
23. J. Felt, *Annals of Salem*, Vol. II, Boston, 1849, p.167.
24. Felt, *Annals of Salem*, Vol. I, p.120.
25. Francis J. Bremer, *John Winthrop*, New York, Oxford University Press, 2003, pp.144–5.
26. C. Bridenbaugh, 'Yankee Use and Abuse of the Forest in the Building of New England, 1620–1660', *Proceedings of the Massachusetts Historical Society*, 3rd series, Vol. 89, 1977, p.27 note 49.
27. *New England's First Fruits*, London, Henry Overton, 1643.
28. Ibid., p.31.
29. Morison, *Founding*, pp.257–62.
30. J. Chaplin, *Life of Henry Dunster*, Boston, Osgood, 1872, p.70.
31. S. E. Morison, 'Precedence at Harvard College in the Seventeenth Century', *Proceedings of the American Antiquarian Society*, new series, Vol. 42, 1932, pp.371–431.
32. A. Forbes (ed.), *Winthrop Papers*, Vol. 5, Massachusetts Historical Society, 1947, pp.42–4.
33. L. Gardener, *Relation of the Pequot Warres*, New Haven, CT, Hartford Press, 1901, p.15.

34. *Winthrop Papers*, Vol. 5, p.38.
35. Ibid., pp.42–4.
36. H. Kilburn, 'Jesuit and gentleman planter: Ingle's rebellion and the litigation of Thomas Copley S.J.', *British Catholic History*, Vol. 34, No. 3, 2019. T. B. Riordan, *The Plundering Time: Maryland and the English Civil War 1645–1646*, Baltimore, Maryland Historical Society, 2004.
37. *Winthrop's Journal*, Vol. II, pp.250–51.

## 2: Army versus Parliament

1. H. G. Tibbutt, *Colonel John Okey 1606–1662*, Publications of the Bedfordshire Historical Record Society, Vol. 35, Streatley, 1955, pp.21–35. S. Ede-Borrett, 'Some Notes on the Raising and Origins of Colonel John Okey's Regiment of Dragoons, March to June, 1645', *Journal of the Society for Army Historical Research*, Vol. 87, 2009, pp.206–13.
2. Beresford, *Godfather*, p.48.
3. 'The third part of Gangræna. Or, A new and higher discovery of the errors, heresies, blasphemies, and insolent proceedings of the sectaries of these times; with some animadversions by way of confutation upon many of the errors and heresies named . . . Briefe animadversions on many of the sectaries late pamphlets, as Lilburnes and Overtons books against the House of Peeres, M. Peters his last report of the English warres, The Lord Mayors farewell from his office of maioralty, M. Goodwins thirty eight queres upon the ordinance against heresies and blasphemies, M. Burtons Conformities deformity, M. Dells sermon before the House of Commons; . . . As also some few hints and briefe observations on divers pamphlets written lately against me and some of my books . . . / By Thomas Edwards Minister of the Gospel,' in the digital collection Early English Books Online, name.umdl.umich.edu/A83515.0001.001, University of Michigan Library Digital Collections.
4. *Winthrop Papers*, Vol. 5, pp.206–8.
5. A. Woolrych, *Soldiers and Statesmen: The General Council of the Army and its Debates, 1647–1648*, Oxford, Clarendon Press, 1987, p.19.
6. Letter from the Commissioners at Holdenby & Examination of Bosville, *Journal of the House of Lords*, Vol. 9, 9 April 1647.

7. I. J. Gentles, *The New Model Army*, Oxford, Blackwell Publishers, 1992, pp.169–73. C. H. Firth, *Clarke Papers*, Vol. 1, Camden Society, 1891, Preface, pp.xxvi–xxxiii, 118–20, 124–5. John Rushworth, 'Historical Collections: Parliamentary proceedings, June 1647', *Historical Collections of Private Passages of State: Volume 6, 1645–47*, London, 1722.
8. *Winthrop Papers*, Vol. 5, pp.206–8.
9. 'Sir Arthur Hesilrige's letter to the honorable committee of Lords & Commons at Derby-House, concerning the revolt and recovery of Tinmouth-castle. In which action, Lieutenant Col. Lilburn (Governor of the castle) was slain, with divers seamen and others', in the digital collection Early English Books Online 2, name.umdl.umich.edu/A86093.0001.001, University of Michigan Library Digital Collections.
10. R. Winthrop (ed.), *Life & Letters of John Winthrop*, Vol. 2, Boston, Little Brown, p.386.
11. T. Carlyle, *Oliver Cromwell's Letters & Speeches: With Elucidations*, Vol. 1, New York, Wiley & Putnam, 1845, pp.296–313.
12. Ibid., p.343.
13. R. Baillie, *Letters & Journals*, Vol. II, Edinburgh, W. Gray, 1775, p.351.
14. J. Morrill (ed.), *The Letters, Writings, and Speeches of Oliver Cromwell: Volume 1: 14 October 1626 to 29 January 1649*, Oxford, Oxford University Press, 2022, p.594.
15. N. Carlin, *Regicide or Revolution? What Petitioners Wanted September 1648–February 1649*, London, Breviary Stuff Publications, 2020, p.68.
16. R. Blair and W. Row, T. M'Crie (ed.), *The Life of Mr Robert Blair*, Edinburgh, printed for the Wodrow Society, 1848, pp.142–4. Rev. W. K. Tweedie (ed.), *Select Biographies*, Volume First, Edinburgh, printed for the Wodrow Society, 1845, pp.153–6. P. Adair, *A True Narrative of the Rise and Progress of the Presbyterian Church in Ireland*, Belfast, Aitchison, 1866, pp.42–6.
17. *Winthrop Papers*, Vol. 3, pp.187, 190–93.
18. Blair and Row, *Life of Mr Robert Blair*, p.210.
19. *Winthrop Papers*, Vol. 5, p.42.
20. For background on the ambiguities and limits of toleration in Cromwell's circle, see J. Coffey, 'Puritanism and Liberty Revisited: The Case for Toleration in the English Revolution', *Historical Journal*, Vol. 41, No. 4, Dec 1998, pp.961–85.

21. H. Guthry, *Memoirs of Henry Guthry Late Bishop of Dunkel in Scotland*, London, J. Nutt, 1702, p.249.
22. P. Crawford, '"Charles Stuart, That Man of Blood"', *Journal of British Studies*, Vol. 16, No. 2, Spring 1977, pp.41–61. See also Ted Vallance, 'The Cromwell Day Address 2019: Cromwell, Blood Guilt and the Trial and Execution of Charles I', *Cromwelliana*, 3rd series, No. 9, 2020, pp.5–21.
23. *A True Account of the Great Expressions of Love . . .*, British Library, Thomason Tracts, E 468 (26).
24. C. R. Hudleston (ed.), *Naworth Estate and Household Accounts 1648–1660*, Durham, Andrews & Co., Bernard Quaritch, 1958, pp. xi, xii, 24, 41.
25. C. H. Firth, *Clarke Papers*, London, Camden Society, 1894, Vol. II, Preface, p.viii.
26. A. Woodhouse (ed.), *Puritanism and Liberty, being the Army Debates (1647–9) from the Clarke Manuscripts with Supplementary Documents*, University of Chicago Press, 1951, p.111.
27. E. Peacock, 'Notes on the Life of Thomas Rainborrowe, Officer in the Army and Navy in the service of the Parliament of England', *Archaeologia*, Society of Antiquaries of London, Vol. XLVI, 1880, Appendix B, p.64.
28. D. Underdown, *Pride's Purge: Politics in the Puritan Revolution*, Oxford, Oxford University Press, 1971, p.141.
29. Ibid. Re the purge itself, see pp.143–8.

## 3: The Breda Mission

1. F. B. Bickley, 'Letters Relating to Scotland, January 1650', *English Historical Review*, Vol. 11, No. 41, Jan 1896, pp.112–17.
2. A seemingly overdue payment was authorized by Cromwell in November 1650 relating to three weeks' pay for Downing as Scoutmaster General in November 1649. This probably results from Downing badgering the Lord General for back pay to cover part of his time in Edinburgh the previous year. See C.H. Firth, *Cromwell's Army*, London, Methuen, 1902, p.65, note 3. Thomas Scot dates Downing's involvement either from the sending of Winram to the King at Jersey or to the dispatch of commissioners to Breda. The Milton State Papers confirm the former to have been the case. A number of assumptions made in this section

are predicated upon Thomas Scot's testimony to the effect that Downing was his sole or primary source of high-level intelligence from Scotland relating to the Treaty of Breda. 'For Scotland I had the service and assistance of Mr Downing who was resident at Edinburgh, from whom I had account of all the transactions of that people with his Majesty, now our Sovereign, I think when at Jersey, but am sure at Breda.' From C. H. Firth and T. Scott, 'Thomas Scot's Account of His Actions as Intelligencer during the Commonwealth', *English Historical Review*, Jan 1897, Vol. 12, No. 45, pp.118–19.

3. G. E. Aylmer, 'Frost, Gualter', 2004, *ODNB* 37436.
4. J. Nickolls (ed.), *Milton State Papers: Original Letters and Papers of State Addressed to Oliver Cromwell*, London, William Bowyer, 1743, p.16.
5. 'A letter from Ireland read in the House of Commons on Friday Septemb. 28. 1649. From Mr Hugh Peters, Minister of Gods word, and Chaplain to the Lord Lieutenant Cromwell. Of the taking of Tredagh in Ireland, 3552 of the enenies slain, amongst which Sir Arthur Aston the governour, Coll. Castles, Cap. Simmons, and other slain. And the losse on both sides. Also the taking of Trim, and Dundalk. And the Lord Leiutenants marching against Kilkenny. A letter from Ireland, Imprimatur Hen. Scobell. Cleric. Parliamenti', in the digital collection Early English Books Online, name.umdl.umich.edu/A90539.0001.001, University of Michigan Library Digital Collections. J. Burke 'Sir Arthur Aston', Dictionary of Irish Biography Online, www.dib.ie/biography/aston-sir-arthur-a0256.
6. G. Warner (ed.), *The Nicholas Papers*, Vol. 1, London, Camden Society, 1887, pp.288–90.
7. *Milton State Papers*, p.2.
8. F. B. Bickley, 'Letters Relating to Scotland, January 1650', p.113.
9. Ibid.
10. *Milton State Papers*, p.4.
11. Ibid., pp.3–4.
12. Ibid., pp.4–5.
13. 'A rejoinder consisting of two parts, the first entituled, The ballance, or, A vindication of the proceedings and judgement of Parliament and their ministers, in the cases of William (called lord) Craven, Christopher Love: From the scandalous allegations

and ironical reflections of Ralph Farmer . . . in a late infamous libel of his, named, The imposter dethron'd, etc . . . Wherein the Commonwealth's case as to the one is briefly stated, and the treasons of the other are rehearsed as a looking-glass for the priests, and an awakening to England. The second, Evil scattered from the throne, and the wheel brought over the wicked: in an examination of that part of The imposter dethron'd as is in way of reply to The throne of truth exalted, etc.', in the digital collection Early English Books Online 2, name.umdl.umich.edu/A76759.0001.001, University of Michigan Library Digital Collections, p.16.

14. M. Brod, 'The Uses of Intelligence: The case of Lord Craven 1650–60', G. Southcombe and G. Tapsell (eds), *Revolutionary England c.1630–c.1660, Essays for Clive Holmes*, Abingdon, Routledge, 2017, pp.132–49. See also: T. B. Howells (ed.), 'The Trial of Major RICHARD FAULCONER, at the Upper Bench Bar in Westminster-hall, upon an Indictment for Perjury', *A Complete Collection of State Trials*, Vol. 5, London, T. C. Hansard et al., 1816, pp.323–65. 'A true and perfect narrative of the several proceedings in the case concerning the Lord Craven, before the Commissioners for Sequestrations and Compositions sitting at Haberdashers-Hall, the Council of State, the Parliament and upon the indictment of perjury, preferred and found against Major Richard Faulconer, the single and material witness against the Lord Craven, concerning the petition to the King of Scots, which as the said Faulconer pretended, was promoted at Breda by the Lord Craven, and wherein, as the said Faulconer deposed, the Parliament of England was stiled by the name of barbarous and inhumane rebels. Shortly after which oath the Lord Cravens estate was voted by Parliament to be confiscate', in the digital collection Early English Books Online 2, name.umdl.umich.edu/A94942.0001.001, University of Michigan Library Digital Collections, pp.1–5.
15. A. Keay, *The Last Royal Rebel: The Life and Death of James, Duke of Monmouth*, London, Bloomsbury, 2016, p.16.
16. Letter J. Trethewy to W. Edgeman, April 1650, S. R. Gardiner (ed.), *Letters & Papers Illustrating The Relations Between Charles II & Scotland 1650*, Edinburgh, Scottish History Society, 1894, p.59.
17. A. Rivet, 'An exact summary, of the transactions in the treaty at Breda: containing, the most remarkable occurrences that hap'ned

in their consultations: and the Scots commissioners proposals to their declared King', London, 1650, BL Thomason.

18. Dorothy Stimson, 'Hartlib, Haak and Oldenburg: Intelligencers', *Isis*, Vol. 31, No. 2, Apr 1940, University of Chicago Press/History of Science Society, pp.309–32 (quotation on p.314).
19. *Letters & Papers Illustrating The Relations Between Charles II & Scotland 1650*, p.88.
20. Rev. W. K. Tweedie (ed.), *Select Biographies*, Volume First, Edinburgh, printed for the Wodrow Society, 1845, p.174.
21. Calendar of State Papers Domestic: Interregnum, 1650, Mary Anne Everett Green. (ed.), London: Her Majesty's Stationery Office, 1876, Vol. 9, Letter from Middelburg, pp.263–314.
22. Sir James Balfour, *The Historical Works of Sir James Balfour*, Edinburgh, 1824, Vol. 4, p.40.
23. *Milton State Papers*, pp.12–13 (in some editions the name Pudsey is misprinted as Dudsey; listed as Pudsey at the Society of Antiquaries of London).
24. G. Hill (ed.), *The Montgomery Manuscripts: (1603–1706)*, Belfast, 1869, p.394. 'Two Letters from William Basil Esq., Attorney General of Ireland', London, The Parliament of England, 1649, British Library, Thomason Tracts, E587 (1).
25. This section relating to the life of Sir James Montgomery is largely based on two versions of the Montgomery Manuscripts: G. Hill (ed.), *The Montgomery Manuscripts: (1603–1706)*, Belfast, 1869; and Montgomery MS, 1830 edition, Belfast Newsletter.
26. F. B. Bickley, 'Letters Relating to Scotland, January 1650', p.117.
27. See review of T. Verbeek, *Descartes and the Dutch: Early Reactions to Cartesian Philosophy 1637–1650*, Southern Illinois University Press, 1992, by Steven M. Nadler, *Journal of the History of Philosophy*, Vol. 32, No.4, 1994, pp.672–3. A. C. Grayling, *Descartes: The Life of René Descartes and Its Place in His Times*, London, Simon & Schuster, 2006, p.213.
28. *Montgomery Manuscripts*, 1869, p.338.
29. *The Life of Mr Robert Blair*, 1848, p.230 and Preface, pp.xv–xvi.
30. J. Ayton, letter to Edward Nicholas, Mary Anne Everett Green (ed.), *Calendar of State Papers Domestic: Interregnum*, Vol. 9, 1 August 1650, London, 1876, pp.263–314.
31. Sir Edward Walker, *Historical Discourses*, London, Keble, 1705, pp.159–61.

32. Sir James Balfour Paul (ed.), *The Scots' Peerage*, Edinburgh, David Douglas, 1907, pp.288–9. See also H. Paton, 'Gray, Andrew (died 1663)', *Dictionary of National Biography, 1885–1900*, Vol. 23, en.wikisource.org/w/index.php?title=Dictionary_of_National_Biography,_1885-1900/Gray,_Andrew_(d.1663)&oldid=10767177.
33. James Johnston Brown, 'Social, political and economic influences of the Edinburgh merchant elite, 1600–1638', PhD thesis, 1985, Edinburgh Research Archive (ERA), Vol. 2, pp.482, 528.
34. Sir J. B. Paul (ed.), 'The Diary of Sir James Hope, 1646–1654' in *Miscellany*, Vol. 3, Second Series, Vol. 9, Edinburgh, Scottish History Society, 1919, pp.113–14.
35. D. Hay Fleming (ed.), *Diary of Sir Archibald Johnston of Wariston*, Vol. 2, Edinburgh, Scottish History Society, 1919, p.310.

## 4: Mr Downing Goes to War

1. S. R. Gardiner, *History of the Commonwealth & Protectorate*, Vol. 1, London, Longmans, 1903, p.271. See also 'A large relation of the fight at Leith neere Edenburgh: Wherein Major Generall Montgomery, Colonell Straughan, with many more of quality of the Scottish party were slaine and wounded. The particulars on both sides fully related, with a list of the prisoners taken, and number kild. Also a perfect account of every dayes transactions and engagements between the armies, since our armies first entring Scotland. Published by authority', in the digital collection Early English Books Online 2, name.umdl.umich.edu/A88700.0001.001, University of Michigan Library Digital Collections.
2. *Diary of Sir Archibald Johnston of Wariston*, Vol. 2, pp.4–5.
3. *Letters & Papers Illustrating The Relations Between Charles II & Scotland 1650*, p.136. (Lops and Covenanters translated to fleas and lice.)
4. Ibid.
5. Firth and Scott, 'Thomas Scot's Account of His Actions as Intelligencer', p.119.
6. *Milton State Papers*, p.16.
7. K. C. Corsar, 'David Leslie's Defence of Edinburgh, July–August 1650', *Journal of the Society for Army Historical Research*, Vol. 25, No. 103, Autumn 1947, pp.96–105. (Corsar's paper, taken together

with W. S. Douglas, *Cromwell's Scotch Campaigns: 1650–51*, London, Elliot Stock, 1898, provides an invaluable guide to the complex manoeuvres by both armies around Edinburgh in 1650 and generally inform this chapter.)

8. J. Lardner, *A Large Relation of the Fight at Leith . . .*, London, 1650, BL Thomason E609 (1).
9. *Diary of Sir Archibald Johnston of Wariston*, Vol. 2, p.14.
10. *A True Relation of the Proceeding of the English Army Now in Scotland*, London, Parliament of England, 1650, BL Thomason E608 (23).
11. Ibid., pp.14–15.
12. *A Large Relation of the Fight at Leith*, final page (not numbered).
13. *True Relation*, p.10.
14. Bulstrode Whitelocke, *Memorials of the English Affairs*, 1732, p.467.
15. R. and W. Kerr, *Ancram-Lothian Correspondence*, Vol. 2, Edinburgh, 1875, p.276.
16. J. Nicoll, *A Diary of Public Transactions*, Edinburgh, Bannatyne Club, 1846, pp.22–3.
17. *Mercurius Politicus*, Issue 13, 1650, p.201.
18. *Severall Letters from Scotland*, London, 1650, BL Thomason E612 (8).
19. *Diary of Sir Archibald Johnston of Wariston*, Vol. 2, p.19.
20. C. H. Firth, 'Monck, George,' *Dictionary of National Biography, 1885–1900*, Vol. 38; T. Gumble, *The life of General Monck, Duke of Albemarle*, London, Thomas Basset, 1671 (unnumbered pages); Mark Stoyle, 'The Honour of General Monck', *History Today*, August 1993.
21. H. Hexham, *A true and briefe relation of the famous seige of Breda etc.*, Delft, James Moxon, 1637, p.27.
22. *Severall Letters from Scotland*, London, 1650, BL Thomason E612 (8).
23. J. Hodgson, *Autobiography of Captain John Hodgson of Coley Hall*, Near Halifax, Brighouse, 1882, p.42.
24. *Severall Letters from Scotland*, London, 1650, BL Thomason E612 (8).
25. *Milton State Papers*, pp.16–17.
26. John Milton, *The Tenure of Kings & Magistrates*, New York, Henry Holt, 1911.
27. N. McDowell, 'Reading Milton reading Shakespeare politically: what the identification of Milton's First Folio does and does not tell us', *The Seventeenth Century*, Vol. 36, No. 4, 2021, pp.509–25, doi: 10.1080/0268117X.2021.1936144.
28. *Severall Letters from Scotland*, London, 1650, BL Thomason E612 (8).

## 5: The Dunbar Fight

1. Gardiner, *History of the Commonwealth and Protectorate 1649–1656*, Vol. I, pp.289–90.
2. A. Barnes, A., *Memoirs of the Life of Mr Ambrose Barnes*, Durham, Surtees Society, 1867, pp.110–11.
3. Letter from Emmanuel Downing to John Winthrop Junior, *Collections of the Massachusetts Historical Society*, Series 4, Vol. 6, p.78.
4. J. Aubrey, *Miscellanies*, London, Edward Castle, 1696, p.87.
5. C. H. Firth, 'The Battle of Dunbar', Transactions of the Royal Historical Society, new series, Vol. 14, 1900, Appendix, p.52. (For a full discussion of the battle and a review of sources, see pp.19–52, 304.)
6. Lady A. Halkett and J. G Nichols (ed.), *The Autobiography of Lady Anne Halkett*, London, Camden Society, 1875. Lady A. Halkett and S. Trill (ed.), *Selected Self-Writings*, London, Routledge, 2007.
7. 'A letter from Sir Arthur Hesilrige, to the honorable committee of the Councel of State for Irish and Scotish affairs at White-Hall, concerning the Scots prisoners. Die Veneris, 8 Novembr. 1650. Ordered by the Parliament, that this letter be forthwith printed and published. Hen: Scobell, Cleric. Parliamenti', in the digital collection Early English Books Online, name.umdl.umich.edu/A86092.0001.001, University of Michigan Library Digital Collections.
8. Ibid.

## 6: Capturing the Castle and Ending the War

1. W. S. Douglas, *Cromwell's Scotch Campaigns: 1650–51*, London, Elliot Stock, 1898, p.121 and footnote.
2. Summons and charge against Colonel Strachan and others, *The Records of the Parliaments of Scotland to 1707*, K. M. Brown et al. (eds), St Andrews, 2007–25 (March 1651, Perth), www.rps.ac.uk/.
3. J. Somerville, *Memorie of the Somervilles*, Vol. 2, Edinburgh, Constable, 1815, pp.442–53.
4. K. C. Corsar, 'The Surrender of Edinburgh Castle December 1650', *Scottish Historical Review*, Vol. 28, No. 105, April 1949, pp.43–54.
5. *Milton State Papers*, p.57.

6. *Mercurius Politicus*, No. 60, 24 July 1651, pp.953–4.
7. 'A great victory God hath vouchsafed by the Lord Generall Cromwels forces against the Scots. Certifyed by several letters from Scotland. Relating the entring of part of the English army into Fife. 2000 of the Scots slaine. With a list of the particulars of the great and glorious successe therein. And the taking of Callender house by storme. Together with a letter from the Lord Generall to the Right Honourable William Lenthal Speaker of Parliament. Imprimatur Hen. Scobel Cleric. Parliamenti', in the digital collection Early English Books Online 2, name.umdl.umich.edu/A85627.0001.001, University of Michigan Library Digital Collections.
8. Ibid.
9. Bulstrode Whitelocke, *Memorials of the English Affairs*, 1853 edition, Vol. 3, p.323. ED business: Wariston, *Diary*, p.xxxiii; p.98.
10. H. Cary (ed.), *Memorials of the Great Civil War in England from 1646 to 1652*, Vol. 2, London, Henry Colburn, 1842, p.357.
11. Ibid., pp.353–5.
12. Ibid., pp.362–4.

## 7: Rump to Barebone's

1. G. F. S. Ellens, 'The Ranters Ranting: Reflections on a Ranting Counter Culture', *Church History*, Vol. 40, No. 1, Mar 1971, pp.91–107, Cambridge University Press on behalf of the American Society of Church History.
2. 'Flagellum, or, The life and death, birth and burial of Oliver Cromwel faithfully described in an exact account of his policies and successes, not heretofore published or discovered / by S. T., Gent.', in the digital collection Early English Books Online, name.umdl.umich.edu/A43211.0001.001, University of Michigan Library Digital Collections, pp.133–4.
3. S. R. Gardiner, *History of the Commonwealth and Protectorate 1649–1656, Vol. II – 1651–1653*, new edn, London, Longmans, 1903, pp.253–64.
4. *The Annual Register*, Vol. 10, 1767, London, J. Dodsley, 1767, pp.212–13.
5. C. H. Firth, 'The Expulsion of the Long Parliament (continued)', *History*, new series, Vol. 2, No. 8, Jan 1918, pp.193–206.

6. F. Henderson (ed.), *The Clarke Papers: Further Selections from the Papers of William Clarke: Secretary to the Council of the Army 1647–1649, and to General Monck and the Commanders of the Army in Scotland, 1651–1660*, London, Cambridge University Press, 2005, p.114 and note 248.
7. Ibid., p.127. (The provenance of this letter is uncertain. It is datelined Axe Yard, Westminster, which is where Downing lived. But so did Gilbert Mabbot, William Clarke's brother-in-law. I think the tone and subject manner support an attribution to Downing.)

## 8: A Marriage and a Settlement

1. This section is based upon Halkett and Nichols (ed.), *Autobiography of Lady Anne Halkett*; and Halkett and Trill (ed.), *Selected Self-Writings.*
2. Beresford, *Godfather*, p.60.
3. J. R. Lowell, *Among My Books*, Boston, James R. Osgood, 1873, p.252.
4. W. H. Miller, 'The Colonization of the Bahamas 1647–1670', *William and Mary Quarterly*, Vol. 2, No. 1, Jan 1945, p.46.
5. Gardiner, *History of the Commonwealth and Protectorate, Vol. IV – 1655–1656*, London, Longmans, 1903, p.140; *Collections* 5, vol.1, p.373.
6. J. Y. Akerman (ed.), *Letters from Roundhead Officers*, Edinburgh, The Bannatyne Club, 1856, p.94.
7. J. Bampfield, *Colonel Joseph Bampfield's Apology, Written by Himself and Printed at His Desire 1685*, Lewisburg, PA, Bucknell University Press, 1993, p.127
8. C. H. Firth (ed.), *Scotland and the Protectorate*, Edinburgh, Scottish History Society 1899, p.155.
9. F. Dow, *Cromwellian Scotland 1651–1660*, Edinburgh, John Donald Publishers, 1979, p.53 and passim.

## 9: A Diplomat Abroad

1. W. C. Abbott (ed.), *The Writings and Speeches of Oliver Cromwell*, Vol. III, Cambridge, MA, Harvard University Press, 1945, p.732.
2. J. A. Wylie, *History of the Waldenses*, London, Cassell, 1880, p.144.
3. T. Birch (ed.), *A Collection of the State Papers of John Thurloe*, August 1655, Vol. 3, London, 1742, pp.724–38, BHO.

4. R. Vaughan (ed.), *The Protectorate of Oliver Cromwell*, Vol. I, London, Henry Colburn, 1839, p.265.
5. Ibid., p.297.
6. *Thurloe State Papers*, Vol. 3, An intercepted letter from Sir George Ratcliffe, 1655: August (3 of 4), pp.724–38, BHO.
7. Ibid., letter from Manning to Thurloe, 1655: March (1 of 8), pp.185–95, BHO; Clarendon, *History*, Vol. 7, pp.207–16.
8. *Nicholas Papers*, Vol. III, p.153. For Manning's full statements and interrogation, see pp.149–87.
9. *Thurloe State Papers*, Vol. 4, Letter of intelligence from The Hague dated 1 May 1656, 1656: April (5 of 7), pp.710–22, BHO.

## 10: Politician and Envoy

1. 'The Diary of Thomas Burton: 3 December 1656', in John Towill Rutt (ed.), *Diary of Thomas Burton Esq: Volume 1*, London, 1828, pp.1–11, BHO.
2. 'The Diary of Thomas Burton: 23 December 1656', ibid., pp.208–21, BHO.
3. 'The Diary of Thomas Burton: 26 December 1656', ibid., pp.244–58, BHO.
4. Beresford, *Godfather*, pp.84–5.
5. R. Vaughan (ed.), *The Protectorate of Oliver Cromwell*, Vol. 2, London, Henry Colburn, 1838, pp.444–5.
6. Ibid., letter from John Pell to George Downing, 30 March 1658, p.324.
7. T. Birch (ed.), *A Collection of the State Papers of John Thurloe*, Vol. 7, 1658: June (3 of 6), London, 1742, pp.180–89, BHO.
8. Keay, *The Last Royal Rebel*, pp.25–8. N. Greenspan, 'Charles II, Lucy Walter, and the Stuart Courts in Exile', *English Historical Review*, Vol. 131, No. 553, 2016, pp.1386–1414.
9. *Thurloe State Papers*, Vol. 7, pp.267–83.
10. J. Jonstonus, *The Idea of practical physick in twelve books in Latin . . .*, London, 1657, Article 1.
11. 'Cromwell's death and funeral order', in John Towill Rutt (ed.), *Diary of Thomas Burton Esq.*, Vol. 2, 1658, pp.516–30.
12. T. Barret, 'A Study in the Secret History of the Interregnum', *English Historical Review*, Vol. 43, p.49.
13. The restaurant later moved to another part of London, but its

original location in Charing Cross has its reference in *The Proceedings of the Old Bailey, 10 December 1690*. Cipher incident: F. J. Routledge (ed.), *Calendar of the Clarendon State Papers, Vol. IV, 1657–1660*, Oxford, Clarendon Press, 1932, p. 182.

14. B. Reay, 'The Quakers, 1659, and the Restoration of the Monarchy', *History*, Vol. 63, No. 208, Wiley, 1978, pp.193–213.
15. J. Addison, *A Collection of Interesting Anecdotes, Memoirs, Allegories, Essays and Poetical Fragments*, London, printed for the author, 1793, p.308.
16. J. P. Vander Motten, 'New light on Lucy Walter 1649–1659', *The Seventeenth Century*, Vol. 37, No. 3, 2021, pp.391–415.
17. *Thurloe State Papers*, Vol. 7, 1658: August (3 of 4), pp.339–52, BHO.
18. Thomas Carte (ed.), *A Collection of Original Letters & Papers Concerning the Affairs of England 1641–1660 Found Among the Duke of Ormonde's Papers*, Vol. II, London, Society for the Encouragement of Learning, 1739, pp.319–23.
19. Earl of Clarendon, *The Life of Edward Earl of Clarendon, in Which is Included A Continuation of His History of The Grand Rebellion*, Vol. II, new edn, Oxford, Clarendon Press, 1761, pp.424–6. See also Beresford, *Godfather*, p.120.
20. Ibid. (Clarendon, *Life*), p.292.

## 11: Rendition

1. M. Brod, 'Politics and Prophecy in Seventeenth-Century England: The Case of Elizabeth Poole, *Albion*, Vol. 31, No. 3, 199, pp.395–412.
2. L. Hutchinson, *Memoirs of the Life of Colonel Hutchinson . . .*, London, Longman, 1806, p.366.
3. V. L. Rouland, 'A Royalist Account of Hugh Peter's Arrest', *Huntingdon Library Quarterly*, Vol. 18, No. 2, University of Pennsylvania Press, 1955, pp.178–82. J. Max Patrick, 'The Arrest of Hugh Peters', *Huntingdon Library Quarterly*, Vol. 19, No. 4, University of Pennsylvania Press, 1956, pp.343–51.
4. Stearns, *Strenuous Puritan*, p.415, see note 59.
5. E. Bradley Peters, *Hugh Peter: Preacher, Patriot, Philanthropist*, New York, privately printed, 1902, p.53.
6. H. Peter, *A Dying Father's Last Legacy to An Onely Child*, London, Calvert, 1660.

7. Diary of Samuel Pepys, online edition, Tuesday 22 January 1660/1.
8. F. J. Routledge (ed.), *Calendar of the Clarendon State Papers, Vol. V, 1660–1726*, Oxford, Clarendon Press, 1970, p.107.
9. Beresford, *Godfather*, p.144.
10. T. H. Lister, *The Life and Administration of Edward First Earl of Clarendon*, Vol. 3, London, Longman, 1837, p.144.
11. R. C. H. Catterall, 'Sir George Downing and the Regicides', *American Historical Review*, Vol. 17, No. 2, 1912, p.273; for context and a full account of rendition, see pp.268, 289.
12. Ibid., p.279. F. J. Routledge (ed.), *Calendar of the Clarendon State Papers, Vol. V, 1660–1726*, Oxford, Clarendon Press, 1970, pp.181–193.
13. 'The speeches, discourses, and prayers, of Col. John Barkstead, Col. John Okey, and Mr. Miles Corbet', in the digital collection Early English Books Online, name.umdl.umich.edu/A30965.0001.001, University of Michigan Library Digital Collections.
14. Downing to the King, March 28/April 9 1662, Clarendon MSS, Bodleian Library, Vol. 106, F. 164, in Catterall, 'Sir George Downing and the Regicides', p.285.
15. Ibid., p.285.
16. M. Jenkinson, *Charles I's Killers in America*, Oxford, Oxford University Press, 2019.

## 12: Rise and Fall

1. K. Wright, 'Tally Sticks and Townhouses', Virtual St Stephen's, St Stephen's Chapel Westminster/York University, www.virtualststephens.org.uk.
2. A. A. Sherman, 'Pressure from Leadenhall: The East India Company Lobby, 1660–78', *Business History Review*, Autumn 1976, Vol. 50, No. 3, 1976, p.339.
3. Earl of Clarendon, *The Life of Edward Earl of Clarendon, in Which is Included A Continuation of His History of The Grand Rebellion*, Vol. II, new edn, Oxford, Clarendon Press, 1827, p.289.
4. Beresford, *Godfather*, p.210.
5. Earl of Clarendon, *The Life of Edward Earl of Clarendon, in Which is Included A Continuation of His History of The Grand Rebellion*, Vol. III, Oxford, Clarendon Press, 1759, p.601.

6. Beresford, *Godfather*, p.211.
7. Diary of Samuel Pepys, online edition, Wednesday 27 March 1667.
8. See R. Shorto, *The Island at the Center of the World: The Epic Story of Dutch Manhattan and the Forgotten Colony That Shaped America*, New York, Doubleday, 2004. L. H. Roper, 'The Fall of New Netherland and Seventeenth-Century Anglo-American Imperial Formation, 1654–1676', *New England Quarterly*, Vol. 87, No. 4, Dec 2014. And H. L. Schoolcraft, 'The Capture of New Amsterdam', *English Historical Review*, Vol. 22, No. 88, Oct 1907, pp.674–93.
9. Clarendon, *Life*, Vol. II, 1761, p.426.
10. Diary of Samuel Pepys, online edition, 8 October 1665.
11. G. A. Rommelse, 'The Second Anglo-Dutch War (1665–1667)', Doctoral thesis, University of Leiden, Verloren, Hilversum, 2006, p.121; for a general account of the run-up to and course of the war, see pp.93–121.
12. H. T. Colenbrander, *Bescheiden uit Vreemde Archieven Omtrent Grootee Nederlandsche Zeeorlogen 1652–76*, 1919, pp.195–9.
13. Ibid., p.195.
14. J. Scott, '"Good Night Amsterdam". Sir George Downing and Anglo-Dutch Statebuilding', *English Historical Review*, Vol. 118, No. 476, Apr 2003, pp.334–56.
15. Beresford, *Godfather*, pp.247–8.
16. J. P. Ferris, 'Downing, Sir George (1623–84) of St Stephen's Court, Westminster and East Hatley, Cambs', in B. D. Henning (ed.), *The History of Parliament: The House of Commons 1660–90*, Boydell and Brewer, 1983, The History of Parliament online.
17. *Collections of the Massachusetts Historical Society*, Series V, Vol. 1, pp.45–7.
18. Ibid., pp.51–2.

## 13: *Si monumentum requiris . . . circumspice*

1. M. H. Cox and G. T. Forrest (eds), 'Downing Street (Hampden House)', *Survey of London*, Vol. 14, pp.105–12, BHO.
2. 'From John Adams to William Tudor, Sr., 14 July 1818', Founders Online, National Archives, founders.archives.gov/documents/Adams/99-02-02-6930.

# Bibliography


Abbott, W. C. (ed.), *The Writings and Speeches of Oliver Cromwell: Volume I, 1599–1649*, Cambridge, MA, Harvard University Press, 1937.

Abbott, W. C. (ed.), *The Writings and Speeches of Oliver Cromwell: Volume III*, Cambridge, MA, Harvard University Press, 1945.

Adair, Rev. P., *A True Narrative of the Rise and Progress of the Presbyterian Church in Ireland*, Belfast, C. Aitchison, 1866.

Addison, J., *A Collection of Interesting Anecdotes, Memoirs, Allegories, Essays and Poetical Fragments*, London, printed for the author, 1793.

Akerman, J. Y., (ed.), *Letters from Roundhead Officers*, Edinburgh, The Bannatyne Club, 1856.

Akkerman, N., *Invisible Agents: Women and Espionage in Seventeenth-Century Britain*, Oxford, Oxford University Press, 2018.

Akkerman, N. and P. Langman, *Spycraft: Tricks and Tools of the Dangerous Trade from Elizabeth I to the Restoration*, New Haven, CT, Yale University Press, 2024.

Armstrong, A., *George Fenwick of Brinkburn 1603–1656: Governor of Saybrook, Connecticut, Berwick upon Tweed and Edinburgh Castle*, Great Britain, privately published by Dr Angus Armstrong, 2009.

Aylmer, G. E., *The King's Servants: The Civil Service of Charles I 1625–1642*, London, Routledge & Kegan Paul, 1961.

Aylmer, G. E., *The State's Servants: The Civil Service of the English Republic 1649–1660*, London and Boston, Routledge & Kegan Paul, 1973.

Baillie, R., *The Letters and Journals of Robert Baillie, A.M.*, Vol. 3, The Bannatyne Club, Edinburgh, 1842.

Bampfield, J., *Colonel Joseph Bampfield's Apology, Written by Himself and*

*Printed at His Desire 1685*, Lewisburg, PA, Bucknell University Press, 1993.

Barnard T., D. O. Croinin and K. Simms (eds), *A Miracle of Learning: Studies in Manuscripts and Irish Learning: Essays in Honour of William O'Sullivan*, London, Routledge, 1998.

Barnes, A., *Memoirs of the Life of Mr Ambrose Barnes*, Durham, Surtees Society, 1867.

Bennett, M., *Historical Dictionary of the British and Irish Civil Wars 1637–1660*, New York, Routledge, 2013.

Beresford, J., *The Godfather of Downing Street: Sir George Downing 1623–1684: An Essay in Biography*, London, Richard Cobden-Sanderson, 1925.

Berkley, Sir J., 'Memoirs of Sir John Berkley' in F. Maseres (ed.), *Select Tracts Relating to The Civil Wars in England in the Reign of King Charles the First*, Part II, London, printed by R. Wilks, 1815.

Blair, R. and W. Row, T. M'Crie (ed.), *The Life of Mr Robert Blair*, Edinburgh, printed for the Wodrow Society, 1848.

Bookbinder A. et al., *The Downing Family and Legacies of Enslavement*, Cambridge, Downing College, 2022.

Bremer, F., *John Winthrop, America's Forgotten Founding Father*, New York, Oxford University Press, 2003.

Brown, D., *Empire and Enterprise: Money, power and the Adventurers for Irish land during the British Civil Wars*, Manchester, Manchester University Press, 2020.

Buchan, J., *Oliver Cromwell*, London, Hodder and Stoughton, 1934.

Burnet, G., *Bishop Burnet's History of His Own Time: From the Restoration of King Charles the Second to the Treaty of Peace at Utrecht, in the Reign of Queen Anne*, London, Henry G. Bohn, 1857.

Burns, J., *Memoirs by James Burns, Bailie of the City of Glasgow 1644–1661*, Edinburgh, Thomas Stevenson, 1832.

Carlin, N., *Regicide or Revolution? What Petitioners Wanted, September 1648–February 1649*, London, Breviary Stuff Publications, 2020.

Carlyle, T., *Oliver Cromwell's Letters and Speeches*, New York, Putnam, 1845.

Carte, T. (ed.), *A Collection of Original Letters & Papers Concerning the Affairs of England 1641–1660, Found Among the Duke of Ormonde's Papers*, Vol. II, London, 1739.

Cary, H. (ed.), *Memorials of the Great Civil War in England from 1646 to 1652*, Vol. 2, London, Henry Colburn, 1842.

Causton, H. K. S., *The Howard Papers: With a biographical pedigree and criticism*, London, Causton and Son, 1862.

Chaplin, J., *The Life of Henry Dunster, First President of Harvard College*, Boston, Osgood, 1872.

Clarendon, Earl of, *The Life of Edward Earl of Clarendon, in Which is Included A Continuation of His History of The Grand Rebellion*, Vol. I, new edn, Oxford, Clarendon Press, 1827.

Clarendon, Earl of, *The Life of Edward Earl of Clarendon, in Which is Included A Continuation of His History of The Grand Rebellion*, Vol. II, new edn, Oxford, Clarendon Press, 1827.

Clarendon, Earl of, *History of the Great Rebellion* (seven volumes), Oxford, Oxford University Press, 1839.

Clark, A., *Aubrey's 'Brief Lives'*, Oxford, Clarendon Press, 1898.

Coleman, D. C. and P. Mathis (eds), *Enterprise and History: Essays in Honour of Charles Wilson*, Cambridge, Cambridge University Press, 1984.

*Collections of the Massachusetts Historical Society*, Vols I–VII, Boston, 1806–65.

*Collections of the Massachusetts Historical Society*, Vol. VII, Boston, 1865.

*Collections of the Massachusetts Historical Society*, Vol. I, 5th series, Boston, MHS, 1871.

Como, D. R., *Radical Parliamentarians and the English Civil War*, Oxford Academic, 2018, doi.org/10.1093/oso/9780199541911.001.0001 (accessed 18 August 2024).

Cressy, D., *Coming over: Migration and communication between England and New England in the seventeenth century*, New York, Cambridge University Press, 1987.

*Cromwelliana: A Chronological Detail of Events in Which Oliver Cromwell was Engaged From the Year 1642 to his Death 1658*, London, Machell Stace, 1810.

De Lisle, L., *White King: Traitor, Murderer, Martyr*, London, Chatto & Windus, 2018.

Denton, B., *Only in Heaven: The Life and Campaigns of Sir Arthur Hesilrige, 1601–1661*, Sheffield, Sheffield Academic Press, 1997.

Douglas, W. S., *Cromwell's Scotch Campaigns: 1650–51*, London, Elliot Stock, 1898.

Dow, F., *Cromwellian Scotland 1651–1660*, Edinburgh, John Donald Publishers, 1979.

Downing, R. and G. Rommelse, *A fearful gentleman: Sir George Downing in The Hague, 1658–1672*, The Hague, Hilversum Verloren, 2011.
Downing, W. C. and R. Wilberforce, *Genealogy of the Downing Family*, Philadelphia, privately published, 1901.
Dunn, R. S., *Puritans & Yankees: The Winthrop Dynasty of New England 1630–1717*, Princeton, NJ, Princeton University Press, 1962.
Durston, C., *Cromwell's major generals, Godly government during the English Revolution*, Manchester, Manchester University Press, 2001.
Ellis, J., *To Walk in the Dark*, Cheltenham, The History Press, 2011.
Evelyn, J., *Diary and Correspondence, Vol. III*, London, Henry G. Bohn, 1859.
Felt, J., *Annals of Salem from Its First Settlement*, Salem, Ives, 1827.
Felt, J., *Annals of Salem Second Edition, Volume II*, Salem, Munroe, 1849.
Firth, C. H. (ed.), *Scotland and the Commonwealth, 1651–53*, Edinburgh, Edinburgh University Press, 1895.
Firth, C. H. (ed.), *Scotland and the Protectorate*, Edinburgh, Scottish History Society, 1899, p.155.
Firth, C. H., *Oliver Cromwell and the Rule of the Puritans in England*, New York, Putnam's, 1900.
Firth, C. H., *Cromwell's Army*, London, Methuen & Co., 1902.
Firth, C. H., *The Last Years of The Protectorate, 1656–1658*, Vol. I, 1656–1657, London, Longmans, Green and Co., 1909.
Firth, C. H., *The Last Years of The Protectorate, 1656–1658*, Vol. II, 1657–1658, London, Longmans, Green and Co., 1909.
Firth, C. H. and G. Davies, *The Regimental History of Cromwell's Army*, Vol. I, Oxford, Clarendon Press, 1940.
Fleming, D. H. (ed.), *Diary of Sir Archibald Johnston of Wariston, Vol. II, 1650–1654*, Edinburgh, Edinburgh University Press, 1919.
Forbes, A. B. (ed.), *Publications of the Colonial Society of Massachusetts*, Vol. XXXII, Transactions 1933–1937, Boston, published by the Society, 1937.
Forster, J., *Lives of Eminent British Statesmen: Henry Vane, Volume IV*, London, Longman's, 1838.
Fraser, A., *Cromwell Our Chief of Men*, London, Weidenfeld & Nicolson, 1973.
Gardener, L., *Relation of the Pequot Warres*, New Haven, CT, Hartford Press, 1901.

Gardiner, S. R. (ed.), *Charles II and Scotland in 1650*, Edinburgh, Edinburgh University Press, 1894.

Gardiner, S. R., *History of the Commonwealth and Protectorate 1649–1656*, Vol. I. – 1649–1650, new edn, London, Longmans, Green and Co., 1903.

Gardiner, S. R., *History of the Commonwealth and Protectorate 1649–1656*, Vol. II. – 1651–1653, new edn, London, Longmans, Green and Co., 1903.

Gardiner, S. R., *History of the Commonwealth and Protectorate 1649–1656*, Vol. III. – 1653–1655, new edn, London, Longmans, Green and Co., 1903.

Gardiner, S. R., *History of the Commonwealth and Protectorate 1649–1656*, Vol. IV. – 1655–1656, new edn, London, Longmans, Green and Co., 1903.

Gaunt, P., *The Cromwellian Gazetteer: An Illustrated Guide to Britain in the Civil War and Commonwealth*, Gloucester, Alan Sutton & the Cromwell Association, 1987.

Gentles, I. J., *The New Model Army*, Oxford, Blackwell Publishers, 1992.

Gentles, I. J., *The English Revolution and the Wars in Three Kingdoms 1638–1652*, London, Routledge, 2017.

Godwin, B. D., *The Civil War in Hampshire (1642–45) and the Story of Basing House*, London, Bumpus Ltd, 1904.

Grainger, J. D., *Cromwell Against the Scots*, Barnsley, Pen and Sword Military, 2021.

Guthry, H., *Memoirs of Henry Guthry Late Bishop of Dunkel in Scotland*, London, J. Nutt, 1702.

Halkett, Lady A. and J. G. Nichols (ed.), *The Autobiography of Lady Anne Halkett*, London, Camden Society, 1875.

Halkett, Lady A. and S. Trill (ed.), *Selected Self-Writings*, London, Routledge, 2007.

Hall, D., *The Puritans: A Transatlantic History*, Princeton, NH, Princeton University Press, 2019.

Hamilton, M., *Social and Economic Networks in Early Massachusetts: Atlantic Connections*, University Park, PA, The Pennsylvania State University Press, 2009.

Hassam, J. T., *The Bahama Islands: Notes on an Early Attempt at Colonization*, Cambridge, John Wilson and Son, 1899.

Healey, J., *The Blazing World: A New History of Revolutionary England*, London, Bloomsbury, 2023.

Henderson, F. (ed.), *The Clarke Papers: Further Selections from the Papers of William Clarke: Secretary to the Council of the Army 1647–1649, and to General Monck and the Commanders of the Army in Scotland, 1651–1660*, London, Cambridge University Press, 2005.

Hill, C., *God's Englishman: Oliver Cromwell and the English Revolution*, London, Penguin Books, 1970.

Hill, G. (ed.), *The Montgomery Manuscripts: (1603–1706)*, Belfast, James Cleeland et al., 1869.

Hill, P. R. and J. M. Watkinson, *Major Sanderson's War: The Diary of a Parliamentary Cavalry Officer in the English Civil War*, Cheltenham, Spellmount, 2008.

Hill, P. R. and J. M. Watkinson, *Cromwell Hath the Honour, But . . . Major-General Lambert's Campaigns in the North 1648*, Barnsley, Frontline Books, 2012.

Holles, D., *Memoirs of Denzil Lord Holles, Baron of Ifield in Sussex, From the Year 1641 to 1648*, London, printed for Tim Goodwin, 1699.

Hopper, A., *Turncoats and Renegadoes: Changing Sides during the English Civil Wars*, Oxford, Oxford University Press, 2012.

Hudleston, C. R. (ed.), *Naworth Estate and Household Accounts 1648–1660*, Durham, Andrews & Co., Bernard Quaritch, 1958.

Hutchinson T., *A History of Massachusetts From the First Settlement Thereof*, Salem, Thomas and Andrews, 1795.

Hutton, R., *The Making of Oliver Cromwell*, London, Yale University Press, 2021.

Hyde, E., *The Life of Edward Earl of Clarendon, Lord High Chancellor of England, and Chancellor of the University of Oxford*, Oxford, Original manuscripts, 1759.

Jaffray, A., *Diary of Alexander Jaffray*, 2nd edn, London, Darton & Harvey, 1833.

Japikse, N., *Der Verwikkelingen Tusschen de Republiek En Engeland van 1660–1665*, Leiden, S. C. Van Doesburgh, 1900.

Jefferson, S., *The History and Antiquities of Carlisle, with an account of the Castles, Gentlemen's Seats and Antiquities, in the vicinity; and biographical memoirs of eminent men connected with the locality*, London, Whittaker and Co., 1838.

Jenkinson, M., *Charles I's Killers in America: The Lives & Afterlives of*

*Edward Whalley & William Goffe*, Oxford, Oxford University Press, 2019.

Jordan, D. and M. Walsh, *The King's Revenge: Charles II and the Greatest Manhunt in British History*, London, Abacus, 2012.

Jordan, D. and M. Walsh, *The King's Bed: Ambition and intimacy in the Court of Charles II*, London, Pegasus, 2017.

Keay, A., *The Last Royal Rebel: The Life and Death of James, Duke of Monmouth*, London, Bloomsbury, 2016.

Keay, A., *The Restless Republic: Britain Without a Crown*, London, Harper Collins, 2022.

Kerr, R. and W. Kerr, *Ancram-Lothian Correspondence – In two volumes: Vol. I. – 1616–1649*, Edinburgh, 1875.

Killen, W. D. (ed.), *A True Narrative of the Rise and Progress of the Presbyterian Church in Ireland*, Belfast, C. Aitchison, 1866.

Lamont, J., *The Diary of Mr John Lamont of Newton, 1649–1671*, Edinburgh, 1830.

Lay, P., *Providence Lost: The Rise & Fall of Cromwell's Protectorate*, London, Apollo, Head of Zeus, 2020.

Lee, M. (ed.), 'Autobiography, 1626–1670, of John Hay, 2nd earl of Tweeddale' in *Miscellany*, Vol. 12, Edinburgh, Scottish History Society, 1994.

Lincoln, M., *London and the 17th Century: The Making of the World's Greatest City*, New Haven, CT, Yale University Press, 2021.

Lipscombe, N., *The English Civil War: An Atlas and Concise History of the Wars of the Three Kingdoms 1639–51*, Oxford, Osprey Publishing, 2020.

Lister, T. H., *Life and Administration of Edward, First Earl of Clarendon*, Vol. II, London, Longman et al., 1837.

Lister, T. H., *Life and Administration of Edward, First Earl of Clarendon*, Vol. III, London, Longman, 1837.

Little, P., *Lord Broghill and the Cromwellian Union with Ireland and Scotland*, Woodbridge, The Boydell Press, 2004.

Locke, J., *The Second Treatise of Government and a Letter Concerning Toleration*, London, Dover Editions, 2002.

Lowell, J. R., *Among My Books*, Boston, James R. Osgood, 1873.

Ludlow, E. and Firth, C. H. (ed.), *The Memoirs of Edmund Ludlow, 1625–1672, Volumes I and II*, Oxford, Clarendon Press, 1894.

Malcolm, N. and J. Stedall, *John Pell (1611–1685) and his correspondence with Sir Charles Cavendish: The mental world of an early modern mathematician*, Oxford, Oxford University Press, 2005.

Manegold, C. S., *Ten Hills Farm: The Forgotten History of Slavery in the North*, Princeton, NJ, Princeton University Press, 2010.

Marshall, A., *Cambridge Studies in Early Modern British History: Intelligence and Espionage in the Reign of Charles II, 1660–1685*, Cambridge, Cambridge University Press, 1994.

Marshall, A., *Intelligence and Espionage in the English Republic*, Manchester, Manchester University Press, 2023.

Marshall, A., *Oliver Cromwell Soldier: The Military Life of a Revolutionary at War*, London, Brassey's, 2004.

Maunde Thompson, E. (ed.), *Correspondence of the Family of Hatton being chiefly letters addressed to Christopher First Viscount Hatton: A.D. 1601–1704*, London, Camden Society, 1878.

Miller, J., *The Lamp of Lothian, Or the History of Haddington*, Haddington, James Allan, 1844.

Milton, J., *Letters of state written by Mr John Milton, to most of the sovereign princes and republicks of Europe*, Early English Books Online, University of Michigan Library Digital Collections, name.umdl.umich.edu/A50909.0001.001 (accessed 19 August 2024).

Montgomery Martin, R., *The British Colonial Library: Comprising A Popular and Authentic Description of All the Colonies of the British Empire*, Vol. 5, London, Henry G. Bohn, 1845.

Montgomery, W., Esq., *The Montgomery Manuscripts*, Belfast, Belfast News-Letter, 1830.

Moore, S. H., *Pilgrims: New World Settlers & the Call of Home*, New Haven, CT, Yale University Press, 2007.

Morison, S. E., *Builders of the Bay Colony*, Boston, Northeastern University Press, 1930.

Morison, S. E., *The Founding of Harvard College*, Cambridge, MA, Harvard University Press, 1935.

Morley, J., *Oliver Cromwell*, London, Macmillan, 1908.

Morrill, J. (ed.)., *The Letters, Writings, and Speeches of Oliver Cromwell: Volume 1: 14 October 1626 to 29 January 1649*, Oxford, Oxford University Press, 2022.

Morrill, J. (ed.)., *The Letters, Writings, and Speeches of Oliver Cromwell: Volume 2: 1 February 1649 to 12 December 1653*, Oxford, Oxford University Press, 2022.

Morrill, J. (ed.)., *The Letters, Writings, and Speeches of Oliver Cromwell: Volume 3: 16 December 1653 to 2 September 1658*, Oxford, Oxford University Press, 2022.

Morrill, J. S., 'The Army Revolt of 1647' in A. C. Duke et al. (eds), *Britain and the Netherlands*, Martinus Nijhoff, The Hague, 1977.

Nickolls, J. (ed.), *Milton State Papers: Original Letters and Papers of State Addressed to Oliver Cromwell*, London, William Bowyer, 1743.

Noble, M., *The Lives of the English Regicides*, Ann Arbor, MI, University of Michigan Press, 2009.

Paul, Sir J. B. (ed.), *The Scots Peerage*, Edinburgh, David Douglas, 1910.

Paul, Sir J. B. (ed.), 'The Diary of Sir James Hope, 1646–1654' in *Miscellany*, Vol. 3, Edinburgh, Scottish History Society, 1919.

Parker, M., *John Winthrop: Founding the City upon a Hill*, New York, Routledge Taylor and Francis Group, 2014.

Parrit, B. A. H., *The Intelligencers: British Military Intelligence from the Middle Ages to 1929*, Yorkshire, Pen & Sword Military, 2011.

Peacey, J., '"My Friend the Gazetier": Diplomacy and News in Seventeenth-Century Europe' in J. Raymond and N. Moxham (eds), *News Networks in Early Modern Europe*, Brill, 2016.

Pearl, V., *London and the Outbreak of the Puritan Revolution*, London, Oxford University Press, 1961.

Peter, H. and T. Weld (attrib.), *New England's First Fruits*, New York, Sabin, 1865.

Pierce, B., *A History of Harvard University*, Cambridge, MA, Brown Shattuck and Co., 1833.

Rawley, J. A. and S. D. Behrendt, *The Transatlantic Slave Trade: A History*, Lincoln, NE, University of Nebraska Press, 2005.

Reece, H., *The Army in Cromwellian England, 1649–1660*, Oxford, Oxford University Press, 2013.

Reece, H., *The Fall: Last Days of the English Republic*, London, Yale University Press, 2024.

Rees, J., *The Leveller Revolution*, London, Verso, 2016.

Reese, P., *Cromwell's Masterstroke, The Battle of Dunbar 1650*, Yorkshire, Pen & Sword Military, 2006.

Riordan, T. B., *The Plundering Time: Maryland and the English Civil War 1645–1646*, Baltimore, Maryland Historical Society, 2004.

Roberts, K., *Cromwell's War Machine: The New Model Army 1645–1660*, London, Leo Cooper, 2006.

Rommelse, G. A., *The second Anglo-Dutch war (1665–1667): international raison d'etat, mercantilism and maritime strife*, Hilversum, Verloren, 2006.

Roseveare, H., *The Treasury 1660–1870*, London, Routledge, 1973.

Routledge, F. J. (ed.), *Calendar of the Clarendon State Papers, Vol. IV, 1657–1660*, Oxford, Clarendon Press, 1932.

Routledge, F. J. (ed.), *Calendar of the Clarendon State Papers, Vol. V, 1660–1726*, Oxford, Clarendon Press, 1970.

Rowen, H. H., *John De Witt, Grand Pensionary of Holland, 1625–1672*, Princeton, Princeton Legacy Library, 1978.

Rushworth, J., *Historical Collections, The Fourth and Last Part Containing the Principal Matters Which Happened From the Beginning of the year 1645, to the Death of King Charles the First 1648*, Vol. VII, London, Walker and Co., 1721.

Sadler J. and R. Serdiville, *Cromwell's Convicts*, Barnsley, Pen and Sword Military, 2021.

Saunders Webb, S., *The Governors-General: The English Army and the Definition of the Empire, 1569–1681*, Chapel Hill, NC, University of North Carolina Press, 1979.

Savage, J. (ed.) and John Winthrop, *The History of New England 1630–1649*, Vol. I, Boston, printed by Phelps & Farnham, 1825.

Savage, J. (ed.) and John Winthrop, *The History of New England 1630–1649*, Vol. II, Boston, Little, Brown, 1853.

Scott, E., *The King in Exile: The Wanderings of Charles II from June 1646 to July 1654*, London, Constable, 1905.

Shorto, R., *The Island at the Center of the World: The Epic Story of Dutch Manhattan and the Forgotten Colony That Shaped America*, New York, Doubleday, 2004.

Sibley, J. L., *Biographical Sketches of Graduates of Harvard University*, Vol. I, Cambridge, MA, Charles William Sever, 1873.

Simmons, F. J., *Emanuel Downing*, New Jersey (privately published), 1958.

Smith, G., *The Cavaliers in Exile 1640–1660*, London, Palgrave Macmillan, 2003.

Smith, G., *Royalist Agents, Conspirators and Spies: Their Role in the British Civil Wars, 1640–1660*, Farnham, Ashgate Books, 2011.

Somerville, Lord J., *Memorie of The Somervilles*, Vol. II, Edinburgh, James Ballantyne and Co., 1815.

Southcombe, G. and G. Tapsell, *Revolutionary England, c.1630–c.1660: Essays for Clive Holmes*, London, Routledge, 2022.

Spencer, C., *Killers of the King: The Men Who Dared to Execute Charles I*, London, Bloomsbury Publishing, 2014.

Stearns, R., *The Strenuous Puritan, Hugh Peter 1598–1660*, Champaign, IL, University of Illinois, 1954.

Stevenson R., *Revolution and Counter-Revolution in Scotland, 1644–51*, Edinburgh, Edinburgh University Press, 2003.

Strickland, A., *Lives of the Last Four Princesses of the Royal House of Stuart*, London, Bell and Daldy, 1872.

Swingen, A., *Competing Visions of Empire, Labor, Slavery and the Origins of the British Atlantic Empire*, New Haven, CT, Yale University Press, 2015.

Terry, C. S., *The Cromwellian Union: Papers relating to the negotiations for an incorporating union between England and Scotland*, Edinburgh, Scottish History Society, 1902.

Tibbutt, H. G., *Colonel John Okey 1606–1662*, Publications of the Bedfordshire Historical Record Society, Vol. 35, Streatley, 1955.

Tinniswood, A., *The Rainborowes: Pirates, Puritans and a Family's Quest for the Promised Land*, London, Vintage Books, 2013.

Tomalin, C., *Samuel Pepys: The Unequalled Self*, London, Penguin Books, 2003.

Truxes, T. M., *The Overseas Trade of British America: A Narrative History*, New Haven, CT, Yale University Press, 2021.

Truxes, T. M., *The Overseas Trade of British America: A Narrative History*, Yale Scholarship Online, 2022, doi.org/10.12987/yale/9780300159882.001.0001 (accessed 15 August 2024).

Tweedie, Rev. W. K. (ed.), *Select Biographies*, Volume First, Edinburgh, printed for the Wodrow Society, 1845.

Underdown, D., *Pride's Purge: Politics in the Puritan Revolution*, Oxford, Oxford University Press, 1971.

Upham, C. W., *Salem Witchcraft, Vol. I*, Boston, Wiggin and Lunt, 1867.

Vaughan, R. (ed.), *The Protectorate of Oliver Cromwell, and the State of Europe During the Early Part of the Reign of Louis XIV: Illustrated in a series of Letters between Dr John Pell, Sir Samuel Morland, Sir William Lockhart, Mr Secretary Thurloe and Other Distinguished Men of the Time*, London, Henry Colburn, 1839.

Warner, G. F. (ed.), *The Nicholas Papers: Correspondence of Sir Edward Nicholas*, Vol. I, 1641–1652, printed for the Camden Society, 1886.

Warner, G. F. (ed.), *The Nicholas Papers: Correspondence of Sir Edward Nicholas*, Vol. IV, 1657–1660, London, Offices of the Society, 1920.

Waters, T. F., *A Sketch of The life of John Winthrop the Younger, Founder of Ipswich, Massachusetts in 1633*, Ipswich Historical Society, 1899.

Whitelock, B., *Memorials of the English Affairs from the Beginning of the Reign of Charles the First to the Happy Restoration of King Charles the Second*, Oxford, Oxford University Press, 1853.

Winthrop, J., J. K. Hosmer (ed.), *Winthrop's Journal: History of New England, 1630–1649*, New York, Scribner's, 1908.

Winthrop, J., *Winthrop Papers*, Massachusetts Historical Society (in various volumes and editions), culminating in Vol. V, 1947.

Winthrop, J. and J. Savage, *The History of New England from 1630 to 1649*, Boston, Little, Brown and Company, 1858.

Winthrop, R. C. (ed.), *Life and Letters of John Winthrop*, Vol. I, Boston, Ticknor & Fields, 1864.

Wodrow, Rev. R., *Analecta*, Vol. II, printed for the Maitland Club, 1842.

Woolrych, A., *Soldiers and Statesmen: The General Council of the Army and its Debates, 1647–1648*, Oxford, Clarendon Press, 1987.

Worden, B., *The Rump Parliament 1648–1653*, Cambridge, Cambridge University Press, 1974.

Worden, B., *Roundhead Reputations: The English Civil Wars and the Passions of Posterity*, London, Penguin Books, 2001.

Worden, B., *God's Instruments: Political Conduct in the England of Oliver Cromwell*, Oxford, Oxford University Press, 2012.

## British Library, Thomason Tracts

'*A great victory God hath vouchsafed by the Lord Generall Cromwels forces against the Scots* . . .', London, printed for Robert Ibbitson, 1651. BL Thomason, Vol. 1, E 638 (2).

'*A Large Relation of the Fight at Leith neere Edenburgh, wherein Major Generall Montgomery, Colonell Straughan, with many more of the Scottish Party, were slaine and wounded* . . .', London, printed by Ed. Griffin, 1650. BL Thomason, Vol. 1, E 609 (1).

'*A true Relation of the Proceedings of the English Army now in Scotland, from 22 July to 1 Aug* . . .', London, printed by Edward Husband and John Field, 1650. BL Thomason, Vol. 1, E 608 (23).

Downing, G., '*A True Relation of the progress of the Parlaments Forces in Scotland . . .*', London, printed by William Du-Gard, 1651. BL Thomason, Vol. 1, E 640 (5).

Downing, G., '*A discourse written by Sir George Downing, the King of Great Britain's envoy extraordinary to the states of the United Provinces vindicating his royal master from the insolencies of a scandalous libel . . .*', Early English Books Online, University of Michigan Library Digital Collections, name.umdl.umich.edu/A36497.0001.001 (accessed 30 August 2024).

Pool, E., '*A Vision wherein is manifested the disease and cure of the Kingdome. Delivered to the Generall Councel of the Army, 29 Dec. Together, with a true copie of what was delivered in writing, 5 Jan., to the Generall Councel, of Divine pleasure concerning the King . . .*', London, 1648. BL Thomason, E 537 (24).

'*More Letters from Scotland of the proceedings of the Army . . .*', London, printed by F. Neile, 1651. BL Thomason, E 638 (3).

'*Musgrave muzl'd: or, the mouth of iniquity stoped. Being a vindication of Sir Arthur Hazelrige from a false accusation of John Musgrave in his late pamphlet intituled "A true and exact relation, etc."*', London, printed by John Macock for L. Lloyd and H. Cripps, 1651. BL Thomason, E 625 (11).

'*Severall Letters from Scotland relating to the Proceedings of the Army there . . .*', London, printed by Robert Ibbitson, 1650. BL Thomason, E 612 (8).

'*A narrative of the late Parliament . . .*' London, printed by a Friend to the Common-Wealth, 1658. BL Thomason, Vol. 2, E 935 (5).

Edwards, T., '*The third part of Gangraena. Or, a new and higher discovery of the errors, heresies, blasphemies, and insolent proceedings of the sectaries of these times; with some animadversions by the way of confutation upon many of the errors and heresies named . . . By Thomas Edwards Minister of the Gospel*', 1646, Early English Books Online, University of Michigan Library Digital Collections, name.umdl.umich.edu/A83515.0001.001 (accessed 19 August 2024). BL Thomason, Vol. 1, E 368 (5).

## Early English Books Online

'*A Perfect Diurnall of some Passages of Parliament And Intelligence from the Armies in England, Scotland and Irelands, And more particularly from the Army under the immediate conduct of his Excellency the Lord General Cromwell*', London, printed by W. Hunt.

'*A solemn engagement of the army under the command of His Excellency Sir Thomas Fairfax with a declaration of their resolutions, as to disbanding, and a briefe vindication of their principles and intentions . . . presented to the generall, and by him to be humbly presented to the Parliament with His Excellencies letter to the speaker, June the 8, sent with the same . . .*', Early English Books Online, University of Michigan Library Digital Collections, name.umdl.umich.edu/A60729.0001.001 (accessed 19 August 2024).

'*The complaint of the boutefeu, scorched in his owne kindlings. Or The backslider filled with his owne wayes*', Early English Books Online 2, University of Michigan Library Digital Collections, name.umdl.umich.edu/A80277.0001.001 (accessed 30 August 2024).

'*A declaration, or representation from His Excellency, Sir Thomas Fairfax, and the Army under his command humbly tendred to the Parliament, concerning the just and fundamentall rights and liberties of themselves and the kingdome. With some humble proposals and desires. By the appointment of his Excellency Sir Thomas Fairfax, with the officers and souldiers of his Army. Signed John Rushworth, secretary*', Early English Books Online, University of Michigan Library Digital Collections, name.umdl.umich.edu/A39976.0001.001 (accessed 30 August 2024).

'*A letter from Colonel Barkstead, Colonel Okey, and Miles Corbet, to their friends in the congregated churches in London with the manner of their apprehension*', Early English Books Online, University of Michigan Library Digital Collections, name.umdl.umich.edu/A30963.0001.001 (accessed 19 August 2024).

'*The speeches, discourses, and prayers, of Col. John Barkstead, Col. John Okey, and Mr Miles Corbet, upon the 19th of April being the day of their suffering at Tyburn: together with an account of the occasion and manner of their taking in Holland: as also of their several occasional speeches, discourses, and letters, both before, and in the time of their late imprisonment: faithfully and impartially collected for a general satisfaction*', Early English Books Online, University of Michigan Library Digital Collections, name.umdl.umich.edu/A30965.0001.001 (accessed 30 August 2024).

'*A letter from Sir Arthur Hesilrige, to the honorable committee of the Councel of State for Irish and Scotish affairs at White-Hall, concerning the Scots prisoners. Die Veneris, 9 Novembr. 1650. Ordered by the Parliament, that this letter be forthwith printed and published. Hen: Scobell, Cleric. Parliamenti*', Early English Books Online, University of Michigan Library Digital Collections, name.umdl.umich.edu/A86092.0001.001 (accessed 19 August 2024).

'*Sir Arthur Hesilrige's letter to the honorable committee or Lords & Commons at Derby-House, concerning the revolt and recovery of Tinmouth-castle. In which action, Lieutenant Col: Lilburn (Governor of the castle) was slain, with divers seamen and others*', Early English Books Online, University of Michigan Library Digital Collections, name.umdl.umich.edu/A86093.0001.001 (accessed 19 August 2024).

'*A true relation of the routing the Scotish army near Dunbar, Sept. 3. instant . . .*', Early English Books Online 2, University of Michigan Library Digital Collections, name.umdl.umich.edu/A95269.0001.001 (accessed 30 August 2024).

'*Letters of state written by Mr John Milton, to most of the sovereign princes and republicks of Europe, from the year 1649, till the year 1659; to which is added, an account of his life; together with several of his poems, and a catalogue of his works, never before printed*', Early English Books Online, University of Michigan Library Digital Collections, name.umdl.umich.edu/A50909.0001.001 (accessed 30 August 2024).

'*Hosanna, or, A song of thanks-giving sung by the children of Zion, and set forth in three notable speeches at Grocers Hall, on the late solemn day of thanksgiving, Thursday June 7, 1649: the first was spoken by Alderman Atkins, the second by Alderman Isaac Pennington, the third by Hugh Peters (no alderman, but) clericus in cuerpo*', Early English Books Online, University of Michigan Library Digital Collections, name.umdl.umich.edu/A26129.0001.001 (accessed 30 August 2024).

'*The Lord Gen. Cromwel's letter: with a narrative of the proceedings of the English Army in Scotland: and a declaration of the General Assembly, touching the dis-owning their King and his interest. Published by authority*', Early English Books Online 2, University of Michigan Library Digital Collections, name.umdl.umich.edu/A80949.0001.001 (accessed 30 August 2024).

'*Strange newes from the north: Containing a true and exact relation of a great and terrible earth-quake in Cumberland and Westmerland. With the miraculous apparition of three glorious suns that appeared at once. And other wonderful appearances that happened in Yorkeshire, of divers bodies of armed men marching, and riding through every town for twelve miles compass about Malton, with the strange accidents that befel the cattel therabout through fright thereof, to the admiration of many thousand beholders. Together with, the charge against Charles Howard Esquire High Sheriff of the county of Cumberland. Verefied by severall gentlemen of known and approved credit*', Early English Books Online 2, University of Michigan Library Digital Collections, name.umdl.umich.edu/A78347.0001.001 (accessed 30 August 2024).

'*A faithful memorial of that remarkable meeting of many officers of the Army in England, at Windsor Castle, in the year 1648 . . . By William Allen, late Adjutant-General of the Army in Ireland*', Early English Books Online 2, University of Michigan Library Digital Collections, name.umdl.umich.edu/A74991.0001.001 (accessed 30 August 2024).

'*A true and perfect narrative of the several proceedings in the case concerning the Lord Craven, before the Commissioners for Sequestrations and Compositions sitting at Haberdashers-Hall, the Council of State, the Parliament and upon the indictment of perjury, preferred and found against Major Richard Faulconer . . . Shortly after which oath the Lord Cravens estate was voted by Parliament to be confiscate*', Early English Books Online 2, University of Michigan Library Digital Collections, name.umdl.umich.edu/A94942.0001.001 (accessed 30 August 2024).

'*A letter from Ireland read in the House of Commons on Friday Septemb. 28. 1649. From Mr Hugh Peters, Minister of Gods word, and Chaplain to the Lord Lieutenant Cromwell . . . A letter from Ireland, Imprimatur Hen: Scobell. Cleric. Parliamenti*', Early English Books Online, University of Michigan Library Digital Collections, name.umdl.umich.edu/A90539.0001.001 (accessed 30 August 2024).

'*A true and perfect narrative of the several proceedings in the case concerning the Lord Craven, before the Commissioners for Sequestrations and Compositions sitting at Haberdashers-Hall, the Council of State, the Parliament and upon the indictment of perjury, preferred and found against Major Richard Faulconer . . . Shortly after which oath the Lord Cravens estate was voted by Parliament to be confiscate*', Early English Books Online 2, University of Michigan Library Digital Collections, name.umdl.umich.edu/A94942.0001.001 (accessed 30 August 2024).

'*The life of General Monck, Duke of Albemarle, &c. with remarks upon his actions / by Tho. Gumble . . .*', Early English Books Online 2, University of Michigan Library Digital Collections, name.umdl.umich.edu/A42329.0001.001 (accessed 30 August 2024).

'*A declaration of the English army now in scotland* [sic]. *To the people of Scotland, especially those among them, that know and fear the Lord; we the officers and souldiers of the English army do send greeting*', Early English Books Online 2, University of Michigan Library Digital Collections, name.umdl.umich.edu/A82142.0001.001 (accessed 28 August 2024).

'*A declaration of the army of England upon their march into Scotland as also a letter of His Excellency the Lord Generall Cromwell to the General Assembly of the Kirk of Scotland: together with a vindication of the aforesaid declaration from the uncharitable constructions, odious imputations, and scandalous aspersions of the General Assembly of the Kirk of Scotland, in their reply thereto: and an answer of the under-officers and souldiers of the army, to a paper directed to them from the people of Scotland*', Early English Books Online 2, University of Michigan Library Digital Collections, name.umdl.umich.edu/A37365.0001.001 (accessed 30 August 2024).

'*The advance of Sir Arthur Hasilrigg, from the garrison of Portsmouth, toward the city of London: and his letter to the Lord Mayor, aldermen, and Commoun Council . . .*', Early English Books Online 2, University of Michigan Library Digital Collections name.umdl.umich.edu/A75903.0001.001 (accessed 25 August 2024).

'*A true relation of the daily proceedings and transactions of the Army in Scotland under his Excellency the Lord Gen. Cromwell. / Certified by letters from the Head-quarters at Stonehill in Scotland, Aug. 23. And published by authority*', Early English Books Online 2, University of Michigan Library Digital Collections, name.umdl.umich.edu/A95197.0001.001 (accessed 23 August 2024).

'*Mercurius publicus: comprising the sum of forraign intelligence . . . [no.29 (12 July–19 July 1660)]*', Early English Books Online, University of Michigan Library Digital Collections, name.umdl.umich.edu/A71350.0001.001 (accessed 20 August 2024).

'*A letter from General Monck from Dalkeith, 13 October 1659. Directed as followeth. For the Right Honorable William Lenthal, Esquire, Speaker; to be communicated to the Parliament of the Common-wealth of England, at Westminster*', Early English Books Online 2, University of Michigan Library Digital Collections, name.umdl.umich.edu/A76003.0001.001 (accessed 24 August 2024).

'*A chronicle of the late intestine war in the three kingdoms of England, Scotland and Ireland with the intervening affairs of treaties and other occurrences relating . . . to which is added a continuation to this present year 1675: being a brief account of the most memorable transactions in England,*

*Scotland and Ireland, and forreign parts / by J.P.*', Early English Books Online, University of Michigan Library Digital Collections, name.umdl.umich.edu/A43206.0001.001 (accessed 1 September 2024).

'*A True copy of the journal of the High Court of Justice for the tryal of K. Charles I as it was read in the House of Commons and attested under the hand of Phelps, clerk to that infamous court / taken by J. Nalson Jan. 4, 1683: with a large introduction*', Early English Books Online, University of Michigan Library Digital Collections, name.umdl.umich.edu/A63490.0001.001 (accessed 1 September 2024).

'*An exact summary, of the transactions in the treaty at Breda*', Early English Books Online 2, University of Michigan Library Digital Collections, name.umdl.umich.edu/A91850.0001.001 (accessed 1 September 2024).

'*A Catalogue of the names of all such who were summon'd to any Parliament (or reputed Parliament) from the year 1640 . . .*', Early English Books Online 2, University of Michigan Library Digital Collections, name.umdl.umich.edu/A31297.0001.001 (accessed 1 September 2024).

'*An exact and most impartial accompt of the indictment, arraignment, trial, and judgment (according to law) of twenty nine regicides, the murtherers of His Late Sacred Majesty of most glorious memory begun at Hicks-Hall on Tuesday, the 9th of October, 1660, and continued (at the Sessions-House in the Old-Bayley) until Friday, the nineteenth of the same moneth: together with a summary of the dark and horrid decrees of the caballists, preperatory to that hellish fact exposed to view for the reader's satisfaction, and information of posterity*', Early English Books Online, University of Michigan Library Digital Collections, name.umdl.umich.edu/a52526.0001.001 (accessed 2 September 2024).

'*A collection of several passages concerning his late highnesse Oliver Cromwell, in the time of his sickness; wherein is related many of his expressions upon his death-bed. Together with his prayer within two or three dayes before his death. Written by one that was then groom of his bed-chamber*', Early English Books Online, University of Michigan Library Digital Collections, name.umdl.umich.edu/A96977.0001.001 (accessed 2 September 2024).

'*Articles of peace, friendship & entercourse, concluded and agreed between England and France, in a treaty at Westminster, bearing date the third of November, new stile, in the year of our Lord God, 1655*', Early English Books Online 2, University of Michigan Library Digital

Collections, name.umdl.umich.edu/A80875.0001.001 (accessed 1 September 2024).

'*Sir Arthur Hasilrig's meditations, or, The Devil looking over Durham*', Early English Books Online, University of Michigan Library Digital Collections, name.umdl.umich.edu/A60296.0001.001 (accessed 1 September 2024).

Carew, G., Esq., '*Fraud and oppression detected and arraigned . . . Faithfully recollected and digested into a method by G.C. a lover of his countrey. Whereunto are added some necessary advertisements concerning the improvement of navigation and trade*', Early English Books Online, University of Michigan Library Digital Collections, name.umdl.umich.edu/A34059.0001.001 (accessed 30 August 2024).

Gent, S. T. (J. Heath), '*Flagellum, or, the Life and death, birth and burial of Oliver Cromwel faithfully described in an exact account of his policies and successes, not heretofore published or discovered/ by S. T., Gent*', Early English Books Online, University of Michigan Library Digital Collections, name.umdl.umich.edu/A43211.0001.001 (accessed 25 August 2024).

Ligon, R., '*A true & exact history of the island of Barbados illustrated with a mapp of the island, as also the principall trees and plants there, set forth in their due proportions and shapes, drawne out by their severall and respective scales: together with the ingenio that makes the sugar, with the plots of the severall houses, roomes, and other places that are used in the whole processe of sugar-making . . . / by Richard Ligon, Gent*', Early English Books Online, University of Michigan Library Digital Collections, name.umdl.umich.edu/A48447.0001.001 (accessed 1 September 2024).

Lilly, W., '*A peculiar prognostication astrologically predicted according to art: Whether, or no, His Majestie shall suffer death this present yeere 1649. / The possibility thereof discussed and divulged, by William Lilly, student in astrologie*', Early English Books Online 2, University of Michigan Library Digital Collections, name.umdl.umich.edu/A88288.0001.001 (accessed 29 August 2024).

Peters, H., '*A dying fathers last legacy to an onely child, or, Mr Hugh Peter's advice to his daughter written by his own hand, during his late imprisonment in the Tower of London, and given her a little before his death*', Early English Books Online, University of Michigan Library Digital Collections, name.umdl.umich.edu/A54501.0001.001 (accessed 30 August 2024).

Peters, H., '*Gods doings, and mans duty opened in a sermon preached before both Houses of Parliament, the Lord Major and aldermen of the city of London, and the assembly of divines at the last thanksgiving day, April 2, for the recovering of the West, and disbanding 5000 of the Kings horse, &c., 1645 /1645 / by Hugh Peters . . .*' Early English Books Online, University of Michigan Library Digital Collections, name.umdl.umich.edu/A54509.0001.001 (accessed 30 August 2024).

Peters, H., '*The tales and jests of Mr Hugh Peters collected into one volume / published by one that hath formerly been conversant with the author in his life time . . .; together with his sentence and the manner of his execution*', Early English Books Online, University of Michigan Library Digital Collections, name.umdl.umich.edu/A54514.0001.001 (accessed 30 August 2024).

Sikes, G., '*The life and death of Sir Henry Vane, Kt., or, A short narrative of the main passages of his earthly pilgrimage together with a true account of his purely Christian, peaceable, spiritual, gospel-principles, doctrine, life and way of worshipping God, for which he suffered contradiction and reproach from all sorts of sinners, and at last, a violent death, June 14. Anno, 1662: to which is added, his last exhortation to his children, the day before his death*', Early English Books Online, University of Michigan Library Digital Collections, name.umdl.umich.edu/A60227.0001.001 (accessed 30 August 2024).

## Journal Articles

Anthony, H. S., 'Mercurius Politicus under Milton', *Journal of the History of Ideas*, Vol. 27, No. 4, Oct–Dec 1966, pp.593–6, 598–609.

Barbour, V., 'Dutch and English Merchant Shipping in the Seventeenth Century', *Economic History Review*, Vol. 2, No. 2, Jan 1930, pp.261–90.

Beckles, H. McD, 'Plantation Production and White "Proto-Slavery": White Indentured Servants and the Colonisation of the English West Indies, 1624–1645', *The Americas*, Vol. 41, No. 3, Jan 1985, pp.21–45.

Bickley, F. B., 'Letters Relating to Scotland, January 1650', *English Historical Review*, Vol. 11, No. 41, Jan 1896, pp.112–17.

Bolton, C. K., 'Lord Saye and Sele', *New England Quarterly*, Vol. 10, No. 2, Jun 1937, pp.345–6.

Boxer, C. R., 'Public Opinion and the Second Anglo-Dutch War, 1664–1667', *History Today*, Vol. 16, No. 9, Sep 1966.

Boyle, J. R., 'Katy's Coffee House, Newcastle', *Monthly Chronicle of North-Country Lore and Legend*, Vol. 3, No. 30, Aug 1889, pp.369–70.

Bremer, F. J., 'In Defense of Regicide: John Cotton on the Execution of Charles I', *William and Mary Quarterly*, Vol. 37, No. 1, Jan 1980, pp.103–24.

Bridenbaugh, C., 'Yankee Use and Abuse of the Forest in the Building of New England, 1620–1660', *Proceedings of the Massachusetts Historical Society*, 3rd series, Vol. 89, 1977, pp.3–35.

Brod, M., 'Politics and Prophecy in Seventeenth-Century England: The Case of Elizabeth Poole', *Albion: A Quarterly Journal Concerned with British Studies*, Vol. 31, No. 3, Autumn 1999, pp.395–412.

Burgess, G., 'Was the English Civil War a War of Religion? The Evidence of Political Propaganda', *Huntington Library Quarterly*, Vol. 61, No. 2, 1998, pp.173–201.

Burrell, S. A., 'The Covenant Idea as a Revolutionary Symbol: Scotland, 1596–1637', *Church History*, Vol. 27, No. 4, Dec 1958, pp.338–50.

Canny, N., 'Migration and Opportunity: Britain, Ireland and the New World', *Irish Economic and Social History*, Vol. 12, 1985, pp.7–32.

Clark, D. L., 'John Milton and William Chappell', *Huntington Library Quarterly*, Vol. 18, No. 4, Aug 1955, pp.329–50.

Clemens, P. G. E., 'The World of Maurice Thomson', review of R. Brenner, *Merchants and Revolution: Commercial Change, Political Conflict, and London's Overseas Traders, 1550–1653*, in *Reviews in American History*, Vol. 21, No. 4, Dec 1993, pp.575–83.

Coffey, J., 'Puritanism and Liberty Revisited: The Case for Toleration in the English Revolution', *Historical Journal*, Vol. 41, No. 4, Dec 1998, pp.961–85.

Cohen, R. D., 'Puritan Education in Seventeenth Century England and New England', review of R. L. Greaves, *The Puritan Revolution and Educational Thought: Background for Reform*, and R. Middlekauff, *The Mathers: Three Generations of Puritan Intellectuals, 1596–1728*, in *History of Education Quarterly*, Vol. 13, No. 3, Autumn 1973, pp.301–7.

Como, D. R., 'Printing the Levellers: Clandestine Print, Radical Propaganda, and the New Model Army', *The Library*, Vol. 22, No. 4, 2021, pp.441–86.

Corsar, K. C., 'David Leslie's Defence of Edinburgh July–August, 1650',

*Journal of the Society for Army Historical Research*, Vol. 25, No. 103, Autumn, 1947, pp.96–105.

Corsar, K. C., 'The Surrender of Edinburgh Castle December, 1650', *Scottish Historical Review*, Vol. 28, No. 105, Apr 1949, pp.43–54.

Crawford, P., '"Charles Stuart, That Man of Blood"', *Journal of British Studies*, Vol. 16, No. 2, Spring 1977, pp.41–61.

Crawford, P., 'The Savile Affair', *English Historical Review*, Vol. 90, No. 354, Jan 1975, pp.76–93.

Crow, S. D., '"Your Majesty's Good Subjects": A Reconsideration of Royalism in Virginia', *Virginia Magazine of History and Biography*, Vol. 87, No. 2, Apr 1979, pp.158–73.

Davies, G., 'The Army and the Downfall of Richard Cromwell', *Huntington Library Bulletin*, No. 7, Apr 1935, pp.131–67.

Durston, C., 'The Fall of Cromwell's Major-Generals', *English Historical Review*, Vol. 113, No. 450, Feb 1998, pp.18–37.

Ede-Borrett, S., 'Some Notes on the Raising and Origins of Colonel John Okey's Regiment of Dragoons, March to June, 1645', *Journal of the Society for Army Historical Research*, Vol. 87, 2009, pp.206–13.

Engstrom, H. R., Jr., 'Sir Arthur Hesilrige: The Forgotten Knight of the Long Parliament', *Albion: A Quarterly Journal Concerned with British Studies*, Vol. 8, No. 4, Winter 1976, pp.320–32.

Fatovic, C., 'The Anti-Catholic Roots of Liberal and Republican Conceptions of Freedom in English Political Thought', *Journal of the History of Ideas*, Vol. 66, No. 1, Jan 2005, pp.37–58.

Faul, D., 'Cromwell in Ireland: The Massacres', *Seanchas Ardmhacha: Journal of the Armagh Diocesan Historical Society*, Vol. 20, No. 1, 2004, pp.293–8.

Fea, A., 'Portraits of Lucy Walter', *Burlington Magazine for Connoisseurs*, Vol. 87, No. 509, Aug 1945, pp.19, 194–6.

Firth, C. H., 'Cromwell and the Insurrection of 1655', *English Historical Review*, Vol. 3, No. 10, Apr 1888, pp.323–50.

Firth, C. H., 'The Battle of Dunbar', *Transactions of the Royal Historical Society*, new series, Vol. 14, 1900, pp.19–52, 304.

Firth, C. H., 'Cromwell and the Crown', *English Historical Review*, Vol. 17, No. 67, Jul 1902, pp.429–42.

Firth, C. H., 'Cromwell and the Crown', *English Historical Review*, Vol. 18, No. 69, Jan 1903, pp.52–80.

Firth, C. H., 'The Expulsion of the Long Parliament (continued)', *History*, new series, Vol. 2, No. 8, Jan 1918, pp.193–206.

Firth, C. H. et. al., 'Unpublished Letters of Oliver Cromwell', *English Historical Review*, Vol. 2, No. 5, Jan 1887, pp.148–52.

Firth, C. H. and Scott, T., 'Thomas Scot's Account of His Actions as Intelligencer during the Commonwealth', *English Historical Review*, Vol. 12, No. 45, Jan 1897, pp.116–26.

Fisher, L. D., '"Dangerous Designes": The 1976 Barbados Act to Prohibit New England Slave Importation', *William and Mary Quarterly*, Vol. 71, No. 1, Jan 2014, pp.99–124.

Gaunt, P. G. I., review of P. Little, *Lord Broghill and the Cromwellian Union with Ireland and Scotland*, in *Journal of British Studies*, Vol. 45, No. 1, Jan 2006, pp.153–5.

Gentles, I., 'The Struggle for London in the Second Civil War', *Historical Journal*, Vol. 26, No. 2, Jun 1983, pp.277–305.

Gentles, I., 'The New Model Officer Corps in 1647: A Collective Portrait', *Social History*, Vol. 22, No. 2, May 1997, pp.127–44.

Gragg, L. D., 'A Puritan in the West Indies: The Career of Samuel Winthrop', *William and Mary Quarterly*, Vol. 50, No. 4, Oct 1993, pp.768–86.

Green, S. A. and Winthrop, R. C., Jr., 'December Meeting, 1893; Letter of Emmanuel Downing; Elegy on John Foster; Miscellaneous Business', *Proceedings of the Massachusetts Historical Society*, 2nd series, Vol. 8, 1892–4, pp.370–95.

Greenspan, N., 'Charles II, Lucy Walter, and the Stuart Courts in Exile', *English Historical Review*, Vol. 131, No. 553, 2016, pp.1386–1414.

Heath, G. D., III, 'Cromwell and Lambert, 1653–1657', *The Historian*, Vol. 21, No. 4, Aug 1959, pp.372–91.

Holmes, C., 'The Trial and Execution of Charles I', *Historical Journal*, Vol. 50, No. 2, Jun 2010, pp.289–316.

Hutton, R., review of A. Hopper, *Turncoats and Renegadoes: Changing Sides During the English Civil Wars*, in *English Historical Review*, Vol. 129, No. 538, Jun 2014, pp.719–21.

Johns, A., 'Coleman Street', *Huntington Library Quarterly*, Vol. 71, No. 1, Mar 2008, pp.33–54.

Kelsey, S., 'The Death of Charles I', *Historical Journal*, Vol. 45, No. 4, Dec 2002, pp.727–54.

Kelsey, S., 'Politics and Procedure in the Trial of Charles I', *Law and History Review*, Vol. 22, No. 1, Spring 2004, pp.1–5.

Kelsey, S., '"The Now King of England"', *English Historical Review*, Vol. 132, No. 558, Oct 2017, pp.1077–1109.

Kelsey, S., 'King Charles His Case: The Intended Prosecution of Charles I', *Journal of Legal History*, Vol. 39, No. 1, 2018, pp.58–87.

Kelsey, S., 'Instrumenting the trial of Charles I', *Historical Research*, Vol. 92, No. 255, Feb 2019, pp.119–38.

Kilburn, H., 'Jesuit and gentleman planter: Ingle's rebellion and the litigation of Thomas Copley S.J.', *British Catholic History*, Vol. 34, No. 3, 2019, pp.374–95.

Kishlansky, M., 'The Sales of Crown Lands and the Spirit of the Revolution', *Economic History Review*, Vol. 29, No. 1, Feb 1976, pp.125–30.

Kishlansky, M., 'Mission Impossible: Charles I, Oliver Cromwell and the Regicide', *English Historical Review*, Vol. 125, No. 515, Aug 2010, pp.844–74.

Kishlansky, M., 'Martyrs' Tales', *Journal of British Studies*, Vol. 53, No. 2, Apr 2014, pp.334–55.

Lake, P., review of C. S. R. Russell, *The Causes of the English Civil War; The Fall of the British Monarchies, 1637–1642; Unrevolutionary England*, in *Huntington Library Quarterly*, Vol. 57, No. 2, Spring 1994, pp.167–97.

Lindley, K. J., 'Riot Prevention and Control in Early Stuart London', *Transactions of the Royal Historical Society*, Vol. 33, 1983, pp.109–26.

Little, A. M., '"Shoot That Rogue, for He Hath an Englishman's Coat On!": Cultural Cross-Dressing on the New England Frontier, 1620–1760', *New England Quarterly*, Vol. 74, No. 2, Jun 2001, pp.238–73.

Little, P., 'Monarchy to protectorate: re-drafting the Humble Petition and Advice, March–June 1657', *Historical Research*, Vol. 79, No. 203, Feb 2006, pp.144–9.

Mahony, M., 'Presbyterianism in the City of London, 1645–1647', *Historical Journal*, Vol. 22, No. 1, Mar 1979, pp.93–114.

Martin, J. W., 'The Pre-Quaker Writings of George Bishop', *Quaker History*, Vol. 74, No. 2, Fall 1985, pp.20–7.

Morison, S. E., 'Precedence at Harvard College in the Seventeenth Century', *Proceedings of the American Antiquarian Society*, new series, Vol. 42, 1932, pp.371–431.

Miller, L., 'Before Milton Was Famous: January 8, 1649/50', *Milton Quarterly*, Vol. 21, No. 1, Mar 1987, pp.1–6.

Onnekink, D., 'Symbolic Communication in Early Modern Diplomacy: Naval Incidents and the Third Anglo-Dutch War (1667–1672)', *English Historical Review*, Vol. 135, No. 573, Apr 2020, pp.337–58.

Peacey, J. T., 'Order and Disorder in Europe: Parliamentary Agents and Royalist Thugs 1649–1650', *Historical Journal*, Vol. 40, No. 4, Dec 1997, pp.953–76.

Peacey, J. T., 'John Lilburne and the Long Parliament', *Historical Journal*, Vol. 43, No. 3, Sep 2000, pp.625–45.

Peacey, J. T., 'Cromwellian England: A Propaganda State?', *History*, Vol. 91, No. 2, Apr 2006, pp.176–99.

Pestana, C. G., 'A West Indian Colonial Governor's Advice: Henry Ashton's 1646 Letter to the Earl of Carlisle', *William and Mary Quarterly*, Vol. 60, No. 2, 2003, pp.382–421.

Pincus, S. C. A., 'Popery, Trade and Universal Monarchy: The Ideological Context of the Outbreak of the Second Anglo-Dutch War', *English Historical Review*, Vol. 107, No. 422, Jan 1992, pp.1–29.

Polizzotto, C., 'Speaking Truth to Power: The Problem of Authority in the Whitehall Debates of 1648–9', *English Historical Review*, Vol. 131, No. 548, Feb 2016, pp.31–63.

Pope, T. S., 'Court-Martial Held Two Centuries Ago, at Portaferry, County Down', *Ulster Journal of Archaeology*, 1st series, Vol. 8, 1860, pp.62–9, www.jstor.org/stable/20608897 (accessed 5 March 2023).

Prestwich, M., 'Diplomacy and Trade in the Protectorate', *Journal of Modern History*, Vol. 22, No. 2, Jun 1950, pp.103–21.

Reay, B., 'The Quakers, 1659, and the Restoration of the Monarchy', *History*, Vol. 63, No. 208, 1978, pp.193–213.

Rommelse, G., 'The role of mercantilism in Anglo-Dutch political relations, 1650–74', *Economic History Review*, new series, Vol. 63, No. 3, Aug 2010, pp.591–611.

Roper, L. H., 'The Fall of New Netherland and Seventeenth-Century Anglo-American Imperial Formation, 1654–1676', *New England Quarterly*, Vol. 87, No. 4, Dec 2014, pp.666–708.

Rossiter, C., 'Thomas Hooker', *New England Quarterly*, Vol. 25, No. 4, Dec 1952, pp.459–88.

Rostenberg, L., 'Robert Stephens, Messenger of the Press: An Episode in 17th-Century Censorship', *Papers of the Bibliographical Society of America*, 2nd quarter, Vol. 49, No. 2, 1955, pp.131–52.

Ruland, V. L., 'A Royalist Account of Hugh Peters' Arrest', *Huntington Library Quarterly*, Vol. 18, No. 2, Feb 1955, pp.178–82.

Sachse, W. L., 'The Migration of New Englanders to England, 1640–1660', *American Historical Review*, Vol. 53, No. 2, Jan 1948, pp.251–78.

Schoolcraft, H. L., 'The Capture of New Amsterdam', *English Historical Review*, Vol. 22, No. 88, Oct 1907, pp.674–93.

Schroeder, J. T., 'London and the New Model Army, 1647', *The Historian*, Vol. 19, No. 3, May 1957, pp.245–61.

Scott, D., 'The "Northern Gentlemen", the Parliamentary Independents, and Anglo-Scottish Relations in the Long Parliament', *Historical Journal*, Vol. 42, No. 2, Jun 1999, pp.347–75.

Scott, J., '"Good Night Amsterdam". Sir George Downing and Anglo-Dutch Statebuilding', *English Historical Review*, Vol. 118, No. 476, Apr 2003, pp.334–56.

Solt, L. F., 'The Fifth Monarchy Men: Politics and the Millennium', *Church History*, Vol. 30, No. 3, Sep 1961, pp.314–24.

Staffell, E., 'The Horrible Tail-Man and the Anglo-Dutch Wars', *Journal of the Warburg and Courtauld Institutes*, Vol. 63, 2000, pp.169–86.

Stimson, D., 'Hartlib, Haak and Oldenburg: Intelligencers', *Isis*, Vol. 31, No. 2, Apr 1940, pp.309–26.

Taft, B., 'The Council of Officers' Agreement of the People, 1648/9', *Historical Journal*, Vol. 28, No. 1, Mar 1985, pp.169–85.

Underdown, D., 'The Problem of Popular Allegiance in the English Civil War: The Prothero Lecture', *Transactions of the Royal Historical Society*, Vol. 31, 1981, pp.69–94.

Vallance, Ted, 'The Cromwell Day Address 2019: Cromwell, Blood Guilt and the Trial and Execution of Charles I', *Cromwelliana*, 3rd series, No. 9, 2020, pp.5–21.

Vander Motten, J. P., 'New Light on Lucy Walter, 1649–1659', *The Seventeenth Century*, Vol. 37, No. 3, 2022, pp.391–415.

Walker, J., 'The Secret Service under Charles II and James II', *Transactions of the Royal Historical Society*, Vol. 15, 1932, pp.211–42.

Wedgewood, C. V., 'European Reaction to the Death of Charles I', *American Scholar*, Vol. 34, No. 3, Summer 1965, pp.431–46.

Worden, B., 'Oliver Cromwell and The Protectorate', *Transactions of the Royal Historical Society*, 6th series, Vol. 20, 2010, pp.57–83.

# Acknowledgements

I PAY TRIBUTE TO John Beresford, the pioneer of Downing studies, whose 1925 'essay in biography' provided a sure and broad foundation of fact. I am obliged too to all those scholars who spotted something particularly interesting in George Downing – including, but not only – Gijs Rommelse, Roger Downing, Jonathan Scott, Henry Roseveare and Ralph Catterall. In making sense of Downing's times, I have been chiefly guided by the work of Samuel Rawson Gardiner and Charles Harding Firth, David Underdown, Austin Woolrych, Patrick Little, Anna Keay, Paul Lay, Manfred Brod and Ian Gentles.

Many thanks to Patrick Walsh and Cora MacGregor at Pew Literary for their patient diligence, constant support and being so good at what they do. Patrick fully understood the character of George Downing from the off and helped nurse this project through Covid and other crises. I am hugely grateful to Drummond Moir and all his team at Atlantic Books – especially James Nightingale, Harry O'Sullivan and the copyeditor, Mandy Greenfield; and to Jessica Case and Claiborne Hancock at Pegasus Books in the United States.

It was the infectious enthusiasm of Professor Christopher

Andrew that first inspired my interest in the history of intelligence. I keep *The Secret World* always close to hand.

My wife, Laura Cumming, introduced me to The Hague and Delft (the latter she has made her own with her wonderful book, *Thunderclap*). She has been first reader, editrix of early drafts, champion of rigour, dispenser of encouragement and true collaborator. She also chose the pictures. Thanks too to Hilla Sewell and Thea Sewell for their internships in the bibliography department and to William Sewell for watching the door. All my family deserve extra thanks for putting up with my prolonged absences in the 17th century.

# List of Illustrations

| | |
|---|---|
| p.232 | John Pell, from a lost portrait by Sir Godfrey Kneller (public domain, via The Picture Art Collection / Alamy) |
| p.242 | James Naylor, British Museum (public domain, via Wikimedia Commons) |
| p.246 | View of the Binnenhof, The Hague, Gerrit Adriaensz Berckheyde, Museo Nacional Thyssen-Bornemisza, Madrid |
| p.250 (1) | Mary, Dowager Princess of Orange, Gerrit van Honthorst, National Trust (public domain via Wikimedia Commons) |
| p.250 (2) | Elizabeth, Queen of Bohemia, Gerrit van Honthorst, National Gallery, London (public domain via Wikimedia Commons) |
| p.251(1) | Lady Stanhope, Anthony Van Dyck, private collection, (public domain via ART Collection / Alamy) |
| p.251(2) | Lucy Walter (possibly a depiction of Louise de Kérouaille, Duchess of Portsmouth), after Peter Lely, Abbotsford House, (public domain via Danvis Collection / Alamy) |
| p.265 | Edward Hyde, Lord Clarendon, after Peter Lely, National Trust, (public domain via Wikimedia Commons) |
| p.270 | Hugh Peter with the devil (public domain via Wikimedia Commons) |
| p.274 | Hanging of dead regicides – Cromwell, Bradshaw & Ireton (public domain via Wikimedia Commons) |
| p.297 | Battle of Lowestoft, Hendrick van Minderhout, National Maritime Museum, (public domain via Wikimedia Commons) |
| p.298 | Voorhout (public domain, via The History Collection / Alamy) |
| p.302 | The Corpses of the De Witt Brothers, Jan de Baen, Rijksmuseum, Amsterdam |

# Index